# Modern China and International Economic Law

This book series offers an essential forum for Chinese economic law scholars, as well as international scholars interested in China's practice in the context of international economic law. It is thus the aim of this book series to publish essential monographs/ compilations in the field of international economic law that focus on China, or on uniquely Chinese characteristics. This book series above all focuses on research that closely relates current practices with past history, and future policies with current circumstances, pursuing a philosophy of understanding legal practices by combining the past and present. Accordingly, top scholars in China and beyond its borders will be invited to contribute to this project from their respective areas of focus, which can cover broad topics related to international law in the current context of China's peaceful rise, such as China's economic policy with various countries, its participation in the WTO legal system and bilateral investment treaty practices, etc.; as well as more specific topics such as China's domestic legislation regarding foreign business, its unique "one country, two systems" policy and its implications on external economic interactions between different "systems" within China.

Huiping Chen

# China's Practice in International Investment Law

中国国际经济法学会
Chinese Society of International Economic Law, CSIEL

Springer

Huiping Chen
Professor of International law
Xiamen University School of Law
Xiamen, Fujian, China

ISSN 2364-8317 ISSN 2364-8325 (electronic)
Modern China and International Economic Law
ISBN 978-981-96-5015-6 ISBN 978-981-96-5016-3 (eBook)
https://doi.org/10.1007/978-981-96-5016-3



This Springer imprint is published by the registered company Springer Nature Singapore Pte Ltd.
The registered company address is: 152 Beach Road, #21-01/04 Gateway East, Singapore 189721, Singapore

# Acknowledgments

This monograph is published in the book series of Modern China & International Economic Law. The author would like to thank Prof. An Chen, my former Ph.D. supervisor and colleague at Xiamen Law School, who is the series Editor-in-Chief and author of the first monograph of this series, for his kind organization of this series and strong encouragement and support to me in writing this book. Gratitude is given to Springer Nature colleagues for their patience, cooperation and careful editing of this book. I would also like to thank my husband and daughter for their understanding, support and love.

# Introduction

This book intends to discuss China's practice in international investment law from two aspects, that is, China's practice in international investment treaties and China's practice in international investment dispute settlement. Many ideas of this book originate from the author's personal experience and research when she has opportunities to participate indirectly in and continually follow up China's concluding of some investment agreements and the resolution of some investment disputes that China is a disputing party or Chinese investors are involved. The research team of international investment law of Xiamen University School of Law has longstanding research and rich accumulation in this area, and often offers advisory reports to Chinese Government in the conclusion of investment agreements as well as resolution of investment disputes. The author is lucky enough to be in this team, and witnesses the whole journey that China develops in investment agreements from toddle to grownup, and also witnesses China's achievements in active participation in the rule of law in international investment agreements.

For the aspect of China's investment treaty practice, this book focuses on the specific and special historical period as of the beginning of the twenty-first century when China developed from mere major capital-import economy to major economy of both capital-import and export, and at the same time, the international investment treaty practice was in a crossroad for the whole world. This book tries to elaborate the heatedly discussed issues, the compromise eventually reached as well as the characteristics of the treaties that China negotiated with the Association of Southeast Asian Nations (ASEAN) states (Chap. 1), Korea (Chap. 2), African countries (Chap. 3) and the US (Chap. 4). China proposed the Belt and Road Initiative as early as 2012, and this Initiative has far-reaching impacts on China's international investment law practice (Chap. 5).

For the aspect of China's investment dispute settlement practice, it is important to probe into China's position toward the legitimacy crisis of international investment arbitration and the currently undergoing ISDS reform. On the domestic level, China made some creative ISDS mechanisms under its Belt and Road Initiative (Chap. 5). On international level, this book tries to reflect on the expansion of jurisdiction by tribunal (Chap. 6) and the new developments of ISDS in the early twenty-first century (Chap. 7). China cautiously responds to the ISDS reform in the international level (Chap. 8). Till August 30, 2023, there have been eight cases that China is challenged by foreign investors to international investment arbitration, and there have been 25 international investment arbitration and conciliation cases that had been formally initiated by Chinese investors pursuant to international investment agreements signed between China (including Hong Kong) and other countries or investment contracts signed between the investors and foreign governments. Among all the above cases, two cases were initiated by Chinese investors pursuant to the China-ASEAN Investment Agreement (Chap. 1). Two cases were commenced on the basis of the China-Korean BIT where in one case China was challenged while in the other case Chinese investor is the claimant (Chap. 2). Two other cases were brought by Chinese investors against African countries (Chap. 3). The final chapter goes through some selected cases where China acted as the respondent state and Chinese investors acted as the claimants (Chap. 9).

To conclude, on the one hand, this book follows and analyzes China's investment treaty conclusion practice within the last twenty years, and thus reflects the whole journey that China changes its position from majorly protecting its own rights and interests as host state, to tryingly to balance the rights and interests of both host state and foreign investor. On the other hand, China's participation in the international ISDS reform and the creation of its domestic ISDS mechanisms also shows that China is trying to balance the rights and interests of both host state and foreign investor so as to provide sufficient protection to Chinese overseas investors.

# Contents

# Chapter 1
# China-ASEAN Investment Agreement Practice

The China-ASEAN[1] Free Trade Area (FTA) was established in 2010,[2] based on several agreements including the Framework Agreement on Comprehensive Economic Co-operation between ASEAN and China ("the CAFTA Framework Agreement") signed in November 2002,[3] Agreement on Trade in Goods signed in 2004, Agreement on Trade in Services signed in 2007, the Agreement on Investment signed in 2009, etc. The negotiations on the investment agreement between China and ASEAN were the most difficult one and lasted for several years.

The finally concluded Agreement on Investment is a high-standard investment agreement. It offers better treatment and provides better protection to investors than those BITs that China concluded with individual ASEAN states in early time. The signing of a comprehensive and open investment agreement has and will continue to benefit investors from both China and ASEAN.

The Agreement on Investment allows foreign investors to submit any investment dispute with the host state to international arbitration. So far, there are two cases that

[1] ASEAN (the Association of South East Asian Nations) was formed in 1967 by Indonesia, Malaysia, the Philippines, Thailand and Singapore, joined by Brunei in 1984 (known as the ASEAN-6), and by Cambodia, Laos, Myanmar and Vietnam in the 1990s (known as CLMV or the new ASEAN members).

[2] The China-ASEAN FTA was updated in 2019 to further open up markets to the other party. As of 2022, the two parties are negotiating to update it further.

[3] The full title of the agreement is "the Framework Agreement on Comprehensive Economic Co-operation between the Association of South East Asian Nations and the People's Republic of China" (China-ASEAN Framework Agreement). It was signed in Phnom Penh, Cambodia on November 4, 2002. Since the purpose of the Agreement is to create a "China-ASEAN Free Trade Area (CAFTA)", the agreement is also referred to as the "CAFTA Framework Agreement".

The part on the negotiations of China-ASEAN investment agreement in this chapter was previously published in the title of China-ASEAN Investment Agreement Negotiations—The Substantive Issues in the Journal of World Investment & Trade, Vol. 7, No. 1, February 2006.



H. Chen, *China's Practice in International Investment Law*, Modern China and International Economic Law, https://doi.org/10.1007/978-981-96-5016-3_1

have been referred to international arbitration, both of which are brought by Chinese investors.

This chapter will first discuss several issues related to the negotiations of the investment agreement, and then briefly discuss the investor-state dispute settlement by referring to the two arbitration cases.

## 1.1 Overview of the Investment Agreement Negotiations

In accordance with the CAFTA Framework Agreement signed in 2002, China and ASEAN planned to establish the China-ASEAN Free Trade Area (CAFTA) by 2010 with the ASEAN-6 and by 2015 with the four new ASEAN members. The CAFTA negotiations were primarily in the fields of trade in goods, services and investment. The negotiations on trade in goods have resulted in an agreement in 2004,[4] while the investment negotiations had been in stalemating for several years. Not until the August of 2009 did the China and ASEAN concluded the Agreement on Investment of the Framework Agreement on Comprehensive Economic Cooperation.

The CAFTA Framework Agreement has set up basic contents and guidelines for the prospective investment agreement but leaves details for future negotiations. So far, preliminary negotiations have achieved a comprehensive framework, due also to the legal foundation established by the bilateral investment agreements (BITs) between China and the ten ASEAN countries. However, although China and ASEAN easily came to a general consensus as to investment facilitation and investment protection, there were substantial controversies over investment liberalization. Reasons for these controversies included: first, investment liberalization per se is a global contentious issue; second, the vague term "progressively liberalize" used by the CAFTA Framework Agreement[5] induces differentiated understanding; and third, approaches and modalities to investment liberalization vary. China had also enumerated several constraints and difficulties for her; investment liberalization is directly related to substantive provisions of the agreement, such as the definition of "investor" and "investment", market access (opening up of industries), national treatment and pre-establishment national treatment. Therefore, these substantive controversies had deferred and even deadlocked the investment negotiations for a long time.

In the author's opinion, these controversies should be discussed and resolved in a broad context. The process of progressive liberalization should be limited and restricted taking into account both China and ASEAN countries as developing countries. In this context, careful and restricted definitions of "investor" and "investment", limited market access, as well as qualified national treatment should be acceptable for both sides.

---

[4] The full title of the Agreement is "Agreement on Trading in Goods of the Framework Agreement on Comprehensive Economic Cooperation between ASEAN and China" which was signed on November 29, 2004.

[5] See the China-ASEAN Framework Agreement, Article 5(a).

The following firstly examines the general consensus between China and ASEAN on the framework of the prospective investment agreement; then discusses the key controversies over investment liberalization; and finally proposes specific provisions or modalities.

## 1.2 General Consensus Between China and ASEAN on the Framework of the Prospective Investment Agreement

### *1.2.1 Basic Contents of the Prospective Investment Agreement Set up by the CAFTA Framework Agreement*

The CAFTA Framework Agreement serves as a roadmap for the negotiations on the China-ASEAN Free Trade Area.[6] By the same token, its provisions regarding investment function as guidelines for the proposed agreement and negotiations. Article 5 is the only article which deals specifically with investment, in addition to other articles which have some relevance to investment. They set up basic contents for the future agreement, including objectives, main elements and approaches for agreement.

Article 5 specifies that "to promote investment and to create a liberal, facilitative, transparent and competitive investment regime, the parties agree to: (a) enter into negotiations in order to progressively liberalize the investment regime; (b) strengthen cooperation in investment, facilitate investment and improve transparency of investment rules and regulations; and (c) provide for the protection of investments".[7]

Although this article is brief, general or even simple, it covers almost all issues an international investment agreement should cover, including objectives, investment promotion and facilitation, investment protection and investment liberalization. Although Article 5 does not mention principles of the agreement, they can be inferred from the context of the Framework Agreement. Therefore, a comprehensive picture for the prospective agreement is clearly provided.

First of all, the objectives of the agreement are clear. The immediate objective is "to create a liberal, facilitative, transparent and competitive investment regime". The overall objective is "to promote investment". In other words, the purpose of creating a comprehensive investment agreement is to promote more inflow of foreign investment into CAFTA, specifically, into both China and ASEAN countries. Therefore, the relationship between the immediate and overall objectives is means and end. Further, these objectives in turn serve to realize the general objectives of CAFTA,

[6] *China-ASEAN FTA Factsheet*, available at: << http://www.mti.gov.sg/public/FTA/frm_FTA_Default.asp?sid=179&cid=1902>>.

[7] See the China-ASEAN Framework Agreement, Article 5.

i.e., to strengthen and enhance a closer economic, trade and investment cooperation between the parties.[8] Therefore, the final objective as well as purpose of the investment agreement is to promote investment and closer economic cooperation between China and ASEAN. Keeping these objectives in mind will foster a sound and acceptable agreement, as well as resolve discrepancies as to specific substantive provisions.

Secondly, the main elements of the future investment agreement are explicitly stipulated. Article 5 enumerates them: investment liberalization, facilitation and promotion; transparency of investment rules and regulations; and investment protection. Given that the purpose of the transparency rule is for investment protection, the proposed agreement has three pillars, i.e., investment promotion, protection and liberalization. Another element a comprehensive agreement should cover is investment dispute settlement mechanism. Although Article 5 is silent here, according to Article 11 of the CAFTA Framework Agreement,[9] this element is supplied by the Agreement on Dispute Settlement Mechanism between ASEAN and China. Therefore, it is clear that both China and ASEAN have general consensus on an overall and comprehensive investment regime.

Thirdly, general principles of the future agreement, though not addressed by Article 5, can still be inferred from the Framework Agreement. The first principle is "forward-looking" because the Framework Agreement itself is forward-looking with the objective of closer economic relations between China and ASEAN in the twenty-first century.[10] Since there are several years left for the realization of CAFTA with old ASEAN member states by 2010 and with new ASEAN states by 2015, the investment arrangements concerning parties' obligations and commitments could be ambitious. The second principle is "flexibility" which means sensitive sectors in the goods, services and investment sectors could be addressed and correspondingly, different policies or options instead of ironclad or monolithic bloc provisions should result, in consideration of the differences among China and ASEAN countries.[11] For example, taking into consideration China's difficulties in liberalizing her investment regime, ASEAN should not require radical changes of China's laws and regulations. The third principle is "special and differential treatment".[12] Cambodia, Laos, Myanmar and Vietnam, the four less developed countries, are newer ASEAN member states. To address their special economic and political needs, special and differential treatment should be given them without requiring reciprocal treatment.

---

[8] See the China-ASEAN Framework Agreement, Article 1(a).

[9] According to Art. 11.1 of the China-ASEAN Framework Agreement, a formal dispute settlement mechanism was to be established to settle disputes arising under the Framework Agreement and its covered future agreements. On November 29, 2004, the Agreement on Dispute Settlement Mechanism between ASEAN and China was signed to be effective from January 1, 2005. The latter Agreement contains an article (Article 2) to the same effect of Art. 11.1 of the former Agreement.

[10] This objective is clearly stated in the Preamble of the China-ASEAN Framework Agreement.

[11] The principle of flexibility is addressed in Art. 2 (d) and (e) and Art. 8 (3) of the China-ASEAN Framework Agreement.

[12] This principle is addressed in the Preamble and Art. 8 (3) of the China-ASEAN Framework Agreement.

Approaches for agreement have also been suggested by Article 5, including "progressive liberalization". Also, mutual benefits, understanding and compromise, successfully used in the BITs between China and the ten ASEAN countries, should also be incorporated into the current investment negotiations.

To sum up, Article 5, together with the Framework Agreement as a whole, has provided basic contents for the future investment agreement. However, the simplicity and generality of the article, as well as the vague term of "progressively liberalize", have also added complexity and difficulty to the investment negotiations.

### *1.2.2 Framework of the Investment Agreement Agreed upon During Early Negotiations*

According to the Framework Agreement, investment negotiations shall commence in 2003.[13] Actually, the negotiations started in June 2003. The China-ASEAN Trade Negotiation Committee Working Group on Investment (TNC-WGI) was established.

Until October 2005, the TNC-WGI has held nine meetings touching upon varied issues. Substantial progress as to the outline of the proposed agreement has been made. In the second meeting, it was agreed that the Framework Agreement on ASEAN Investment Area ("AIA Framework Agreement") would be used as a template for the negotiated investment agreement.[14] The ASEAN Investment Area was initiated in 1995 to promote intra-ASEAN investment flow and enhance ASEAN as an attractive and competitive site for foreign direct investments.[15] The AIA Framework Agreement in 1998 and its Protocol in 2001 constitute legal instruments for investment liberalization among ASEAN countries with the objective of establishing a competitive ASEAN Investment Area containing a more liberal and transparent investment environment, while ensuring the realization of free flow of investments by 2020.[16] This timeframe was later moved up to 2010 by ASEAN members. The AIA Framework Agreement is a comprehensive agreement with comparatively high standards for investment treatment and investment protection. China accepted it as a template for a lack of more suitable one.

In the seventh meeting, it was agreed that the detailed contents of the agreement should include, *inter alia*, the following principles and elements: (1) the definitions of terms such as "investment" and "investor", as well as the scope of coverage and objectives; (2) the liberalization of investments including the opening up of industries, national treatment, MFN treatment and prohibition of performance requirements; (3) protection, facilitation and promotion of investments, including MFN treatment, adequate protection, expropriation, compensation for losses, transfer and

[13] See the China-ASEAN Framework Agreement, Article 8 (2).

[14] *China-ASEAN FTA Factsheet*, available at: <<http://www.mti.gov.sg/public/FTA/frm_FTA_Default.asp?sid=179&cid=1902>> .

[15] See the Framework Agreement on the ASEAN Investment Area, Preamble.

[16] See the Framework Agreement on the ASEAN Investment Area, Article 3.

repatriation of profits, subrogation and transparency; (4) dispute settlement mechanisms including state-to-state and investor-to-state mechanisms; and (5) general provisions including safeguard measures, general exceptions, institutional arrangements, consultations, relations with other agreements, modification of schedules, annexes and action plans, amendments, entry into force, duration and termination, and programs and action plans. These elements can be categorized into substantive provisions (investment promotion and facilitation, investment protection and investment liberalization—the three pillars of investment agreement), procedural provisions (dispute settlement mechanisms) and general provisions, among which the substantive provisions constitute the core of the agreement. As a result, the substantive provisions are the focus of the investment negotiations.

With regard to rules for investment promotion and facilitation, and investment protection, there are few problems for both China and ASEAN since the BITs between them have provided a common and sound legal foundation. The main function of most BITs in the world (except for the BITs signed by the US and Canada) is to provide promotion and protection to foreign investors.[17] So China and ASEAN can easily and simply transplant the main relevant rules of the BITs between them into the proposed investment agreement with minor adjustments.

Therefore, the crucial problem between China and ASEAN lied in investment liberalization which is not covered by the BITs between them. The investment liberalization issue was debated from the very beginning and had led to deadlock for some years.

## 1.3 Crucial Substantive Controversies Over Investment Liberalization

At the beginning of the negotiations, China was not willing to discuss liberalization while ASEAN insisted on this. Later on, China compromised on this. During early negotiations, China and ASEAN disagreed over the necessity of investment liberalization, and a regime for it. Specific issues related to investment liberalization include the definition of "investor" and "investment", market access (opening up of industries), national treatment and pre-establishment national treatment, etc.

### *1.3.1 Main Reasons for These Substantive Controversies*

There are two main reasons for the conflict over investment liberalization between China and ASEAN. The first concerns the international environment and the second one concerns the specific situation between China and ASEAN.

---

[17] In the last decade, the United States and Canada have strongly advocated investment liberalization through BITs. Therefore, the BITs signed by them contain rules regarding investment liberalization.

The first reason is that investment liberalization per se is a newly contentious global issue. Traditionally, BITs focused on investment promotion and protection. However, for the past two decades the US has strongly advocated free movement of capital flows. From the beginning, many countries, especially developing nations, have objected to investment liberalization. Today only BITs signed by the US and Canada cover investment liberalization, and very limited regional agreements of free trade areas such as NAFTA (both the US and Canada are parties to it) have similar provisions. ASEAN countries have partially accepted investment liberalization in the AIA Framework Agreement but this is strictly limited to ASEAN countries. In the WTO framework, most developing countries including India, China, Malaysia, Indonesia, Thailand and Philippines—the latter four countries are ASEAN members—are strongly opposed to it.[18] China has never accepted it in either her national laws or regulations, or the BITs.

Although ASEAN as a whole opposes investment liberalization in an international arena, they insisted on it in the China-ASEAN Free Trade Area. They reasoned that investment liberalization in a limited area is acceptable, and their ultimate purpose in establishing CAFTA is the opening up of the Chinese market.[19] For China, this is her first time to negotiate liberalization in a multilateral investment agreement. Her hesitation, prudence and caution are quite understandable.

The second reason for the conflict between China and ASEAN over investment liberalization is that the Framework Agreement itself is ambiguous and uses vague language, namely "progressively liberalize the investment regime".[20] This vague language has led to different understandings as to what "progressively liberalize the investment regime" means and how to "progressively liberalize the investment regime". In China's opinion, "progressively liberalize the investment regime" does not necessarily mean investment liberalization. Further, the focus of "progressively liberalize the investment regime" should be "progressively" which means gradual, not immediate liberalization. In contrast, ASEAN has insisted that investment liberalization is a clear target of the future investment agreement.[21]

---

[18] For the position of developing countries, see WTO (2002-3), p. 21. For the positions of Malaysia, Indonesia, Thailand and Philippines, see WTO (2002-1).

[19] This purpose was first addressed in *Forging Closer ASEAN-China Economic Relations in the Twenty-first Century*: A Report Submitted by the ASEAN-China Expert Group on Economic Cooperation, October 2001, p. 12, available at the ASEAN Secretariat website. In the 6th TNC-WGI meeting, ASEAN made it clearer.

[20] See the China-ASEAN Framework Agreement, Article 5(a).

[21] The debate on "progressively liberalize the investment regime" was addressed in the 5th TNC-WGI meeting. Relevant meeting report is confidential.

### *1.3.2 Substantive Arguments on Investment Liberalization of the Two Parties*

Investment liberalization is the key issue in the investment negotiations between China and the ASEAN countries. Different aspects of investment liberalization have been debated during different TNC-WGI meetings. All the debates may be categorized into three main arguments, i.e., whether it is necessary to cover investment liberalization in the future investment agreement, whether it is feasible and practicable to realize investment liberalization, and how to address progressive liberalization in the future investment agreement. Substantial progress has been made—though very slowly—from the necessity debate to probability debate and then to the modality debate. The current deadlock is on the modalities of progressive investment liberalization. The past experience of the TNC-WGI meetings in consensus-building regarding progressive liberalization shows that it is very likely for the two sides to work out creative but acceptable and appropriate ways to settle the modality controversies over liberalization.

The first argument focused on the necessity of covering investment liberalization in the future investment agreement.[22] China contended that the future investment agreement should only cover investment facilitation and investment protection but exclude investment liberalization for two reasons. The first reason is that the flows of investment between China and ASEAN are comparatively small. The second reason is that investment liberalization should be carefully dealt with since the Asian Financial Crisis among ASEAN countries in 1997 led people to cautiously and thoughtfully revisit the significance of foreign investment on their national economies. In contrast, ASEAN insisted that investment liberalization is an important element for the future agreement, because its purpose in establishing CAFTA is to open up Chinese industries for investment. ASEAN argued that if liberalization were not included, there was no need to negotiate a separate investment protection agreement because the existing ten BITs between China and ASEAN countries are enough to promote and protect investments. ASEAN further contended that investment liberalization will increase mutual investment and attract investment from other countries. As to the lessons of the Asian Financial Crisis, ASEAN contended that the real reason for the crisis was the lack of control on short-term foreign investment. Foreign direct investment was not the reason. Moreover, the goal of the CAFTA investment regime is to promote direct investment in the free trade area.

The second argument focused on the feasibility and practicability of investment liberalization.[23] During these negotiations, China enumerated several current constraints and difficulties. The first is that China is in economic transition, and the adjustment of her domestic industries has involved serious difficulties. The second is that China's current different registration systems for foreign-invested enterprises and

[22] Contentions of both China and ASEAN as to this necessity argument were expressed in the 5th TNC-WGI meeting. Relevant meeting report is confidential.

[23] Contentions of both China and ASEAN as to this probability argument were addressed in the 5th and 6th TNC-WGI meetings. Relevant meeting reports are confidential.

domestic enterprises block the conferment of pre-establishment national treatment (national treatment at the market access phase). In China, foreign-invested enterprises can be set up only with approval from the government while domestic enterprises can be set up by registration. If the approval system for the setting up of foreign-invested enterprises is not changed, national treatment in the pre-establishment phase cannot be realized. Therefore, China insisted that national treatment in the investment agreement should be limited to national treatment in the post-establishment phase. As to the difficulties faced by China's industrial adjustment, ASEAN is of the opinion that the inflows of foreign investment created by the CAFTA investment regime will ameliorate the industrial adjustment of both China and ASEAN.

After several TNC-WGI meetings and negotiations, China finally agreed to cover investment liberalization in the future agreement, with the pre-condition of progressive liberalization.

Therefore, the third argument focused on approaches and modalities to be employed to address progressive liberalization in the prospective investment agreement. ASEAN insisted on a negative approach (also called "top-down" approach) while China only agreed to a positive approach (also called "bottom-up" approach).[24] ASEAN also suggested that the principle of "standstill, rollback and no backtracking" be adopted by the investment agreement so as to progressively realize the target of investment liberalization.[25]

### 1.3.3 Specific Issues Related to Investment Liberalization

In the author's opinion, investment liberalization should be handled judiciously instead of being restricted. In the global context, it is not prudent to realize full liberalization for developing countries. But in certain specific areas, such as the ASEAN Investment Area or CAFTA, limited liberalization will benefit the economic development of contracting parties. For both China and ASEAN countries, immediate and full investment liberalization is not likely to be realized currently, but since the target of CAFTA is to be established by 2010, there is enough time for gradual and progressive liberalization.

The problems and difficulties of liberalization raised by China are reasonable but not irresolvable. It is true that the flows of investment between China and ASEAN are comparatively small, since the sources of FDI for both sides are Japan, the US, Europe, etc. However, there is great potential for the fast increase of flows between China and ASEAN for the reason that China is encouraging her private enterprises to invest abroad with the "Going out" policy. Moreover, the establishment of CAFTA

[24] The negative or positive modality issue was heatedly discussed in the 7th TNC-WGI meeting. The following two TNC-WGI meetings focused on the modality argument again without any result. Relevant meeting reports are confidential.

[25] This principle was suggested by ASEAN in the 5th TNC-WGI meeting.

with free investment will not only attract investment among the contracting parties, but attract FDI from outside the contracting parties.

With regard to the current structural difficulties in China's domestic laws, possible and sound ways might be worked out to change the situation. For example, when China entered the WTO, she undertook seemingly burdensome commitments with regard to investment at that time. However, her inconsistent laws and regulations concerning investment have since been abolished or changed. By the same token, China's now seemingly inconsistent investment provisions with the proposed investment liberalization can be overcome in the near future. Moreover, experience shows that once China agrees to undertake certain international obligations, she will make every effort to fulfill them. There will not be an exception for the CAFTA investment agreement to be signed by the two parties.

The deadlock of China-ASEAN investment negotiations thus is caused by the modality debate as how to gradually liberalize investment. This debate should be resolvable because in international agreement negotiations, compromise is necessary. The successful experiences of investment multilateral agreements like MIGA Convention[26] and ICSID Convention[27] show that compromise among different parties is an essential element.

Because the two sides disagreed on progressive investment liberalization, many related issues could not be resolved, e.g., the definition of "investor" and "investment", market access (opening up of industries), national treatment and pre-establishment national treatment, etc. Therefore, these specific issues should be addressed.

## 1.4 Suggested Approaches for Specific Issues with Regard to Investment Liberalization and the Final Concluded Provisions in the Investment Agreement

In this part, the author suggests provisions regarding liberalization-related issues, specifically definitions for "investor" and "investment", market access (opening up of industries), national treatment and pre-establishment national treatment in order to resolve the discrepancies between China and ASEAN on the investment liberalization. These suggestions are based on a review of general practice in international investment agreements, and a comparison of the practice of both ASEAN and China. The author believes that an investment agreement could be successfully concluded. In fact, the Investment Agreement was finally concluded in August 2009, and the China-ASEAN FTA was officially established in 2010, as estimated.

[26] The full title of the MIGA Convention is "the Convention Establishing the Multilateral Investment Guarantee Agency" which was signed in 1985.

[27] The full title of the ICSID Convention is "the Convention on the Settlement of Investment Disputes between States and Nationals of Other States" which was signed in 1965.

### 1.4.1 Methodologies

Firstly, keeping the objectives and principles stated in the CAFTA Framework Agreement in mind will help overcome obstacles and difficulties in the negotiations.

Secondly, relevant specific provisions in some existing legal investment instruments between developing countries (specifically by either China or ASEAN) can be referred to as examples for the proposed CAFTA investment agreement. These instruments include the BITs between China and ASEAN countries, by China or ASEAN with other countries, and between other main developing countries, the AIA Framework Agreement, the ASEAN Agreement for the Promotion and Protection of Investment (1987 ASEAN Agreement),[28] and the free trade agreements concluded between developing countries as well.

Thirdly, when discussing and drafting the relevant specific provisions for the future CAFTA investment agreement, the broad context must be considered. For example, positions of developing countries in the debates over investment liberalization in the WTO framework, in the regional and bilateral investment agreements between developing and developed countries, should be taken into account.

Fourthly, successful experience of the "compromise" principle in concluding international investment agreements can be a guiding principle for the CAFTA investment agreement. The above-mentioned ICSID and MIGA conventions, as well as the BITs between China and ASEAN countries, were concluded on the basis of compromise. To be specific, differing opinions of different countries and the specific requirements of individual countries can be skillfully addressed and dealt with during relevant negotiations.

Fifthly, interests of home and host countries—including the issue of flow of funds—should be taken into account in a balanced manner when drafting the definition and other treatment standards.[29]

Sixthly, since the CAFTA is a free trade area between developing countries, and can be regarded as an experimental or trial model, China should make some concessions in agreeing upon a certain degree of investment liberalization. But there are two conditions. The first is that the liberalization obligation does not exceed what China can bear. The second is that an exception clause of MFN treatment as to the liberalization obligation should be included in the investment agreement so that the liberalization obligation does not apply to other foreign investors or investment.

[28] The full title of the Agreement is "Agreement among the Government of Brunei Darussalam, the Republic of Indonesia, Malaysia, the Republic of the Philippines, the Republic of Singapore and the Kingdom of Thailand for the Promotion and Protection of Investments". The title of the Agreement was amended to "The ASEAN Agreement for the Promotion and Protection of Investments" by the 1996 Protocol. This Agreement was acceded to by Vietnam, Myanmar, Cambodia and Laos when they became members of ASEAN.

[29] WTO Report (2002-3), p. 3.

### *1.4.2 Definition of "Investor"*

The definition of investor is directly related to investment liberalization. The scope of investor helps to delimit the boundary of the investment agreement, thus the broader the definition of investor, the broader the scope of the investment agreement, and more people are qualified to invest abroad.

Generally speaking, in international investment agreements, "investor" is defined to cover both natural persons and artificial or legal persons (or judicial persons) or called "companies" or "entities" in general,[30] with the condition that they have the nationality of one of the contracting states. The nationality of natural persons is determined by reference to the domestic law of the parties concerned that could be called nationals or citizens. Most countries consider that permanent residents should not be included in the definition.[31] The nationality of entities can be determined according to three different criteria, including the place of incorporation or constitution, the location of the seat (or the principal place of business) and the nationality of ownership or control.[32] Some treaties combine the criteria of place of incorporation and the location of the seat together,[33] and some other treaties require the three criteria be met at the same time.[34] Such qualifications were employed in part to prevent companies from setting up "mail-box" operations in order to benefit from an investment agreement.[35]

In practice, "investor" is sometimes strictly qualified according to the country's degree of economic development or to serve the country's specific economic target. China used to have a narrow scope of investor in its BITs. With regard to natural persons, not all of them with Chinese nationality are qualified to be investors in the BITs. For example, in her BIT with Sweden, only those Chinese natural persons with authorization to make an investment from the government are qualified investors. By the same token, not all legal persons (not to mention other economic entities without legal status) with incorporation, constitution and location are qualified. Other elements such as "be entitled to undertake activities of economic cooperation with foreign countries" or "have the legal capacity to invest abroad" are used to restrict the scope of investors.[36] However, in the BITs between China and ASEAN countries, "investor" requires fewer qualifications.

---

[30] See UNCTAD (1998), p. 37; see also UNCTAD (1999-2), p. 32.

[31] Some countries such as the United States and Canada insist that permanent residents should be included in the definition of investor.

[32] See UNCTAD (1998), p. 39.

[33] Both China and ASEAN have such practice. One example is the BIT between China and France. Another example is Art. I(2) of the ASEAN Agreement for the Promotion and Protection of Investments.

[34] One example is Art. 1 of the Charter on a Regime of Multinational Industrial Enterprises in the Preferential Trade Area for Eastern and Southern African States. See *Scope and Definition*, United Nations, New York and Geneva, 1999, p. 40.

[35] WTO (2002-3), p. 6.

[36] For examples, please refer to the BITs between China and Romania, and between China and Sweden, respectively.

For ASEAN, "investor" is also confined to some qualifications. Since the purpose of the AIA Framework Agreement is to liberalize investment among ASEAN countries, ASEAN prefers to have a comparatively narrower definition of investor. The AIA Framework Agreement differentiates between the ASEAN investor and non-ASEAN investor with respect to national treatment and industries open to foreign investment.[37] ASEAN investors cover the nationals of a member state and juridical persons of a member state.[38] For both natural persons and juridical persons to be investors, the criterion of nationality is adopted along with the qualifications of "making an investment in another member state" and minimum equity requirement.[39] But in the ASEAN Agreement for the Promotion and Protection of Investments, nationals as investors do not have these qualifications.

The above analysis and comparison show that ASEAN and China did not have substantial differences with respect to the definition of "investor" (including nationals and companies) in past years.

However, with the gradual establishment of the market economy in China, her quick economic development and the "Going out" strategy as well, China is encouraging her natural persons and economic entities to invest abroad. Therefore, less and less qualifications are attached to investors in respect of China in her new BIT model and in the BITs recently signed with other countries.

In the current situation, during the CAFTA investment negotiations, China suggests defining "investor" as (a) natural persons who have nationality of a contracting party in accordance with the laws of that contracting party, and (b) economic entities including companies, corporations, associations, partnerships and other organizations incorporated and constituted under the laws and regulations of a contracting party and having their seats in that contracting party, irrespective of whether or not for profit and whether their liabilities are limited or not.[40] This proposed definition was drafted by reference to the BITs and FTAs concluded by the US and EU which represent the international trend with regard to the definition of "investor". This definition is slightly broader than that in the BITs by China and ASEAN countries, and the ASEAN investment instruments. Therefore, it should be acceptable for both sides. Also, the wording of the definition can be subject to further discussion.

Whether "potential investors" should be covered by the future investment agreement is not stated by China's proposed definition. This question is closely related to the issue of pre-establishment treatment which will be specifically discussed in Part III. D. If pre-establishment treatment is conferred, an agreement's provisions apply to the process of investing—before and after the point in time at which an investment

---

[37] See the Framework Agreement on the ASEAN Investment Area, Article 4 (b) (c).

[38] See the Framework Agreement on the ASEAN Investment Area, Article 1.

[39] See the Framework Agreement on the ASEAN Investment Area, Article 1. This Article states that juridical person means any legal entity, including any corporation, trust, partnership, joint venture, sole proprietorship or association.

[40] See the China-ASEAN Framework Agreement on Investment (draft proposal by China), Article 1(3).

was made—as well as during the life of an investment, and the potential investors should be covered in the definition of investor. If pre-establishment treatment is not accorded, the agreement's provisions are limited to regulating the actual entry of investment, without conferring any rights to either potential investors or investors seeking entry.[41]

Eventually, in the finally concluded Agreement on Investment, the definition of investor is quite broad. The Agreement provides that "investor of a Party" means a natural person of a Party or a juridical person of a Party that is making or has made an investment in the territories of the other Parties.[42] "Natural person" is broad to cover not only national or citizen of a Contracting Party, but also permanent resident of a Contracting Party.[43] "Juridical person" is also broad to mean any legal entity duly constituted or otherwise organized under the applicable law of a Party, whether for profit or otherwise, and whether privately-owned or governmentally-owned, and engaged in substantive business operations in the territory of that Party, including any corporation, trust, partnership, joint venture, sole proprietorship or association.[44] The definition of investor does not cover potential investors who plans to make an investment, but it seems to cover investors seeking entry by using the term "is making". But actually, not all investors seeking entry is covered. The Agreement on Investment uses a footnote to indicate that the phrase "is making" shall refer only to Article 5 (Most-Favored-Nation Treatment) and Article 10 (Transfers and Repatriation of Profits).[45]

### *1.4.3 Definition of "Investment"*

Since the definition of investment interacts with other substantive provisions like national treatment and the investor-state dispute settlement mechanism, it plays an important role in shaping any overall investment framework,[46] and thus its importance and significance are obvious.[47] Therefore, when discussing this definition, not only articles concerning this definition should be considered, but also other articles as well. However, so far there is no generally accepted definition of "investment".[48]

---

[41] WTO (2002-3), p. 6.

[42] Article 1.1.e of the Agreement on Investment.

[43] Article 1.1.i of the Agreement on Investment provides that "natural person of a Party" means any natural person possessing the nationality or citizenship of, or right of permanent residence in the Party in accordance with its laws and regulations.

[44] Article 1.1.f of the Agreement on Investment.

[45] Footnote 3 of the Agreement on Investment.

[46] WTO (2002-3), p. 3.

[47] For further information, please refer to Huiping Chen (2002), p. 34.

[48] UNCTAD (1998), p. 32.

The definition of investment is directly related to investment liberalization. For purposes of investment liberalization, a comparatively narrowly defined "investment" is normally preferred, while for purposes of investment protection, a broadly defined "investment" is preferred. The former is called the "narrow approach" while the latter is called the "broad approach". The narrow approach is the enterprise-based or transaction-based definition focused on FDI. The broad approach is the asset-based definition with options for including or excluding various categories of investment[49]; portfolio investment is sometimes included. Most bilateral investment treaties adopt the broad approach because a broad definition will provide comprehensive, rules-based protection and guarantee high standards of treatment for all categories of foreign investment, thereby encouraging increased international investment flows and creating more efficient international capital markets.[50] However, since a broad definition of investment will entail the liberalization of all forms of capital movement, and increase the risk of destabilizing short-term flows,[51] a narrow definition is normally adopted by investment liberalization-oriented agreements. Further, FDI is a more stable form of foreign capital flow than portfolio investment at the post-establishment stage, so it is possible for developing countries to allow the free movement of FDI at the post-establishment stage. For the unstable portfolio investment, in particular speculative short-term capital flows, developing countries want to maintain the right to regulate instead of free movement.

Whether an investment agreement adopts a broad or narrow definition depends on the nature of the agreement, for example, for investment liberalization or investment protection. Since modern investment agreements cover both investment liberalization and investment protection, which approach to adopt is problematic. If the narrow definition is adopted, this definition can be used throughout the whole agreement and make it unnecessary to further delineate any agreement's scope and coverage through operative provisions.[52] If a broad definition is adopted, flexibility is needed. Flexibility could be achieved through an agreement's substantive provisions and the structure of its specific commitments including provisions dealing with pre-establishment commitments.[53] Recently, a compromised hybrid approach has been suggested. This approach uses different definitions for the pre-establishment and post-establishment stages of investment—a narrow approach for market access and investment liberalization (pre-establishment), covering FDI only, and a broad approach, covering a wide range of assets, for the protection of investment once it is established locally (post-establishment).[54]

In terms of ASEAN, a broad definition was employed in the 1987 ASEAN Agreement,[55] because its purpose was investment promotion and protection. In

49 WTO (2002-3), p. 3.

50 WTO (2002-3), p. 4.

51 WTO (2002-3), p. 4.

52 WTO (2002-3), p. 3.

53 WTO (2002-3), p. 5.

54 WTO (2002-3), p. 5.

55 See the 1987 ASEAN Agreement, Article I.3.

contrast, a narrow definition was adopted in the AIA Framework Agreement covering only FDI and excluding portfolio investments and matters relating to investments covered by other ASEAN Agreements, such as the ASEAN Framework Agreement on Services,[56] the reason being that AIA Agreement is for the liberalization of investment.

China has adopted a broad asset-based definition in her BITs with some qualifications and limitations. Until 2005, she has not yet signed any liberalization-oriented investment agreement and thus does not have a mature narrow definition.

China also suggests the hybrid approach to define investment in the future investment agreement with ASEAN. This definition distinguishes the situations of pre-establishment and post-establishment. For admission and establishment, a narrow definition of investment is adopted to cover only FDI excluding portfolio investment and matters relating to investment covered by other ASEAN-China agreements such as the service agreement. The wording of the definition is borrowed almost directly from the corresponding article of the AIA Agreement. Therefore, we can see China is willing to compromise by incorporating acceptable AIA Agreement provisions into the prospective investment agreement. For post-establishment investment treatment and protection, a broad investment is adopted to cover almost every kind of asset.

In the author's opinion, the hybrid approach of investment is suitable for the agreement which focuses on both investment protection and liberalization.

Eventually, in the final concluded Agreement on Investment, a broad asset-based definition of investment is adopted, with an open-ended list of elaboration. "Investment" means every kind of asset invested by the investors of a Party in accordance with the relevant laws, regulations and policies of another Party in the territory of the latter including, but not limited to, the following:

(i) movable and immovable property and any other property rights such as mortgages, liens or pledges;
(ii) shares, stocks and debentures of juridical persons or interests in the property of such juridical persons;
(iii) intellectual property rights, including rights with respect to copyrights, patents and utility models, industrial designs, trademarks and service marks, geographical indications, layout designs of integrated circuits, trade names, trade secrets, technical processes, know-how and goodwill;
(iv) business concessions conferred by law, or under contract, including concessions to search for, cultivate, extract or exploit natural resources; and
(v) claims to money or to any performance having financial value.

Further, returns that are invested are also treated as investments.[57]

56 See the Framework Agreement on the ASEAN Investment Area, Article 2.

57 The Agreement on Investment, Article 1.1.d.

### 1.4.4 Opening up of Industries

During investment negotiations, ASEAN insisted that China open up industries for foreign investment and that the pre-establishment national treatment be conferred to foreign investors and investment.[58] The opening up issue and the pre-establishment national treatment are closely related. The opening up of industries concerns the admission/entry or market access of foreign investment, or the rights of establishment. The pre-establishment treatment refers to the laws and regulations of a host country that govern the entry of foreign investment. These laws and regulations determine whether admission or market access is possible, and if so, on what terms and conditions foreign investment can be established locally. For example, they will decide whether foreign investment is permitted only in certain sectors and industries, or economy-wide.[59]

However, there are differences between these two issues. And further, because pre-establishment is directly related to national treatment, it will be further discussed in the next part with the issue of national treatment. This part will discuss the opening up of industries.

There is no rule of customary international law requiring a state to open her industries and to allow entry by foreign investment. Therefore, the host state has the right to decide whether her industries are open to foreign investors and investment, and what industries to open. In international investment treaties, some countries do agree to open part or all of their industries to foreign investment. For example, the US requires opening up of industries in the BITs with her agreement partners. However, the agreement to open up industries is subject to exceptions or limitations. Therefore, in practice, the concept of an unconditional right of entry does not exist.[60]

When negotiating comprehensive investment rules in the framework of the WTO, great debate exists between developing and developed countries as to the entry of foreign investment. It is generally agreed that from a developing country perspective, creating a right of entry for foreign investors is inappropriate and unnecessary.[61] However, in some economic integration agreements which aim for deep and ultimately complete integration among parties, a narrower concept of right of establishment is used.[62]

In those investment agreements agreeing upon the right of establishment, two different approaches can be found to deal with the opening up of industries: one is the positive list approach—open up some specific industries and sectors at the outset and then extend to more industries and sectors. The other is the negative list approach—open up all industries as a general principle but with exclusions, exceptions and restrictions, and then gradually reduce or eliminate these exceptions and restrictions.

[58] The opening up of industries and the pre-establishment national treatment were heatedly discussed in the 5th and 6th TNC-WGI meetings. Relevant meeting reports are confidential.

[59] WTO (2002-2), p. 1.

[60] WTO (2002-2), p. 3.

[61] Howard Mann et al. (2005), p. 9.

[62] WTO (2002-2), p. 3.

The degree of liberalization of investment with respect to the negative list approach is much higher than that with respect to the positive list approach. Therefore, the state's commitments under the negative list approach are much stronger than those under the positive list approach.

The ASEAN countries adopted the negative list approach in the AIA Framework Agreement at the beginning but later on changed to the positive list approach. In 1998, the AIA Agreement stipulates that all industries are open to all ASEAN investors[63] and subject to a negative list of exceptions which are listed in the Temporary Exclusion List and Sensitive List.[64] However, later practice proved that this economic-wide opening up was too ambitious, hasty and impractical. In 2001, a Protocol was signed to use a positive list approach to open only five industries to foreign investment, i.e., manufacturing, agriculture, forestry, fisheries, and mining and quarrying.[65]

China, being a developing country, never promised the entry of foreign investment in her BITs with other countries by 2005. But China has undertaken some international obligations to open up certain service sectors according to her WTO commitments (to be specific, the GATS commitments). In general, the entry of foreign investment is dealt with in China's domestic laws and regulations. According to the new Regulation on Guiding Foreign Investment in 2002 and the fourth version of the Industrial Catalogue for Guiding Foreign Investment, all industries and sectors related to foreign investment projects are divided into four categories: encouraged sectors, restricted sectors, forbidden sectors and permitted sectors. Only the encouraged sectors, restricted sectors and permitted sectors are open to foreign investment but nevertheless subject to many conditions and national approval by competent authorities. These sectors cover manufacturing, service and agriculture.

During negotiations, ASEAN demanded the opening up of all industries while China only agreed to opening up the manufacturing sector. ASEAN wants China's doors open for ASEAN investors. However, China is negotiating for its service sector in a separate agreement and the agriculture sector is a complicated sector which could not even be satisfactorily tackled in the WTO. Therefore, China made a great concession by agreeing to open up her manufacturing sector on the basis of the positive list approach. However, ASEAN insisted on the negative list approach.[66]

In the author's opinion, the positive list approach should be acceptable for both China and ASEAN. On the one hand, normally the opening up of industries is a progressive process requiring much time (even for developed countries). On the other hand, the positive list approach better fits the reality of both China and ASEAN.

Experience shows that the negotiation process reaching agreement on entry of foreign investment is often long and complicated. The OECD members took more

---

[63] See the Framework Agreement on the ASEAN Investment Area, Article 7(1) (a).

[64] See the Framework Agreement on the ASEAN Investment Area, Article 7(2).

[65] The full title of the Protocol is "the Protocol to Amend the Framework Agreement on the ASEAN Investment Area". The five opening up industries are stipulated in Art. 1(2) of the Protocol.

[66] See the China-ASEAN Framework Agreement on Investment (draft proposal by China), Article 2; the China-ASEAN Framework Agreement on Investment (ASEAN counter-draft proposal), Article 2.

than 20 years to agree on commitments on the right of establishment in the Code of Liberalization of Capital Movements and Current Invisible Operations.[67] When the US was negotiating with Canada for the US-Canada Free Trade Agreement, one of the most difficult issues was that the US sought unfettered access for its investors to the Canadian market but Canada disagreed. Finally, the US gave up.[68] The Multilateral Agreement on Investment (MAI) proposed by OECD failed, one reason being that no agreement could be reached as to the right of establishment.

The ASEAN countries themselves are conservative in respect of the entry of foreign investment in their BITs. ASEAN's experience in the AIA proves that the positive list approach is a practical one for her. If the positive list approach is adopted, China should extend the industries open to foreign investment from manufacturing to agriculture, and they should be broader than those stipulated by the fourth version of the Industrial Catalogue for Guiding Foreign Investment.

### *1.4.5 National Treatment and Pre-Establishment National Treatment*

National treatment means a host country extends to foreign investors treatment that is at least as favorable as the treatment that it accords to national investors in like circumstances.[69] National treatment available at international investment agreements is subject to the domestic rules and regulations of host countries. The host countries preserve their right to make or modify their rules and regulations on foreign investment.[70] National treatment is generally applicable only at the post-establishment stage in almost all international investment agreements.

Applying the right to national treatment in a pre-establishment phase ("pre-establishment national treatment") is rare practice. Nowadays, only the US and Canada insist on pre-establishment national treatment provisions in their bilateral investment treaties.[71] However, in the past, there was disagreement as to this provision even between the two countries. During the Canada-US free trade negotiations, the US sought unfettered access for its investors to the Canadian market at the beginning but failed. The final compromise was that national treatment for US firms is limited to post-establishment.[72]

Other agreements involving pre-establishment national treatment provisions are essentially in the context of regional trading agreements.[73] Examples are NAFTA,

---

[67] Malcolm Bosworth and Leanne Holmes (2003), p. 81.

[68] Michael Hart et al. (1994), p. 382.

[69] UNCTAD (1999-1), p. 1.

[70] WTO (2002), Communication from India (WT/WGTI/W/150).

[71] WTO (2002), Communication from India (WT/WGTI/W/150).

[72] Michael Hart et al. (1994).

[73] WTO (2002), Communication from India (WT/WGTI/W/150).

OECD's Code of Liberalization of Capital Movements and Current Invisible Operations, and the AIA Framework Agreement.

Pre-establishment national treatment accords rights to foreign investors even though they have not yet become economic citizens of the host state.[74] It guarantees, in principle, a very liberal investment regime that can amount to an open-door policy toward foreign investment. Moreover, it places foreign investors on an equal footing with national investors to compete for investment opportunities in the host country.[75] According to UNCTAD, no country has yet found itself in a position to do this.[76]

In the context of investment, the extension of national treatment from the post- to pre-establishment stage has been considered to be a "revolution" by many countries.[77]

The position of developing countries toward pre-establishment national treatment is likely to be rejection.[78] According to one WTO report, developing countries are not in a position to accept pre-establishment treatment as a general commitment.[79] In India's opinion, binding rules on "pre-establishment commitments" will neither be feasible nor necessary. On the contrary, developing countries need to retain the ability to screen and channel FDI in tune with their domestic interests and priorities.[80]

Even in APEC where both China and ASEAN are members, only post-establishment national treatment is accorded. APEC leaders and ministers have committed their economies to create free and open investment by 2010 and 2020. However, since they recognize the diversity existing among APEC economies, the progressive liberalization approach is adopted. Economies may, on a voluntary basis, choose progressively extending national treatment in one or more sectors, or eliminating exceptions to national treatment.[81]

ASEAN countries in a multilateral context (i.e., WTO) have emphasized a need for flexibility of national treatment in a future multilateral investment agreement, particularly with respect to the pre-establishment national treatment.[82] However, in the regional context, they accord pre-establishment national treatment. The AIA Framework Agreement stipulates that national treatment applies to both pre-establishment and post-establishment phases.[83] But exceptions to national treatment are allowed by way of temporary exclusion and sensitive lists, which have to be phased out by 2010 for ASEAN investors and 2020 for non-ASEAN investors in ASEAN-6 countries, with later deadlines for new ASEAN countries. In 2002, in an effort to

[74] Howard Mann and Konrad von Moltke (2005), p. 7.

[75] WTO (2002-2), p. 8.

[76] UNCTAD (1999-1).

[77] This comment was made by Patrick Juillard, which was quoted by an UNCTAD document on national treatment. See WTO (2002), Communication from India (WT/WGTI/W/150).

[78] Howard Mann and Konrad von Moltke (2005), p. 7.

[79] WTO (2002-2), p. 3.

[80] WTO (2002), Communication from India (WT/WGTI/W/150).

[81] APEC, *Options for Investment Liberalization and Business Facilitation to Strengthen the APEC Economies—For Voluntary Inclusion in Individual Action Plans.*

[82] The Swedish National Board of Trade (1999), p. 5.

[83] See the Framework Agreement on the ASEAN Investment Area, Article 7(1) (b).

further improve the investment climate, Brunei, Indonesia, Myanmar, Philippines and Thailand agreed to accelerate the phase-out of the Temporary Exception List for manufacturing by January 2003.[84]

For China, according national treatment to foreign investors is a huge problem, not to mention pre-establishment national treatment. In the past, China did not promise national treatment in the BITs with other countries. In her 2005 Model BIT, national treatment will be accorded but subject to her laws and regulations.[85] However, it is still quite a challenge to confer national treatment to foreign investors because China's unique ownership system (public-owned enterprises, private-owned enterprises and mixed ownership enterprises) allows for different treatment even among domestic investors. Thus, discrepancies in investment policies and practices already exist between and among various governments of different levels and provinces. Under such circumstances, discussions over national treatment and investment liberalization with ASEAN countries remain at bay for China. China has made a concession to accord post-national treatment in the future China-ASEAN Investment Agreement but reserves the right to regulate the entry of foreign investment.

To bridge the gap between China and ASEAN, the two-tier structure proposed by the Swedish National Board of Trade can be referred to as an acceptable model.[86] The two-tier structure was suggested to settle the debate between developed and developing countries on the commitments on pre-establishment and post-establishment national treatment for the future international investment rules in the WTO. This structure suggests that all WTO members accept a base agreement with commitments on post-establishment national treatment, while member country obligations are extended on a voluntary basis to cover national treatment in the pre-establishment phase.[87] Although this structure is designed for a multilateral investment agreement with more than three parties, the core of it, i.e., flexibility and different schemes for pre- and post-establishment, might be borrowed by China and ASEAN to tackle their debate on the pre- and post-establishment national treatment. In the author's opinion, both China and ASEAN should undertake the obligation of according post-establishment national treatment. As to the pre-establishment national treatment, it is up to the choice of either party.

In the following part, the author would like to further discuss the modalities of according post- and pre-establishment national treatment, given that China and ASEAN disagree on the modalities of national treatment as a general obligation.

There are two approaches for national treatment as modalities for the progressive liberalization of investment. One is the negative list approach ("top-down" approach)—list exceptions to the general obligation of national treatment—and the other is the positive list approach ("bottom-up" approach)—list the specific sectors to which national treatment applies. A strength of the positive list approach is that it gives signatories discretion over what to include and when. Politically sensitive

---

[84] Chia Siow Yue (2004), p. 3.

[85] See China's 2005 BIT Model, Article 3.3.

[86] The Swedish National Board of Trade (1999), p. 5.

[87] The Swedish National Board of Trade (1999), p. 5.

areas can be kept outside the scope of the agreement.[88] The negative list approach can automatically include new types of investment while the positive list approach cannot. Some regard it as the weakness of the positive list approach while many regard it as a strong point, depending on the policy choice of relevant countries.

Investment agreement members may reduce or eliminate the industries or measures in the negative list, or broaden the positive list, so as to achieve a progressively higher level of liberalization of investment by periodically entering into successive rounds of negotiations. However, the process of liberalization shall take place with due respect for national policy objectives and the level of development of individual members.[89]

Experience with GATS showed that a positive list approach was preferable when a new area was for the first time the subject of liberalization at a multilateral level.[90] It allowed for selective liberalization of entry and establishment in specific activities under defined conditions, giving countries more control over the liberalization and rule-making process. It also minimized the chances of making unforeseen mistakes in binding entry and establishment rights in key sectors.[91] Therefore, in the context of WTO investment rules negotiations, the positive list approach is suggested to schedule market access commitments and related policy obligations as a realistic way.[92] This way will provide balance between policy discipline and flexibility for developing countries, allow them to undertake commitments commensurate with their individual development needs and circumstances and pursue their national economic and social objectives.[93]

However, the AIA Framework Agreement uses the negative list approach. Specifically speaking, each member country can submit a Temporary List and a Sensitive List to exclude the industries and measures to which national treatment cannot be accorded.[94] The above commitments were not undertaken immediately when the Agreement was signed. Progressive approaches are adopted to realize liberalization of investment. First, national treatment is extended to ASEAN investors by 2010 and to all investors by 2020.[95] Second, the Temporary Exclusion List shall be reviewed every two years and shall be progressively phased out by 2010 by all member states except Vietnam, Laos and Myanmar.[96] This timeframe was accelerated to 2003 by the Protocol.[97] The Sensitive List shall be first reviewed by January 1, 2003, and then reviewed by periodic intervals.[98]

---

[88] Malcolm Bosworth and Leanne Holmes (2003), p. 89.

[89] WTO (2002-2), p. 14.

[90] WTO (2002-2), p. 4.

[91] WTO (2002-2), p. 4.

[92] WTO (2002-2), p. 2.

[93] WTO (2002-2), p. 2.

[94] See the AIA Framework Agreement on the ASEAN Investment Area, Article 7.

[95] See the AIA Framework Agreement on the ASEAN Investment Area, Article 4.

[96] See the AIA Framework Agreement on the ASEAN Investment Area, Articles 7.4 & 7.5.

[97] See the AIA Framework Agreement on the ASEAN Investment Area, Article 2.

[98] See the AIA Framework Agreement on the ASEAN Investment Area, Articles 7.4 & 7.5.

Based on the above analysis, the author suggests that the positive list approach should be acceptable by China and ASEAN whether national treatment applies to post- or pre-establishment phase.

Eventually, in the finally concluded Agreement on Investment, post-establishment national treatment with negative list approach is adopted. The Agreement provides that "Each Party shall, in its territory, accord to investors of another Party and their investments treatment no less favourable than it accords, in like circumstances, to its own investors and their investments with respect to management, conduct, operation, maintenance, use, sale, liquidation, or other forms of disposal of such investments".[99] It further provides that "Article 4 (National Treatment) …… shall not apply to:

(a) any existing or new non-conforming measures maintained or adopted within its territory;

(b) the continuation or amendment of any nonconforming measures referred to in Subparagraph (a)".

It also requires Parties to endeavor to progressively remove the non-conforming measures.[100]

## 1.5 The China-ASEAN Investment Agreement Practice Regarding Investor-State Dispute Settlement

A major feature of the China-ASEAN Investment Agreement regarding dispute settlement is that it allows investors to refer any investment dispute with the host state to international arbitration, including referring to the International Centre for Settlement of Investment Disputes (ICSID), ICSID Additional Facilities, other arbitration institutions or any ad hoc arbitration.[101] This is quite different from many other BITs that China concluded with individual ASEAN states.

After a decade of the signing of the China-ASEAN Investment Agreement, there are two cases that have been brought to international arbitration based on the Agreement. The first case is Qiong Ye and Jianping Yang v. Cambodia[102] brought to ICSID in 2021. The second one is PowerChina and China Railway v. Viet Nam (I)[103] brought to ICSID in 2022. Both cases are still in the arbitration proceedings. Both cases are brought by Chinese investors. The following will provide an overview of the two cases.

---

99 The Agreement on Investment, Article 4.

100 The Agreement on Investment, Article 6.

101 The Agreement on Investment, Article 14.4.

102 Qiong Ye and Jianping Yang v. Kingdom of Cambodia (ICSID Case No. ARB/21/42) https://icsid.worldbank.org/cases/case-database/case-detail?CaseNo=ARB/21/42.

103 PowerChina HuaDong Engineering Corporation and China Railway 18th Bureau Group Company Ltd v. Socialist Republic of Viet Nam (ICSID Case No. ARB(AF)/22/7), (AF)/22/7.

### 1.5.1 Qiong Ye and Jianping Yang V. Cambodia

This is the first arbitration lodged under the 2009 China-ASEAN Investment Agreement. According to IA Reporter's database, it is also the first treaty-based claim brought against Cambodia. There are two main reasons for the Chinese claimants to choose to base the China-ASEAN Investment Agreement to bring the case for arbitration. The first is that this Agreement allows any investment dispute to be referred to international arbitration. In contrast, the China-Cambodia BIT only allows the "dispute involving the amount of compensation for expropriation" be referred to international arbitration.[104] The other reason is that the China-ASEAN Investment Agreement offers better investment treatment to foreign investors. The current dispute is related to expropriation and the breach of other investment treatment.

The case was registered in ICSID on September 1, 2021 by two Chinese nationals Qiong Ye and Jianping Yang (collectively referred as "Claimants"). The dispute is alleged to arise from Cambodia's violation of the China-ASEAN Investment Agreement through the treatment of Claimants' investment in a telecommunications enterprise, although the precise nature of the dispute remains undisclosed. The Claimants appear to be co-directors of a Cambodian (but Chinese-owned) telecoms company, Emaxx Telecom. Emaxx Telecom was reportedly operating a 4G mobile network in Cambodia, reportedly signing a contract with China's Huawei for the construction of additional 4G base stations in eight Cambodian cities in 2014. However, in October of 2020, Cambodia's Ministry of Posts and Telecommunications (MPTC) reportedly revoked Emaxx's mobile service operator license as part of a decision to sanction 17 telecoms operators which had failed to pay income taxes, were inactive or had reported incorrect revenue figures. In March of 2021, the MPTC then reportedly announced that it had granted new licenses to 49 internet service providers—but Emaxx was not on this list. In 2021, the Claimants raised this arbitration proceeding. From January 29, 2024, to February 2, 2024, the Tribunal held a hearing on jurisdiction and the merits in Singapore and the case is still pending.

### 1.5.2 PowerChina and China Railway V. Viet Nam (I)

This is the second arbitration lodged under the 2009 China-ASEAN Investment Agreement. The claimants are two Chinese investors, i.e., PowerChina HuaDong Engineering Corporation and China Railway 18th Bureau Group Company Ltd (collectively referred as "Claimants"). The Claimants also brought a parallel arbitration proceeding to ad hoc arbitration that is administered by ICSID on the basis of China-Viet Nam BIT (1992).[105] The China-Viet Nam BIT only allows the "dispute

[104] China-Cambodia BIT, Article 9.3.

[105] PowerChina HuaDong Engineering Corporation and China Railway 18th Bureau Group Company Ltd v. Socialist Republic of Viet Nam (ICSID Case No. ADM/23/1).

involving the amount of compensation for expropriation" be referred to international arbitration.[106]

The case was registered in ICSID (using ICSID Additional Facility) on November 29, 2022. The Tribunal was constituted on April 26, 2023. By April 15, 2024, the Tribunal has issued three Procedural Orders. The Respondent requested to address the objections to jurisdiction as a preliminary question, but as a result, the objections to jurisdiction are joined to the merits of the dispute. The case is still pending now. No other details of the case are available so far.

## References

Chia Siow Yue (2004) China-ASEAN free trade area, paper for presentation at the AEP Conference, Hong Kong, April 12-13

China-ASEAN Framework Agreement

Howard Mann, Konrad von Moltke (2005) A Southern Agenda on Investment? Promoting Development with Balanced Rights and Obligations for Investors, Host States and Home States, IISD

Howard Mann, Konrad von Moltke, Luke Eric Peterson, Aaron Cosbey (2005) IISD model international agreement on investment for sustainable development: Negotiators' handbook, April

Huiping Chen (2002) OECD's multilateral agreement on investment: a Chinese perspective. Kluwer Law International

Malcolm Bosworth, Leanne Holmes (2003) Pre-establishment commitments in a multilateral investment agreement—the GATS approach. In International Investment Instruments and Their Legal Interpretations, APEC

Michael Hart, Bill Dymond, Colin Robertson (1994) Decision at midnight: inside the Canada-US free-trade negotiations. UBC Press

The Swedish National Board of Trade (1999) WTO: rules on investment in a new round, Report of May 3 1999

UNCTAD (1998) Bilateral investment treaties in the mid-1990s. United Nations, New York and Geneva

UNCTAD (1999-1) National treatment. United Nations, New York and Geneva

UNCTAD (1999-2) Scope and definition. United Nations, New York and Geneva

WTO (2002-1), Working Group on the Relationship between Trade and Investment, Report on the Meeting Held on 3–5 July 2002: Note by the Secretariat (WT/WGTI/M/18)

WTO (2002-2), Working Group on the Relationship between Trade and Investment, Modalities for Pre-establishment Commitments Based on A GATS-type, Positive List Approach (WT/WGTI/W/120)

WTO (2002-3), Report of the Working Group on the Relationship between Trade and Investment to the General Council (WT/WGTI/6)

---

[106] China-Viet Nam BIT, Article 8.3.

# Chapter 2
# The China-Korea International Investment Agreements Practice

International investment agreements (IIAs) include not only bilateral investment treaties, but also plural investment agreements, investment chapter in a free trade agreement, etc. China has concluded several IIAs with Korea including the China-Korea bilateral investment treaty (BIT) 1992, China-Korea BIT 2007, China-Japan-Korea Trilateral Investment Agreement (2012), the investment chapter of the China-Korea Free Trade Agreement (2015), as well as the Investment Chapter of the RECP (2020). All these IIAs contribute to the mutual investment between China and Korea. Further, both China and Korea were challenged by an investor from the other country before ICSID on the basis of the 2007 China-Korea BIT.

This chapter will review the China-Korea IIAs as well as the ISDS cases.

## 2.1 The 1992 China-Korea BIT

China signed the first BIT with Korea on September 30, 1992, (1992 China-Korea BIT) which came into force as of December 4, 1992.

This part will first briefly examine the background of the signing of the BIT, that is, the mutual investment situation between China and Korea before the 1992 China-Korea BIT. Korea started to attract foreign direct investment ever since 1962 but the scale of inward investment was very small. In 1970s, the Korean Government established free export areas and set priority for export-oriented heavy industry. In 1980s, the Korean Government changed its economic development strategy and took measures to attract FDI and to liberalize domestic economy. The policy of absorbing foreign investment to develop domestic economy has made Korea one of the Four Asian Dragons. This set a successful example for China which started the Opening Up policy at the end of 1970s.

However, the foreign direct investment from Korea to China before 1992 was in small scale and sort of experimental. Most Korean investment projects in China were

 
H. Chen, *China's Practice in International Investment Law*, Modern China and International Economic Law, https://doi.org/10.1007/978-981-96-5016-3_2

made via the institutions in Hong Kong or other places. On the other hand, there was almost no Chinese company that invested in Korea in that same period.

The main reasons lied in two aspects: firstly, China and Korea had not yet established diplomatic relations which made folk communication and mutual investment more difficult. Secondly, before 1992, the Korean Government's policy was focusing on absorbing foreign investment to develop its own economy, rather than encouraging outward investment, before it became a strong economy power.

When the Chinese Government and Korean Government established the official diplomatic relations on August 24, 1992, the BIT between China and Korea was signed on September 30, 1992, as a result. Before the signature of an official China-Korea BIT, an investment agreement was signed by civil organizations of the two countries. That is, the Agreement on the Encouragement and Reciprocal Protection of Investments between the China Chamber of International Commerce and the Korea Trade Promotion Corporation was signed on May 2, 1992. Such a civil agreement expired when the official BIT came into effect on December 4, 1992.

This part will then examine the characteristics of the 1992 China-Korea BIT. Entering into 1990s, China has accumulated enough experience in absorbing foreign investment, formulating laws and regulations on foreign investment, and concluding BITs with other countries. Moreover, China's economy has developed into a relatively mature and increasing stage. As a consequence, the 1992 China-Korea BIT is more open compared to the BITs China concluded with other countries in 1980s.

The 1992 BIT confers national treatment to investors (Art. 3.2). Both national treatment and MFN treatment apply to domestic procedures including access to the courts of justice and administrative tribunals and authorities. Disputes concerning expropriation and the amount of expropriation should be submitted to domestic courts or administrative tribunal or authorities for review (Art. 5.5), and only dispute concerning the amount of compensation may be submitted to the World Bank's International Center for Settlement of Investment Disputes (ICSID) for conciliation or arbitration (Art. 9.3). Any other dispute may be submitted to ICSID for arbitration on the basis of mutual agreement reached by the two disputing parties.

The 1992 China-Korea BIT had great impact on mutual investment between China and Korea. The 1992 BIT greatly promoted the inward investment to China from Korea. During 1985 to 1992, the average amount of investment projects by Korean enterprises in China was only USD 0.66 million. However, in 1996, the amount reached USD 2.67 million.[1] Since 1994, large group companies in Korea carried out large-scale investments in China. Ever since 2002, Korea has become the fourth biggest home country of foreign investment in China. After comparison, it is clear that there is more investment from Korea to China than from China to Korea. Therefore, we can say the investment has the characteristic of "one street". Korean investment in China contributed a lot to the foster of China's economy.

[1] Guan Wang (2006).

## 2.2 The 2007 Updated China-Korea BIT

15 years later, in 2007, China and Korea updated their BIT into the new BIT (2007 China-Korea BIT) which came into force as of December 1, 2007.

This part will briefly examine the economic background of the update. During 1990s, Korea has developed into a developed economy and joined the OECD. After the 1997 Asian Financial Crisis, Korea loosed the limits on the fields opened to foreign investment, and carried out cross board liberalization and encouraging policy. In addition to absorbing foreign investment, Korea also encourages outward investment to escalate its industries. Due to the facts that China and Korea are adjacent countries that share similar cultures, and their economy has complementary characteristics, China becomes the ideal target country of Korea's outward investment.

On the part of China, with China's quick economic development and its heavy foreign exchange reserves, China seriously carried out the new policy of "Going Abroad" as of early 2000s. For many Chinese companies, Korea is an ideal place to invest, in addition to those South-East Asian countries.

Although China was late to attract foreign investment compared to Korea, after around thirty years of development, the two countries gradually come to the convergence: both stress the absorbing of high quality foreign investment and encouraging outward investment.

In 2005, China-Korea Economic Cooperation Forum was held. This arose new round of mutual investment. The two countries decided to expand cooperation fields, enlarge cooperation scale, create new cooperation modes, strengthen cooperation basis, enhance cooperation level and fasten cooperation pace.

This part will then briefly examine the characteristics of the 2007 updated China-Korea BIT. After 15 years of successful operation of the 1992 BIT, the two governments, considering the new development of each country's, and to advance with the times, decided to update the 1992 BIT in 2007.

The new BIT is more similar to the Western BITs and more detailed with more articles. This also shows China's new policy to be both capital-importing country and capital-exporting country. The new BIT also borrows several articles from Korea-Japan BIT.

In the Preamble, it is stressed that the Korea-China Comprehensive Cooperative Partnership would be enhanced. National treatment is reiterated, it is also promised that the existing non-conforming measures will not be increased (ratchet effect) (Art. 3.2). The new BIT adds new articles concerning treatment of foreign investors including fair and equitable treatment and full and constant protection and security (Art. 2.2). Each contracting party also promises not to take any unreasonable or discriminatory measures on foreign investment (Art. 2.3). New articles on transparency and application of the Agreement are also added.

The new BIT eliminated the restriction that only the dispute concerning amount of compensation of expropriation can be submitted to international arbitration. Now any dispute arising from investment may be submitted to international arbitration. But the new BIT sets a time limit of three years for the investor to submit the dispute for international arbitration (Art. 9.7). It also clearly provides that the new BIT does not apply to the dispute arose before its entry into force (Art. 12). The new BIT also adds several new articles concerning investor-state dispute settlement procedures.

The new BIT substantially promotes mutual investment between China and Korea. By the end of September 2009, the two countries' mutual investment totaled about 450 billion US dollars, an increase of nearly 100 times the initial establishment of diplomatic relations in 1992.[2] As of June 2009, Korea's accumulated actual outward investment is USD 137.5 billion, USD 28.6 billion of which was invested in China. This accounted for 41.78% of Korea's all outward investment. China has become the biggest host country of Korea's outward investment.[3] The second biggest one is the USA that accounted for 18.83% of Korea's all outward investment. In the same token, Korea becomes the important host country of China's outward investment.

## 2.3 The 2012 China-Japan-Korea Trilateral Investment Agreement

China, Japan and Korea are neighboring countries located in the Northeast Asia. China and Japan are among the three biggest economies in the world (the biggest is the USA), and Korea is among the ten biggest. The combined GDP of the three countries accounted for 16.7 percent of the global total in 2010.[4] As of 2008, the three key Northeast Asian neighboring countries had been considering to strengthen regional economic cooperation among the three countries. This was restated in the First Japan–China-Korea (Republic of Korea) Trilateral Summit Meeting on December 13, 2008. The tripartite cooperation is regarded as a dramatic development that will contribute significantly to the stability and prosperity of this region and the entire world.[5] Investment will be part of the above-mentioned economic cooperation. The three countries have agreed to conclude a China-Japan-Korea trilateral investment agreement. Official negotiations in this regard are in process, while various studies and formal communications have been finished. If such an agreement is finalized, the Northeast Asia will become a bloc for mutual investment and absorb more foreign investment from outside the area.

The three countries have signed bilateral investment treaties (BIT) with each other. The three BITs have played important role in promoting mutual investment among the three countries. They also constitute sound and solid bases for the currently

[2] South Korea Investment Cooperation Committee 6th joint meeting was held in Beijing, available at http://www.sourcejuice.com/1278463/2009/11/23/South-Korea-Investment-Cooperation-Committee-6th-joint-meeting-held, last visited on September 30, 2010.

[3] Yihao Wei, Guowei Wu.

[4] First Japan-China-ROK Trilateral Summit Meeting Held, available at www.gov-online.go.jp/pdf/hlj_img/vol_0018et/18-19.pdf, *last visited on September 15, 2010.*

[5] First Japan-China-ROK Trilateral Summit Meeting Held, available at www.gov-online.go.jp/pdf/hlj_img/vol_0018et/18-19.pdf, *last visited on September 15, 2010.*

undergoing China-Japan-Korea trilateral investment agreement. The three countries have bilateral investment agreements with each other. If all of these BITs can be integrated into one comprehensive agreement, it will do good to all the three countries.

Firstly, let us look at the China-Japan BIT. Japan has become a world economy power after two decades of economic development with the assistance from the USA. When China carried out its Opening Up policy at the end of 1970s, Japan became the main home country of foreign investment in China. On August 27, 1988, Chinese Government and Japanese Government signed an Agreement on the Promotion and Protection of Investments which came into force on May 14, 1989. The 1988 China-Japan BIT have been promoting and protecting Japanese investment in China ever since. Thereafter, Chinese investment in Japan is increasing compared to the past as a result of China's new policy of "Going abroad".

Then, let us look at the Korea-Japan BIT. The Korea-Japan BIT was signed on March 22, 2002, and entered into force on January 1, 2003. The BIT gives national treatment to investors from the other country in both pre-establishment and post-establishment (Article 2). This is quite different from the China-Japan BIT and the China-Korea BIT that give limited national treatment only in the post-establishment stage. The Korea-Japan BIT allows a lot of exceptions and exclusions to national treatment. The BIT also includes a transparency article (Article 7), performance requirement (Article 9), non-expropriation guarantee (Article 10) and a detailed article on investor-state dispute settlement (Article 15).

The Korea-Japan BIT is a typical type of BIT between developed countries. Its purpose is to promote liberalization of mutual investment.

The BITs between the three countries have set strong basis for a trilateral investment agreement for them, which would further promote and protect the mutual investment for the benefits of the three countries. Moreover, the three countries have many industries and fields to be complementary each other and suitable for mutual investment. For example, for Korea's outward investment in China, Korean companies can invest in such industries as green industry, motor, steel, electronics, communication, new energy and ecology environment. They can also invest in the areas in China, for instance, the Middle and West part of China and the old industrial bases such as the Northeast part of China. For China's investment in Korea, Chinese companies can invest in the air space and cosmos industries, life science and nuclear energy.

The decision to negotiate a trilateral investment agreement was made at the Summit Meeting among the leaders of China, Japan and Korea on January 14, 2007.[6] The first round of the negotiation on the trilateral investment agreement took place in Tokyo on March 22 and 23, 2007.[7] Six rounds of negotiations have been held till April 2009. Negotiations on the trilateral investment agreement among the three countries have made positive progress. On May 23, 2010, the ministers of trade and commerce

---

[6] Joint Press Statement of the Seventh Summit Meeting among the People's Republic of China, Japan and the Republic of Korea, available at http://www.mofa.go.jp/region/asia-paci/pmv0701/joint070114.pdf, last visited on September 16, 2010.

[7] The First Round of the Negotiation on the Trilateral Investment Agreement among the People's Republic of China, Japan and the Republic of Korea, available at http://www.mofa.go.jp/announce/event/2007/3/1172855_844.html, last visited on September 16, 2010.

of the three countries agreed to conclude a trilateral investment agreement within 2010 the earliest so as to strengthen the economic partnership of the three countries. Altogether, 13 rounds of negotiations have been conducted by May 2012, when the Agreement was finally signed. The Agreement came into force on May 17, 2014. The purpose of the agreement is to actively promote regional investment of enterprises within the respective countries and also provide a favorable legal, institutional and procedural environment for investment in order for regional investors to manage successful businesses. Moreover, the three countries will endeavor to provide the necessary infrastructures to facilitate the free movement of investment capital of the region.[8]

The Trilateral Investment Agreement borrows a lot of high-standard protection provisions from the US model BIT. The Agreement consists of 27 articles and one Protocol. Post-establishment national treatment was provided. It is made clear that most-favored-nation treatment (Art. 4) does not apply to dispute settlement. Provisions on fair and equitable treatment as well as full protection and security (Art. 5) are clearly defined in the way similar to what the US model BIT provides. Expropriation (Art. 11) is generally provided in the text of the Agreement, but detailed in the Protocol, again in the way similar to what the US model BIT provides. The Agreement also has detailed provisions on the protection of intellectual property (Art. 9). Investor-state dispute settlement (Art. 15) is also provided in detail.

## 2.4 The Investment Chapter of the 2015 China-Korea FTA

The substantial economic ties and close cultural relations between the two countries necessitate the establishment of free trade area between them. The two governments initiated studies on the feasibility of China-Korea FTA since 2006. The Joint China-Korea FTA Feasibility Study involving industry, government and academia was jointly declared by the two governments on May 28, 2010. The two countries launched formal negotiations on China-Korea Free Trade Agreement (FTA) in 2012, just after the formal signature of the Trilateral Investment Agreement. After 13 rounds of negotiations, the FTA was concluded on June 1, 2015, and came into force on December 20, 2015.

The FTA covers provisions majorly on trade in goods, trade in service, investment and others. The structure of the Investment Chapter (Chapter 12) is basically similar to the Trilateral Investment Agreement, but some provisions are more detailed and similar to the US model BIT. For example, the provisions on fair and equitable treatment as well as full protection and security (Art. 12.5), and the provisions and annexes (Annex 12-A and 12-B) on expropriation (Art. 12.9) are almost directly copied from the US model BIT.

---

[8] Japan–China-ROK Trilateral Summit: Trilateral Cooperation VISION 2020, available at http://www.mofa.go.jp/region/asia-paci/jck/summit1005/vision2020.html, last visited on September 15, 2010.

We can say that the Investment Chapter provides very high standard of protection to investors.

## 2.5 The Investment Chapter of the Regional Comprehensive Economic Partnership

In addition to the above agreements, both China and Korea are also members of the Regional Comprehensive Economic Partnership (RCEP) which also provides legal protection to investors from the two countries. RCEP is a regional trade agreement that is one of the most notable mega-regional economic agreements signed in recent years.[9]

The RCEP negotiations were initiated in November 2012, and concluded on November 15, 2020. It came into force on January 1, 2022. The parties to RECP include the ten ASEAN members plus China, Japan, Korea, Australia and New Zealand. The contents of RCEP cover not only the traditional areas such as trade in goods, trade in service and investment, but also new areas such as intellectual property and competition.

Chapter 10 of RCEP is the Investment Chapter. The chapter contains boilerplate provisions on protection, facilitation and liberalization of investment sectors.[10] Among the investment agreements that both China and Korea are parties, the RECP Investment Chapter provides the highest standard for investors. For example, it provides to investors the pre-establishment national treatment (Art.3.1) in the negative list approach (Art. 8) and pre-establishment MFN treatment (Art. 4) which excludes its application to investor-state dispute settlement. The provisions on fair and equitable treatment, full protection and security, and expropriation and its annexes (10 A and 10 B) are almost copied from the US model BIT. It also has new provisions on prohibited performance requirements (Art. 6).

It is worth noting that the Investment Chapter does not have any provisions on investor-state dispute settlement (ISDS). That means if there is any investment dispute between foreign investor and the host state arising from this chapter, the foreign investor could not bring the dispute to international arbitration for resolution. Actually, the ISDS was included in the initial negotiating drafts, but excluded during the final negotiations.[11] The omission of the investor-state dispute settlement is a compromise of the negotiating parties during the negotiations for two major reasons. Firstly, in the past years ISDS is backlashed and some countries decided to terminate or renegotiate IIAs with ISDS clauses. Secondly, within the UNCITRAL, countries have been discussing for years the reform of ISDS without a consensus outcome. Considering the far-reaching impact of the potential ISDS reform to be concluded by UNCITRAL, many countries and investment agreements choose to wait for the

[9] Lugg et al. (2024), p. 1.

[10] Lugg et al. (2024), p. 1.

[11] Lugg et al. (2024), pp.2 & 21.

final result. According to Lugg A et al., the reasons for RCEP not to include ISDS in the final stage are because over the course of the negotiations, mounting ISDS cases, including most notably the Phillips Morris case in Australia, as well as the politicization of the TPP and the weakening of the ISDS norm there, led to increased skepticism among the parties. Further, Malaysia abruptly changed positions to be in strong opposition to ISDS after the election of a new government there, which led to a strong push for abandoning the idea of ISDS in the final rounds of the negotiations.[12]

However, ISDS is not eternally abandoned by RCEP. It is only postponed for future negotiations. According to Article 10.18, the Parties shall, without prejudice to their respective positions, enter into discussions on ISDS no later than two years after the date of entry into force of RCEP. The Parties shall conclude the discussions within three years from the date of commencement of the discussions. The two-year condition for ISDS discussions is suffice now, and it is expected that the RCEP Parties will open the discussions soon.

## 2.6 Practice of the ISDS

Although the 1992 China-Korea BIT was terminated in 2006, for the investments and returns acquired prior to the date of termination of it, the provisions of Article 1 to 14 shall continue to be effective for a further period of fifteen years from the date of termination (Art. 16). In other words, the treatment to investors and the ISDS available to investors are still applicable to investments made prior to January 1, 2007, until December 31, 2021, should investors choose so. Further, the 2007 China-Korea BIT, the 2012 China-Japan-Korea Trilateral investment agreement, the Investment Chapter of the 2015 China-Korea Free Trade Agreement, as well as the Investment Chapter of the 2020 RECP are currently and equally applicable to investors from China and Korea.

So far, there is only two cases that have been brought to international arbitration for resolution. One case is shortened as Ansung Housing v. China.[13] The other is shortened as Min v. Korea.[14] Both cases are initiated on the basis of the 2007 China-Korea BIT, and both have been concluded.

### *2.6.1 Ansung Housing V. China*

Ansung Housing Co., Ltd. is a Korean company. On November 4, 2014, it instituted an arbitration proceeding against China at ICSID on the basis of China-Korea BIT (2007). Claims arose out of the local government's alleged actions in relation

[12] Lugg et al. (2024), p. 22.

[13] Ansung Housing v. China, Award (2017).

[14] Fengzhen Min v. Korea, Decision (2021).

to Ansung's investment in the construction of a golf and country club and luxury condominiums in Sheyang-Xian, Jiangsu Province. On December 12, 2006, the South Korean company Ansung Housing entered into an investment agreement on a golf course and condominium development project in Sheyang-Xian with the Sheyang Harbor Industrial Zone Administration Committee (the Committee). The project construction consisted of two phases, each of which would occupy 1,500 mu (100 hectares) of land. After the commencement of the first phase of the project, Chinese policies on real estate development changed, the Committee could no longer provide the 1500 mu of land for the second phase at the price agreed in the investment agreement and Ansung would have to apply for land use rights through a public sale at higher prices. After the completion of the first phase, the Committee didn't provide the additional land necessary for the second phase. At latest by October 2011, Ansung had knowledge of loss or damage incurred on the project. On December 17, 2011, Ansung had to sell its shares in the golf business to a Chinese purchaser at a low price. Ansung sent its Request for Arbitration with ICSID electronically on October 7, 2014, and physically on October 8, 2014, on the basis of the 2007 China-Korea BIT. On November 4, 2014, the ICSID Secretary-General registered the institution of arbitration proceedings.

The tribunal was constituted on September 2, 2016. The case is about expropriation. But China filed preliminary objections to dismiss the claim that it thinks it is manifestly without legal merits pursuant to ICSID Arbitration Rule 41(5), because Ansung instituted this ICSID arbitration more than three years after it first acquired knowledge that it had incurred loss or damage, rendering the claim time-barred under Article 9(7) of the China-Korea BIT. Ansung responded that the China-Korea BIT's MFN clause applies so as to allow Ansung to take advantage of more favorable treatment in third-party BITs with respect to the time requirement.

This dispute mainly focuses on the following two legal issues: 1. Does the claim that beyond arbitration limitation period constitute "manifestly without legal merit"? 2. Does the MFN clause apply to the question of time limitation?

For the first issue, since Article 9(7) of China-Korea BIT explicitly sets up 3-year time limitation, so the tribunal accepted the preliminary objection advanced by China's representatives by a decision regarding manifest without legal merit due to a lack of temporal jurisdiction according to Article 41(5) of the ICSID Convention. For the second issue, the Tribunal supported China's representative's view that the wording of Article 3 limits MFN treatment to the host state's territory and covers only "investment and business activities" which is defined as "the expansion, operation, management, maintenance, use, enjoyment, and sale or other disposal of investments", and does not include dispute settlement.

Eventually, the Tribunal finds Ansung's claim to be time-barred and not protected by operation of the MFN Clause. The Tribunal finds the claim hence to be manifestly without legal merit. The tribunal issued the award on March 9, 2017, in favor of China and rejected all the claims made by Ansung.[15]

---

[15] Ansung Housing v. China, Award (2017).

This is the second case that China is challenged. With the experience of and deep thoughts after the Ekran case, this time China shows more self-confidence and calm. It decided to respond instead of seeking settlement with foreign investor. Moreover, China's performance in the case shows that it has more research and a sound understanding of the arbitration rules and is more tactful. It invoked time bar in the fast-track procedure in the jurisdiction issue and succeeded. Further, its interpretation of the MFN clauses not to cover procedural provisions is more accurate and finally accepted by the tribunal.

### 2.6.2 *Min V. Korea*

On August 3, 2020, the ICSID Secretary-General registered a request from imprisoned Chinese investor Fengzhen Min ("Claimant" or "Min") for the institution of arbitration proceedings against Republic of Korea ("Respondent") under China - Korea, Republic of BIT (2007).

A press release dated July 30, 2020, described the dispute as relating to a domestic company which was pursuing real estate investments in South Korea. Min was the sole shareholder of a Korean company called Pi Korea, which became the ultimate owner of a valuable building in central Beijing in 2008. To finance this acquisition, Pi Korea took out two loans, which were eventually assigned to the Korean state-owned Woori Bank. When Mr. Min failed to repay the loans, Woori Bank seized the collateral and sold them to foreign investors. Mr. Min unsuccessfully sued to prevent the sale. In 2010, a criminal investigation was lodged against Mr. Min, which culminated with the Claimant being charged with embezzlement, bribery, making false accusations and breach of fiduciary duty. In 2016, Mr. Min was convicted of embezzlement and other offenses, and sentenced to six years in prison. Afterward, Woori Bank took steps to enforce its security, removing Mr. Min as director of Pi Korea. In December of 2013, Woori Bank entered into a share purchase agreement (SPA) with Manner International Trading, a BVI-incorporated company. The shares were transferred to Manner in March 2014 and January 2015. Korean courts eventually found that the SPA was valid.

On July 16, 2020, Mr. Min submitted his request for arbitration, arguing that the Korean proceedings were "fraught with procedural flaws and irregularities", and thus violated the China - Korea, Republic of BIT (2007). Mr. Min further claimed that South Korea failed to admit and protect his investment, and that the legal proceedings were in breach of the BIT's fair and equitable treatment standard, as well as a denial of justice. According to IA Reporter, in February of 2021, South Korea filed preliminary objections pursuant to ICSID Arbitration Rule 41(5), arguing that some of Mr. Min's claims were manifestly without legal merit. Then in a June 18, 2021, decision, the tribunal of Ian Glick (chair, party-appointed), Stephen L. Drymer (Claimant's appointee) and Donald M. McRae (Respondent's appointee) unanimously dismissed the bulk of Korea's Rule 41(5) objections.[16] The Tribunal ruled against Korea's preliminary objections.

Korea then requested for bifurcation of jurisdiction and merits but rejected. Finally, the tribunal found that Pi Korea was constituted for the illegal purpose of receiving bad loans from Woori Bank, and thus Min's shares of the Pi Korea are not fallen into the scope of investment protected by the 2007 China-Korea BIT. The tribunal finally decided that it has no jurisdiction over the case on May 30, 2024.[17]

## References

Ansung Housing Co., Ltd. v. People's Republic of China (ICSID Case No. ARB/14/25), Award (2017)

Fengzhen Min v. Republic of Korea (ICSID Case No. ARB/20/26), Decision on the Respondent's Preliminary Objection Pursuant to Rule 41(5) of the ICSID Arbitration Rules (2021)

Guan Wang (2006) An analysis of the situation of mutual investment between China and Korea and the selection for countermeasure. Northern Economy and Trade, No.11, 2006, General No.264

Joint Press Statement of the Seventh Summit Meeting among the People's Republic of China, Japan and the Republic of Korea. Available at http://www.mofa.go.jp/region/asia-paci/pmv0701/joint070114.pdf

Lugg A, Ganeson K, Elsig M, Chaisse J, Jusoh S (2024) Why is there no investor-state dispute settlement in RCEP? bargaining and contestation in the investment regime. Bus Polit 1–28. https://doi.org/10.1017/bap.2024.8

Yihao Wei, Guowei Wu, A study on the possible effect of China-Korea FTA. Available at http://www.gotoread.com/mag/9110/contribution142790.html

[16] Fengzhen Min v. Korea, Decision (2021).

[17] The Award of the case is not made public. Information about the case is available from Fengzhen Min v Republic of Korea - ICSID Case No. ARB/20/26 - Press Release Ministry of Justice Republic of Korea - 12 June 2024, at https://www.transnational-dispute-management.com/legal-and-regulatory-detail.asp?key=35118, last visited January 4, 2025.

# Chapter 3
# China-African BITs Practice

## 3.1 Introduction

Traditionally, bilateral investment treaties (BITs) are negotiated and concluded between a capital-export country (the developed countries) and a capital-import country (the developing countries). The industrialized developed countries tend to use BITs to seek market access and to provide strong legal protection for their investments. Generally, the BITs accord foreign investors and their investments a portfolio of protection provisions such as national treatment, most-favored-nation treatment (MFN) and other absolute treatments such as fair and equitable treatment. The BITs also provide various means, including international arbitration, to resolve investor-state disputes. In the past, developed countries generally took the initiative to negotiate BITs with developing countries; in this scenario, the former is in an aggressive position and the latter, defensive. BITs reflected the "West vs. Rest" (North vs. South) power dynamic. To date, Germany is the country that has concluded the largest number of BITs in the world.

China is a special and exceptional case. China started to carry out its "Open up" policy in early 1980s to absorb foreign investment to develop its economy. Now China is a major destination for foreign investment. During this period, China entered into BITs with both developed and developing countries, concluding the second greatest number of BITs (just behind Germany). Since 2000, China carried out the "Going Abroad" strategy to encourage outward investment. Then since 2013, China proposed the Belt and Road Initiative, which has greatly promoted international trade and overseas investment. Now China is one of the world's major capital-export countries and continues to conclude BITs.

---

This chapter was expanded based on a previously published article in the title of Sino-African BITs Practice: A New Legal Paradigm? published in *Soochow Law Journal*, vol. 9, no. 2, July 2012. This chapter updates some information and add a lot of new developments.



H. Chen, *China's Practice in International Investment Law*, Modern China and International Economic Law, https://doi.org/10.1007/978-981-96-5016-3_3

Chinese investment in Africa has increased rapidly over the last few years, especially since the implementation of the Belt and Road Initiative. This has led some scholars to assert that China has placed particular emphasis on African countries in both investment and BITs. It is alleged that with the exponential growth of Chinese investment in Africa, the relevance of investment protection and investor-state dispute settlement gains additional importance and features distinctly for China.[1] In other words, their hypothesis is that China would seek stronger protections and broader dispute resolution clauses in Sino-African BITs.[2]

This hypothesis is neither isolated nor accidental. Western media reports focus on Chinese investments in Africa,[3] and offer mostly negative reviews.[4] Chinese interests in Africa have triggered strong reactions from the West—especially from the US but to a lesser extent also from Europe.[5] Chinese presence in Africa is perceived as a threat to US hegemony as well as complication of "the tussle between the EU and the USA over the 'who controls Africa.'"[6]

This chapter challenges such a hypothesis. The central thesis here is that the number and substantive content of Sino-African BITs illustrate a South-South model, different from the North–South BITs. Further, African countries have been challenged before international investment arbitration in more than 170 cases based on the BITs they concluded with other countries; only two of them were initiated by Chinese investors. This chapter first presents an overview of China's outward investment in Africa and China-Africa BITs, so as to provide a context for further analysis. It then assesses the correlation of the number of Sino-African BITs and the total amount of China's investment flows to Africa, to see whether China's investment growth in Africa merits the assertion that China places more emphasis on African countries for its BITs. The third part reviews the evolution of China's general BITs development and its practice with African countries, in particular, and analyzes the content and salient features of the Sino-African BITs. The author finds that China has different approaches to BITs when negotiating with developed countries and developing countries. The Sino-African BITs were signed between developing countries and thus categorized as South-South BITs. Then, this chapter explores the impact of

---

[1] Please refer to the Synopsis of the Session Description of the Panel on "China-Africa Investment Treaties and Dispute Settlement: A Piece of the Multipolar Puzzle, in the 2013 ASIL Annual Meeting. The Synopsis was sent to the author by email on November 14, 2012. The email is in file with the author.

[2] Please refer to the introduction to the panel of China-Africa Investment Treaties and Dispute Settlement for the 107th ASIL Annual Meeting, in: the Program of the 107th ASIL Annual Meeting: International Law in a Multipolar World, p. 44.

[3] Ken Davies (2011), p. 242.

[4] Deborah Brautigam describes the negative images but challenged them by giving very real account of the real Chinese investment (aid) in Africa in her book The Dragon's Gift: The Real Story of China in Africa, Oxford University Press, 2009.

[5] Peter Kragelund, Knocking on a wide open door: Chinese investments in Africa, http://gdex.dk/ofdi/24%20Kragelund%20Peter.pdf.

[6] Peter Kragelund, Knocking on a wide open door: Chinese investments in Africa, http://gdex.dk/ofdi/24%20Kragelund%20Peter.pdf.

China's recent approaches to BITs on future Sino-African BITs, so as to see whether they will lead to a significant shift of China-African treaty approach. This paper also suggests that a distinctive and enhanced South-South model for future China-Africa BITs will be adopted. In the final part, this chapter will briefly discuss the two cases that were brought by Chinese investors against African countries.

## 3.2 Overview of Chinese Investments in Africa and Sino-Africa BITs

China has been a major capital-import country in the world ever since the 1980s, with very limited outward investment, until the early twenty-first century. China started to invest in African countries in the 1980s in a very low volume. Chinese investment in Africa has increased over the years as a result of China's "Going Abroad" strategy. From 2009 to 2012, China's direct investment in Africa grew from US$1.44 billion to US$2.52 billion, and its accumulative direct investment in Africa increased from US$9.33 billion to US$21.23 billion.[7] The Belt and Road Initiative suggested since 2013 also strongly encourages Chinese investment to African countries. From 2013 to 2021, China's direct investment in Africa grew from US$3.37 billion to US$ 4.99 billion, and its accumulative direct investment in Africa increased from US$ 26.19 billion to US$ 44.19 billion.[8] The rapid growth of China's direct investment in Africa is indicative of Africa's development potential and investment appeal, and also points to the mutually beneficial nature of China-Africa cooperation.[9] Chinese investments focus on construction, mining, manufacture, finance, lease and business service, and others.[10] Infrastructure (highways, railways, airports, ports and bridges) accounts for a high percentage of China's investment. These investment areas, on the one hand, are complementary with Western investors, and on the other hand, contribute significantly to Africa's development. In contrast, the EU and the US have been investing in African countries for centuries. Their investments are mainly in such areas as natural resources such as energy, mining and others.

Chinese investment in Africa is often challenged in the media, which claim, *inter alia*, that China is trying "to establish firm control to resources-rich countries", and that China is financing "hospitals, water pipelines, dams, railways, airports, hotels, soccer stadiums, parliament buildings—nearly all of them linked, in some

---

[7] China-Africa Economic and Trade Cooperation (2013), a white paper published by the Information Office of the State Council of China, in August 2013 in Beijing. It is available at https://shcas.shnu.edu.cn/e3/68/c18799a516968/page.htm.

[8] MOFCOM (2013), pp. 14, 18; MOFCOM (2021), pp. 17, 23.

[9] China-Africa Economic and Trade Cooperation (2013), a white paper published by the Information Office of the State Council of China, in August 2013 in Beijing. It is available at https://shcas.shnu.edu.cn/e3/68/c18799a516968/page.htm.

[10] MOFCOM (2021), p. 29.

way, to China's gaining access to raw materials".[11] This accusation has been refuted convincingly by Deborah Brautigam in her book, "The Dragon's Gift: The Real Story of China in Africa". The vocal Western concern of Chinese investment in Africa appears to be a deliberate smoke-screen for their intention to maintain vested interests in Africa and to limit China's involvement in Africa. As reported in the World News Journal (Chinese), Western investors have invested in Africa for over a century, while Chinese investors are new to the scene for about thirty years. Currently, almost all the mines and ports in Africa with convenient transport and adequate facilities are occupied or under the control of American or European companies. What is left for Chinese companies are remote locations often with poor quality.[12] This explains why Chinese investors have to finance "hospitals, water pipelines, dams, railways, airports, hotels, soccer stadiums, parliament buildings—nearly all of them linked, in some way, to China's gaining access to raw materials". Take Chinese investment in Zambia as just one example. Chinese corporations are not the only mining companies in Zambia. In fact, the Zambian mining sector is dominated by other transnational corporations (TNCs) than Chinese.[13] Actually, Chinese investments reach most sectors of the African economy. In contrast, "If you look at the West, it's oil, oil, oil, and nothing else".[14]

China concluded its first BIT in 1982, and by 2024 had concluded 146 BITs[15] (including terminated and updated BITs) with 134 countries.[16] Among these BITs, 37 were concluded with 35 African countries (two BITs were replaced by new ones).[17] In the 1980s, China concluded dozens of BITs with European and Asian countries; the only BIT with Africa (Ghana) was signed in 1989. China signed 15 BITs with African countries in the 1990s, and 18 more in the first ten years of the twenty-first century. In the latest one more decade, China only signed three BITs, including with Democratic Republic of Congo in 2011, Tanzania in 2013 and Angola in 2023, respectively. Among all of these BITs, only 22 have entered into force, while 14 are

[11] Deborah Brautigam listed and convincingly opposed to some of the accusations in her book, Deborah Brautigam (2009), pp. 277–281.

[12] World News Journal, The West intends to squeeze China out of Africa and the media hypes China as "loser", February 9, 2012, available at http://news.ifeng.com/mil/4/detail_2012_02/09/12393398_1.shtml.

[13] Peter Kragelund, Knocking on a wide open door: Chinese investments in Africa, http://gdex.dk/ofdi/24%20Kragelund%20Peter.pdf.

[14] Deborah Brautigam (2009), p. 279.

[15] Details could be found in the UNCTAD website https://investmentpolicy.unctad.org/international-investment-agreements/countries/42/china.

[16] MOFCOM, Report on Development of China's Outward Investment and Economic Cooperation 2011–2012, available at http://wenku.baidu.com/view/c6d92ed0ad51f01dc281f1cc.html.

[17] The number is collected by the author from the MOFCOM website, UNCTAD website and others. China signed two BITs with Nigeria and the Democratic Republic of Congo, respectively, with the earlier ones replaced by the later ones. The 34 African countries that have BITs with China are Ghana, Egypt, Morocco, Mauritius, Zimbabwe, Zambia, Algeria, Democratic Republic of Congo, Gabon, Cameroon, Nigeria, Sudan, South Africa, Cape Verde, Ethiopia, Congo, Botswana, Sierra Leone, Mozambique, Kenya, Côte d'Ivoire, Djibouti, Benin, Uganda, Tunisia, Equatorial Guinea, Namibia, Guinea, Madagascar, Seychelles, Mali, Chad, Libya and Tanzania.

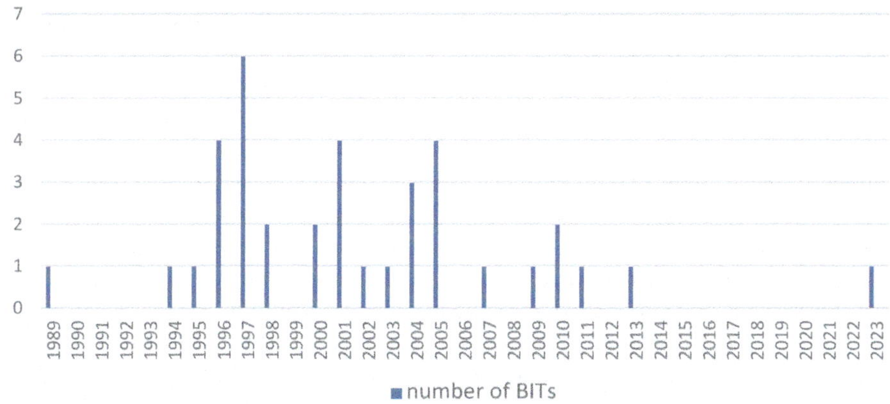


**Chart 3.1** Number of BITs concluded between China and Africa countries

pending, and two were terminated.[18] The 37 Sino-African BITs cover over half (35) of Africa's 56 countries. Chart 3.1 shows the number of BITs concluded between China and African countries on the year basis.

## 3.3 Assessing the Correlation Between the Number of Sino-African BITs and Chinese Investment in Africa and Examining the Driving Forces for Those BITs

### *3.3.1 No Positive Correlation*

Following an empirical study of the relevant data, the author finds that there is no positive correlation between the number of Sino-African BITs and the amount of Chinese investment in Africa.

China began to invest in African countries in the 1980s, on a small scale.[19] From 1979 to the end of 1990, China's total foreign investment in Africa amounted to only 51.19 million USD.[20] During the 1980s, China concluded just one BIT with one African country (Ghana). In the 1990s, while the scale of Sino-African investment increased, it was limited in light of China's policy of "encouraging inward investment

[18] A list of Sino-African BITs is enclosed at the end of the chapter as Annex.

[19] Information Office of the State Council of the People's Republic of China, China-Africa Economic and Trade Cooperation, December 2010, Beijing, available at http://www.scio.gov.cn/zfbps/wjbps/2010/201101/t847811.htm.

[20] Yingji Piao (2006). The author is research fellow at the Institute of West Asia and African Studies of Chinese Academy of Social Science.

while restricting outward investment" during 1990s.[21] During this period, China concluded 15 BITs in Africa.

In 2000, China started to implement its "Going Abroad" strategy to encourage outward investment.[22] As a result, China's outward investment in Africa increased, but not substantially. In 2006, China issued China's African Policy to encourage and support Chinese enterprises to invest in African countries.[23] In the same year, China hosted the Beijing Summit of the Forum on China-Africa Cooperation with delegations from forty-eight African states.[24] As a result of the "China-African cooperation" policy, Chinese investment in Africa has been increasing. From 2003 to 2010, China's total investment flows to Africa amounted to about 12 billion USD.[25] As at 2010, China concluded 18 BITs with African countries. The years of 2011 and 2012 saw a sprint of Chinese investment in Africa, which reached 3.17 billion USD[26] and 2.517 billion USD,[27] respectively. In this period, one BIT (with DR Congo in 2011) was concluded.

As of 2013 when the Belt and Road Initiative was first suggested, more and more Chinese investment goes to African countries. In 2014, Chinese investment in Africa reached USD 3.2 billion,[28] while in 2022, Chinese investment in Africa reduced to USD 1.81 billion.[29] In this period, China concluded one BIT with Tanzania in 2013, and one with Angola in 2023.

The above comparison demonstrates that the number of Sino-African BITs concluded in different periods does not correlate with the amounts of Chinese investments in those corresponding periods.

Further, Africa is not the major destination of China's outward foreign direct investment (OFDI). Statistics demonstrate that Chinese outward foreign investment in Africa remains quite limited and accounts for only a low percentage (about 4%) of its total OFDI. Although China's investments in Africa grow rapidly, this increase appears to be proportionate to the overall increase of China's total outward investment. For instance, in 2011, the Chinese annual investment in Africa was 3.17 billion USD, accounting for only 4.3% of its total outward FDI in that year.[30] Up to the end

---

[21] This policy can be found in the Proposal on Strengthening Administration of Overseas Investment Projects by China's State Council Planning Commission on March 5, 1991, available at http://www.people.com.cn/item/flfgk/gwyfg/1991/112302199101.html.

[22] The "Going Abroad" strategy as Chinese national strategy was first officially raised in the Proposal of the Communist Party of China (CPC) Central Committee for Formulating the 10th Five-Year Plan (2001–2005) for National Economic and Social Development in 2000 and then stated in the 10th Five-Year Plan For National Economic and Social Development in 2001.

[23] The Policy was issued on January 12, 2006, available at http://news.xinhuanet.com/world/2006-01/12/content_4042333.htm.

[24] Deborah Brautigam (2009), p. 1.

[25] MOFCOM (2010), p. 37.

[26] MOFCOM (2011), p. 10.

[27] MOFCOM (2012), p. 11.

[28] MOFCOM (2014), p. 15.

[29] MOFCOM (2022), p. 15.

[30] MOFCOM (2011), p. 10.

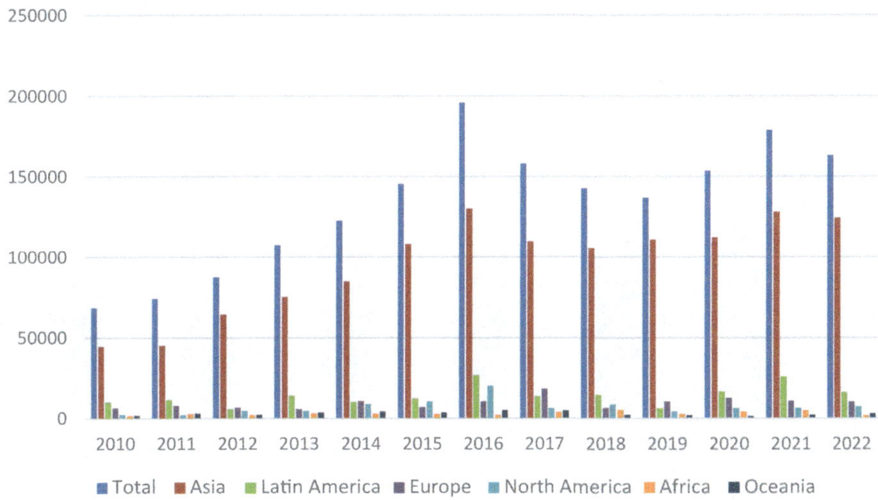


**Fig. 3.1** Chinese FDI outflows by region (millions of USD)[34]

of 2011, China's outward FDI stock in Africa was 16.25 billion USD, accounting for only 3.8% of China's overall outward FDI stock.[31] Further, by the end of 2022, China's outward FDI stock in Africa was USD 40.9 billion, accounting for only 1.5% of China's overall outward FDI stock.[32] In reality, generally speaking, China's general investment in Africa has been increasing over the years, but the percentage of China's overall investment is decreased.

Among the six major regions (shown in Fig. 3.1), Africa receives the least amount of Chinese OFDI (together with Oceania).[33] However, the 37 Sino-African BITs account for over 20% of China's total 150 BITs. Asia receives the largest amount of China's investment, accounting for over 60% of China's overall OFDI; second is Latin America. China has concluded BITs with all 10 ASEAN countries (individually), and Japan, South Korea and India. China also signed the China-ASEAN (as a bloc) Investment Agreement in 2009 as part of China-ASEAN FTA agreements, and China-Japan-Korean Trilateral Investment Agreement in 2012.

The above figure shows China's total OFDI, and its OFDI in the six continents during 2010–2022. It is obvious from this figure that Chinese investment in Africa is generally increasing but still limited, accounting for a small share of China's overall outward FDI flows.

On the other hand, China is not the major source country of foreign investment inflows to Africa, either. The following figure illustrates China's small share

[31] MOFCOM (2011), p. 15.

[32] MOFCOM (2022), p. 21.

[33] Africa received much more China's investment in 2008 as a result of the global financial crisis.

[34] Source: Own compilation based on MOFCOM, Statistical Bulletins of China's Outward Foreign Direct Investment 2010-2022.

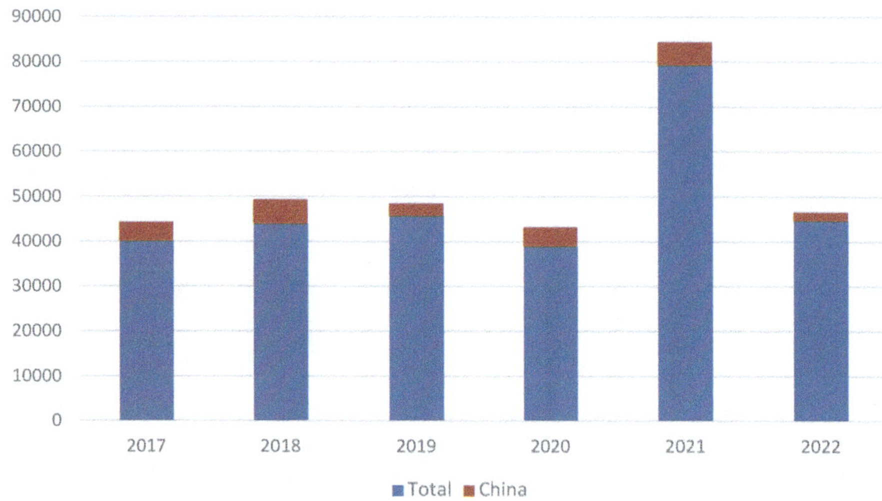


**Fig. 3.2** China's share in Africa's total FDI inflows (millions of USD)[35]

in Africa's total inflows of foreign direct investment during the period 2017–2022 (Fig. 3.2).

Chinese investment in Africa is increasing but still comparatively limited in both amount and percentage share; African investment in China is very little. The nature of mutual investment between China and Africa is a means to promote China-African cooperation, which in nature is a South-South cooperation model. This differs from the North–South cooperation between that China has with Western countries, and that Africa has with Western countries.

To sum up, two things are clear: there is no positive correlation between the number of Sino-African BITs and China's OFDI in Africa; Chinese investment in Africa remains rather limited and insignificant, but it represents a South-South cooperation approach. Therefore, it is questionable to claim that, with the exponential growth of Chinese investment in Africa, Africa is China's major focus for its BITs and that China will place more attention on stronger investor protection and investor-state dispute resolution mechanisms.

### *3.3.2 The Driving Forces for the Conclusion of Sino-African BITs*

Concluding a BIT signals that a country wishes to provide a stable, transparent and predictable investment environment in which investments can thrive—a positive

[35] Source: Own compilation based on World Investment Reports 2023 and MOFCOM, Statistical Bulletins of China's Outward Foreign Direct Investment 2022.

influence, regardless of whether or not the BIT enters into force.[36] This explains the major reason for the comparatively large number of Sino-African BITs while the amount of Chinese investment in Africa is relatively limited. The primary aims of Sino-African BITs, to encourage, promote and protect foreign investment, must be seen within China's overarching strategy of promoting bilateral cooperation.

The other driving forces behind the conclusion of Sino-African BITs include political will and friendly relations. China has maintained good foreign and political relations with African countries ever since its founding in 1949, and has provided a significant amount of economic aid to them. Since the 1990s when some African countries including Zambia,[37] Egypt, Kenya and Nigeria changed their attitude toward foreign investment and started to formulate favorable foreign investment laws to attract more foreign investment, they turned to their old friend—China, which was also keen to attract foreign investment and to sign BITs. The two sides cooperated readily. That is why there were 15 BITs signed in the 1990s. This fact explains the real motivation for the conclusion of the Sino-African BITs; the aim was not to open up African markets or to keenly protect Chinese investors and their investments. Both sides were ready and committed to develop deeper economic cooperation.

Another reason that explains the increased number of Sino-African BITs is the fact that signing an agreement is regarded as a gesture of friendship and diplomatic achievement for leaders when they visit another country. At the time of these first BITs, both parties are developing countries, and China's position toward BITs in the 1990s was still defensive. The contents of those BITs are comparatively simple and focus on the protection of host governments, instead of investor protection. Therefore, they did not include provisions on radical market access or include a high standard of investor protection or stringent investor-state dispute settlement mechanisms.

Further, some Chinese investments have the nature of developmental aid, instead of being strictly commercial undertakings. In the early twenty-first century, China and Africa strengthened their economic relations by holding several China-Africa Cooperation Forums. The Chinese Government committed to set aside special funds to support and encourage investments in Africa. In 2006, the Beijing Action Plan (2007–2009) was adopted, and the Chinese Government issued China's African Policy (2006) to encourage Chinese enterprises to invest in Africa, and to continue to negotiate, conclude and implement BITs. It is worth noting that investment is only one part of China-Africa cooperation which spans political, economic, social and foreign affairs. Considered against this context, the Sino-African BITs were not instruments used to overprotect China's investors and investments in Africa, but instead, represented vehicles for enhanced South-South cooperation.

The above economic, political and diplomatic considerations as driving forces for concluding BITs also reflect the nature of Sino-African BITs as a model of South-South BITs. This broader context must be considered when examining China-African BIT practice.

---

[36] UNCTAD (2005), p. 7.

[37] For example, Zambia passed or updated its 1986 Investment Act, 1991 Investment Act, 1993 Investment Code, 1996 new Investment Act, and 1995 Mines and Minerals Development Act.

## 3.4 Reviewing the Evolution of China's BIT Practice and Analyzing the Contents of Sino-African BITs Through the Three Phases of Development

BITs were originally concluded between developed countries and developing countries, the so-called North–South BITs. There are generally two approaches of North–South BITs: the European approach, represented mainly by the German BITs, and the Western Hemisphere approach, reflected by the Canada and US model BITs. Overall, the European approach tends to cover a narrower scope and focus more on the protection of FDI flows, while the Western Hemisphere approach covers a broader scope and emphasizes more likely both the protection and liberalization of investment.[38] Understandably, the much later developed BITs between developing countries (South-South BITs) follow the more general and less stringent European model, to a large part.[39]

China concluded its first BIT with Sweden in 1982. In the 1980s, China concluded over 20 BITs with many developed countries and some developing countries. In the following decade, China continued to sign BITs. During this period, China's BITs followed the European approach. By 1998, China entered a new phase when it expanded the scope of investor-state disputes eligible for international arbitration in its BIT with Barbados. This signals a significant turn for and the second phase of China's BIT practice. By 2008, China entered a third phase by borrowing some "Americanized" provisions when signing BITs with Mexico and generating its 2010 Model BIT.

This part analyzes China's general BIT practice and the Sino-African BIT practice through the three phases of development—1989–1997; 1998–2008; 2008 to present day. The survey demonstrates that the Sino-African BITs are distinctive from the North–South BITs and shows salient features of South-South BITs.

### *3.4.1 The First Phase of Sino-African BITs (1989–1997)*

As a result of the "Opening Up" policy in early 1980s, China put great effort on absorbing foreign investment and concluding BITs as a tool to show China's friendly legal environment for FDI. Being a major recipient of FDI, China was in a defensive position in negotiating BITs, trying to attract more foreign investment and protect national sovereignty. According to Berger, the Chinese international investment policy until the late 1990s was marked by a reluctance to impose strong legal protection on its foreign investments.[40] Generally speaking, China adopted the more mild European approach in its BITs practice.

---

[38] UNCTAD (2005), p. 31.

[39] UNCTAD (2005), p. 31.

[40] Axel Berger (2011), pp. 162–185.

In terms of Sino-African foreign investment relations in this period, China is capital-export country (though on a very small scale), while Africa recipients. In theory, China should take the aggressive position in Sino-African BITs. This would include provisions such as national treatment aimed at opening up African markets and broad scope of investor-state disputes that protected Chinese investors. While China was well positioned to adopt such an approach, in practice this did not occur.

Early Sino-African BITs such as the China-Ghana BIT (1989), China-Egypt BIT (1994), China- Morocco BIT (1995), China-Mauritius BIT (1996) and China-Nigeria (1997) are very general and rather concise with 11–15 provisions.[41] The number of clauses and structure of these Sino-African BITs are generally similar to those Sino-developing country BITs[42] and Sino-developed country BITs[43] (both are similar to the European BIT approach) in that same period, except for some provisions[44] that will be further elaborated in detail below. Typically, these Sino-African BITs contain provisions covering the following: definitions of investor and investment, investment promotion, MFN treatment, fair and equitable treatment, expropriation and compensation, transfer, subrogation, existing investments, state-state dispute settlement, limited investor-state dispute settlement, consultation and entry into force, duration and termination.

Four points are notable and distinctive in this early treaty practice, compared to North–South BITs in that same period.

Firstly, the Sino-African BITs do not contain some substantive provisions, such as national treatment and performance requirements. These two provisions are important elements for the European approach and the Western Hemisphere approach.[45]

National treatment means that foreign investors of the other contracting party shall be accorded treatment "no less favorable" than that accorded to nationals of the contracting party. The European approach adopts post-establishment national treatment while the Western Hemisphere approach adopts pre-establishment national treatment. The pre-establishment national treatment aims at full market access and investment liberalization. By way of comparison, the Sino-African BITs signed before 1997 generally do not contain a provision on national treatment, while those BITs signed in 1997 accord limited national treatment.[46] This national treatment is generally understood as post-establishment national treatment. Moreover, for those small number of BITs with a national treatment provision, the national treatment is

[41] For example, China-Ghana BIT (the first Sino-African BIT) contains 14 articles; China-Egypt BIT contains 12 articles; China-Morocco BITs contains 12 articles; China-Mauritius BIT contains 15 articles; China-Nigeria BIT contains 11 articles.

[42] One example is China-Philippine BIT (1992) that contains 13 clauses.

[43] For example, China-UK BIT (1986) contains 12 clauses; China-Japan BIT (1988) contains 15 clauses.

[44] National treatment is generally not contained in Sino-African BITs.

[45] The Germany-Liberia BIT (1961) Art. 1(2) and the Germany-Sierra Leone BIT (1965) Art. 2(1) provide for national treatment. The US 1984 Model BIT Article II provides both national treatment and prohibition of performance requirements.

[46] For example, China-Nigeria BIT (1997), Art. 2.4; China-Gabon BIT, Art. 3.1.

accorded *in accordance with the laws and regulations of the host state.*[47] In other words, the host state may decide the scope and extent of national treatment by the maintaining, adopting or modifying of its laws and regulations, giving the host state most of the control and policy space over the admission of foreign investment.

Performance requirements are used by the host state to direct foreign investment to meet domestic economic needs. The BITs concluded by most developed countries prohibit performance requirements,[48] so as to pave way for their investors. On the contrary, Sino-African BITs do not include any provision on performance requirements.

Secondly, the Sino-African BITs developed a distinctive approach to investor-state dispute settlement mechanisms. The North–South BITs allow foreign investors to submit their disputes with host state to ICSID for international arbitration or conciliation.[49] Many BITs between developed countries (such as the US) and African countries provide that *any* investor-state dispute may be submitted to ICSID for settlement by conciliation or binding arbitration.[50] The scope of investor-state disputes that may be submitted for international arbitration is very broad. However, according to Sino-African BITs, amicable settlement through negotiations is the preferred means of dispute resolution, a provision contained in all the Sino-African BITs.[51] If the dispute can't be settled through negotiations within six months, either party to the dispute shall be entitled to submit the dispute to the competent court of the host state.[52] Only the *dispute involving the amount of compensation for expropriation* may be submitted to an ad hoc international arbitral tribunal, within six months after resort to negotiations.[53] This is a unique approach. Moreover, the very narrow scope of disputes eligible for international arbitration tends to favor the host state, and thus is disliked by foreign investors. In addition, Sino-African BITs provide that the governing law of the dispute for international arbitration is the law of the host state, the applicable BIT and the generally recognized principles of international law.[54] The inclusion of host state law as governing law for arbitral tribunal shows a respect for the host state's sovereignty and national interests, and takes the host state's special situation into consideration.

Thirdly, the Sino-African BITs include other provisions that are very friendly to host states. (i) Foreign investment is required to be *in line with the general economic*

---

[47] For example, China-Nigeria BIT (1997), Art. 2.4; China-Gabon BIT, Art. 3.1.

[48] For example, the US 1984 Model BIT Article II.5 provides that "Neither Party shall impose performance requirements as a condition of establishment, expansion or maintenance of investments, which require or enforce commitments to export goods produced, or which specify that goods or services must be purchased locally, or which impose any other similar requirements".

[49] For example, the US 1984 Model BIT Article VI.

[50] For example, the US-Egypt BIT, Art. 7.3(a).

[51] For example, China-Egypt BIT, Art. 9.1; China-Nigeria BIT, Art. 6.1.

[52] For example, China-Egypt BIT, Art. 9.2; China-Nigeria BIT, Art. 6.2.

[53] For example, China-Egypt BIT, Art. 9.3; China-Ghana BIT, Art. 10; China-Mauritius BIT, Art. 13; China-Nigeria BIT, Art. 6.3.

[54] For example, China-Egypt BIT, Art. 9.7; China-Ghana BIT, Art. 10.5; China-Nigeria BIT, Art. 6.7.

*policy of host state.*[55] This ensures that foreign investment will promote the economic development of the host state and closely align with domestic policy. (ii) The BITs provide that the host state shall encourage foreign investors to make investment and admit foreign investment *in accordance with its laws and regulations.*[56] (iii) BITs were agreed *not to apply* to the host state regarding measures related to the protection of its essential security and interests, public health, its environment, or the prevention of diseases and pests in animals or plants.[57] This exception is most favorable to the host state and raises restrictions for foreign investors.

Lastly, all of the Sino-African BITs developed a distinctive institutional framework called "consultation" between the contracting parties to implement the BITs. According to the consultation mechanism, the representatives of the two Contracting Parties shall hold meetings from time to time. The purpose of the consultation includes: (a) reviewing the implementation of this Agreement; (b) exchanging legal information and investment opportunities; (c) resolving dispute arising out of investments; (d) forwarding proposals on promotion of investment; and (e) studying other issues in connection with investments.[58] The consultation mechanism tends to favor the host country and once again reflects China's focus on promoting international cooperation between China and African countries. In contrast, neither the European approach nor the Western Hemisphere approach adopts such a mechanism.

To sum up, the Sino-African BITs during the phase of 1989–1997, while similar to the more mild European approach, displayed several salient features of South-South BIT approach.

### 3.4.2 The Second Phase of Sino-African BITs (1998–2008)

In 1998, China concluded a BIT with Barbados, a small island country in Central America. This marked a significant development in Sino BIT practice. The scope of the investor-state disputes eligible for international arbitration was expanded to include "*Any dispute* concerning an investment between an investor of one Contracting Party and the other Contracting party".[59] This is much broader than China's traditional scope of disputes covered in its earlier BITs which included only disputes related to the amount of compensation for expropriation. The broader coverage of investor-state disputes eligible for international arbitration favors foreign investors vis-à-vis host state. This has been identified as the first time that China consented to submit *any dispute* to ICSID or UNCITRAL for international arbitration and thus marks a significant turn in China's BIT practice.[60] Berger *and* Ofodile

---

[55] For example, China-Mauritius BIT, Art. 3.1.

[56] For example, China-Ghana BIT, Art. 3.1.

[57] For example, China-Mauritius BIT, Art. 11.1.

[58] One example is China-Egypt BIT, Art. 11.

[59] China-Barbados BIT, Art. 9.2.

[60] Norah Gallagher, Wenhua Shan (2008), p.40.

claim that this *significant turn* followed the adoption of China's "Going Abroad" policy encouraging Chinese outbound investment.[61] But this is an incorrect view. China's "Going Abroad" strategy as a Chinese national strategy was first officially raised in *2000*[62] and then adopted in *2001* in China's 10$^{th}$ Five-Year Plan for National Economic and Social Development.

In responding to this broadening, China set up a kind of "safety valve" mechanism to reduce the greater potential risk of more investor-state arbitration. The China-Barbados BIT requires that, prior to arbitration, the parties to the dispute must seek amicable settlement through negotiations. More importantly, it provides that the Contracting Party *may require* the investor to exhaust the local administrative review procedure before the submission of the dispute to international arbitration.[63] Local administrative review allows the host country every opportunity to make redress to foreign victims; this also reduces the number of international claims, and avoids situations that might adversely affect the political relations between the two countries. Since 1998, China has consistently embraced this "safety valve" mechanism in its BIT practice.

This demonstrates that China was very cautious as to the broadening of investor-state disputes eligible for international arbitration. The adoption of a "safety valve" mechanism shows that China remains its defensive position instead of aggressive position in concluding BITs.

This broad investor-state dispute settlement approach is new for China at that time, but always was included in developed countries BITs. Since 1998, China has adopted a similar approach in almost all BITs with no differentiation between China's position as capital-import or capital-export country. This shows China's even-handed approach to international investment.

In fact, China had already broadened the scope of disputes eligible for international arbitration in December 1997 in China-South Africa BIT, before the China-Barbados BIT. This 1997 BIT provided that either disputing party may submit their dispute to an international arbitral tribunal for settlement.[64] However, since South Africa is not a party to the ICSID Convention, the BIT only provides for ad hoc arbitration instead of ICSID arbitration.

Over the next several years following the China-Barbados BIT, China entered into BITs with many African countries which contain similar broad dispute settlement provisions, such as the China-Botswana BIT (2000), China-Republic Congo BIT (2000), China-Kenya BIT (2001), China-Sierra Leone BIT (2001), China- Côte d'Ivoire BIT (2002), China-Djibouti BIT (2003), China-Benin (2004), China-Uganda BIT (2004), China-Equatorial Guinea BIT (2005), China-Namibia BIT (2005), China-Madagascar BIT (2005) and China-Seychelles BIT (2007).

---

61 Axel Berger (2008); *Uche Ewelukwa Ofodile* (2013), p. 156.

62 It was first raised in the Proposal of the Communist Party of China (CPC) Central Committee for Formulating the 10th Five-Year Plan (2001-2005) for National Economic and Social Development.

63 China-Barbados BIT, Art. 9.3.

64 China-South Africa BIT, Art 9.

However, in these Sino-African BITs, China takes an approach that is a bit different from the above China-Barbados BIT approach to dispute settlement. The so-called fork-in-the-road approach provides: (i) any investor-state dispute shall, as far as possible, be settled amicably through negotiations; (ii) if the dispute cannot be settled through negotiations within six months, *the investor may* submit the dispute to the competent court of the host state; (iii) if the dispute cannot be settled within six months after resort to negotiations, it *shall* be submitted *at the request of either party,* to ICSID or an ad hoc arbitral tribunal, provided that the host state *may* require the investor to exhaust the domestic administrative review procedure.[65] This provides the investor with a range of options: foreign investors may opt to have the dispute handled by the domestic court, international arbitration or a combination of the two. In the latter case, the exhaustion of the domestic administrative review procedure is not required. This fork-in-the-road approach is a balanced one for both the foreign investor and host state in that it enables investors a spectrum of options and offers the host state opportunities to settle the disputes in domestic courts.

With regard to dispute settlement mechanisms in these Sino-African BITs, China has not adopted an aggressive approach to provide extra protection to its investors.

The Sino-African BITs concluded in this second phase did not substantially deviate from those concluded in the first stage, except: (i) the change to the investor-state dispute settlement mechanism, as discussed above, and (ii) the containing of a provision on national treatment. Again, the national treatment only applies to post-establishment stage of investment, and the according of national treatment should be "without prejudice to" the host state's laws and regulations.[66]

### 3.4.3 The Third Phase of Sino-African BITs (2008-Present)

After three decades of the "Opening Up" policy, China has become the second largest capital-import country in the world. Correspondingly, most of the BITs between China and other countries were negotiated primarily with defensive concerns in mind. This is reflected primarily in the limited national treatment of foreign investors, which is closely related to market access and international investment liberalization, and the restrictive investor-state dispute resolution mechanism. The investor-state dispute resolution clauses during the first phase limited international arbitration to disputes about the amount of compensation in case of an expropriation, and in the second phase, adopted the "fork-in-the-road" approach which reflected a more balanced one.

With its "Going Abroad" strategy, the Belt and Road Initiative and its rich foreign currency reserves, China has gradually become a major capital-export country. For example, in 2011, China's OFDI flow was 74.56 billion USD, and its total outward

---

[65] Please refer to China-Mozambique BIT Art. 7, China-Botswana BIT Art. 9 and China-Djibouti BIT Art. 9.

[66] For example, China-Uganda BIT Art. 3.2.

FDI stock was 424.78 billion.[67] After ten years, that is, in 2021, China's OFDI net flow was 178.82 billion USD, and its total outward FDI stock was 2785.15 billion USD.[68] Some scholars suggest that China has shifted its policy, during this period, placing more emphasis on protecting its investors' increasing investments abroad and thus negotiating BITs with stronger protections and broader dispute resolution clauses. They assert that China's recent BITs are quite "Americanized".[69] The author does not fully agree with this and argues that China's recent approaches in concluding BITs are influenced by the US 2004 Model BIT, but not fully "Americanized".

The US learned lessons from the extensive NAFTA investment arbitration cases and improved those provisions that were frequently and successfully challenged by investors, such as provisions on fair and equitable treatment, and indirect expropriation. These improved provisions in the US 2004 Model BIT are helpful in the protection of national interests and state sovereignty, and thus are host state friendly. China has borrowed, in part, from these provisions.

---

[67] MOFCOM (2011), p. 3.

[68] MOFCOM (2021), pp. 3, 7.

[69] Congyan Cai (2009), p. 3; Valentina Vadi (2011–2012), pp. 712–713.

The China-Mexico BIT concluded in 2008 borrowed with amendments an article of "Minimum Standard of Treatment" concerning fair and equitable treatment and full protection and security from the US 2004 Model BIT.[70] In China's past BITs, the provision of fair and equitable treatment is rather concise and vague.

China's 2010 Model BIT drafted by MOFCOM has several "Americanized" provisions. For example, China follows several provisions (with amendments) from the

[70] China-Mexico BIT, Article 5, which provides that

1. Each Contracting Party shall accord to investments of investors of the other Contracting Party treatment in accordance with international law, including fair and equitable treatment and full protection and security.
2. For greater certainty, this Article prescribes the international law minimum standard of treatment of aliens as the minimum standard of treatment to be afforded to investments of investors of the other Contracting Party. The concepts of "fair and equitable treatment" and full "protection and security" do not require treatment in addition to or beyond that which is required by the international law minimum standard of treatment of aliens as evidence of State practice and opinio juris. A determination that there has been a breach of another provision of this Agreement, or of a separate international Agreement, does not establish that there has been a breach of this Article.

This Article is very similar to Article 5 of the US 2004 Model BIT, which provides that.

1. Each Party shall accord to covered investments treatment in accordance with customary international law, including fair and equitable treatment and full protection and security.
2. For greater certainty, paragraph 1 prescribes the customary international law minimum standard of treatment of aliens as the minimum standard of treatment to be afforded to covered investments. The concepts of "fair and equitable treatment" and "full protection and security" do not require treatment in addition to or beyond that which is required by that standard, and do not create additional substantive rights ….

US 2004 Model BIT including the criteria for determining indirect expropriation,[71] the exception to indirect expropriation[72] and the denial of benefits.[73]

However, China did not follow the US aggressive approach that favors investors. For example, China does not accept the notion of pre-establishment national treatment, a very important provision in the US Model BIT, which favors foreign investors in terms of market access. China does not take some procedural provisions concerning the international arbitration of investor-state disputes, as in the US Model BIT, such as participation in the dispute by third parties including mediation in the process of negotiation; submission by a non-disputing party and *amicus curiae,* and expert reports; consolidation of arbitration; shareholder's submitting for arbitration in its

---

[71] Article 6.2 provides that.The determination of whether an action or series of actions by a Party, in a specific fact situation, constitutes an indirect expropriation referred to in paragraph 1 above requires a case-by-case, fact-based inquiry that considers, among other factors:

(i) the economic impact of the action or series of actions, although the fact that an action or series of actions by a Party has an adverse effect on the economic value of an investment, standing alone, does not establish that an indirect expropriation has occurred;
(ii) the degree of discrimination to the investors and their investments from the other Contracting Party caused by the action or series of actions in scope or application;
(iii) the extent to which the action or series of actions interferes with distinct, reasonable investment-backed expectations, which arise from the specific commitments to the investor from one Contracting Party; and.
(iv) the character and purpose of the action or series of actions, whether it is taken for public interest in good faith, and whether the above action is appropriate to the purpose of expropriation.

This provision is very similar to the US 2004 BIT Model, Annex B Expropriation, 4 (a), which provides that

The determination of whether an action or series of actions by a Party, in a specific fact situation, constitutes an indirect expropriation, requires a case-by-case, fact-based inquiry that considers, among other factors:

(i) the economic impact of the government action, although the fact that an action or series of actions by a Party has an adverse effect on the economic value of an investment, standing alone, does not establish that an indirect expropriation has occurred;
(ii) the extent to which the government action interferes with distinct, reasonable investment-backed expectations, and.
(iii) the character of the government action.

[72] Article 6.3 provides that "Non-discriminatory regulatory actions by a Party that are designed and applied to protect legitimate public welfare objectives, such as public health, safety, and the environment, do not constitute indirect expropriations. This could be excepted in rare circumstances, for example when the action seriously exceeds what is necessary for the maintaining of legitimate public welfare".

This provision is very similar to the US 2004 BIT Model, Annex B Expropriation, 4 (b), which provides that "Except in rare circumstances, non-discriminatory regulatory actions by a Party that are designed and applied to protect legitimate public welfare objectives, such as public health, safety, and the environment, do not constitute indirect expropriations".

[73] See Article 10 Denial of Benefits, which is similar to Article 17 of the US 2004 BIT Model.

own capacity and in the capacity of the enterprise; and the transparency of arbitral proceedings.[74] Another example is performance requirements that is a key element in the US Model BIT but not appearing in China's BITs.

In 2012, China entered into two important investment agreements, i.e., the China-Japan-Korea Trilateral Investment Agreement and the China-Canada BIT. In these two agreements, China gave concessions to cover prohibitions of performance requirements, for the first time. China agrees that the Trade-related Investment Measures (TRIMs) that prohibit four categories performance requirements in the WTO framework will be incorporated into the agreements and being part of it.[75] An environmental standard is incorporated into the China-Japan-Korean Agreement, for the first time, too.[76] Although the two agreements have detailed provisions which place more emphasis on investor protection and investor-state dispute settlement, compared to China's past BITs, the author argues that this approach reflects the advocacy of Japan, Korea and Canada, instead of China's position. These agreements will equally protect investors in China from Japan, Korea and Canada, and Chinese investors in Japan, Korea and Canada, *vis-a-vis*.

In these negotiations, China did not agree to the pre-establishment national treatment, consistent with its earlier position. In China-Canada BIT negotiations, Canada required national treatment in both pre- and post-establishment stages.[77] However, the final concession is, national treatment only applies to post-establishment stage. In addition, existing non-conforming measures of either Party are excluded from the national treatment.[78] In the China-Japan-Korean Agreement negotiations, both Japan and Korea asked for pre-establishment national treatment with a negative list, while China only agreed with post-establishment national treatment with positive lists. The final compromise is that, Art. 3 provides generally that national treatment applies to investment activities, which seems to include establishment, acquisition and expansion; however, Para. 2 provides that national treatment excludes existing non-conforming measures.[79] China's existing non-conforming measures do not accord national treatment. This clause uses a general way to carve out non-conforming measures without a negative or positive list. To sum up, China only agrees with post-establishment national treatment.

In the China-US BIT negotiations, the US government seeks pre-establishment national treatment with a "negative list" approach. As a USTR official stated, including a market access component, and negotiating it on a "negative list" basis, in the US-China BIT, are "core elements".[80] The pre-establishment national treatment

---

[74] For details, please refer to Karl P. Sauvant and Huiping Chen (2012).

[75] China-Canada BIT, Art 9, China-Japan-Korean Agreement, Art. 7.

[76] China-Canada BIT, Art.18.3, China-Japan-Korea Agreement, Art. 23.

[77] Canada Model BIT, Art. 3.

[78] China-Canada BIT, Art. 8.2. Canada used this Model BIT as a template when negotiating with China.

[79] China-Japan-Korea Agreement, Art. 3.

[80] Market Access Is Key Area In U.S.-China BIT Talks, But Outcome Uncertain, Inside U.S. Trade, October 19, 2012.

was a contested issue between the two governments.[81] However, in 2013, China decided to accept the pre-establishment national treatment with a negative list so as to proceed with the China-US BIT negotiations.[82] Unfortunately, China-US BIT negotiations failed when President Donald Trump took office.

China's above treaty practice can be categorized as North–South BIT approach, which is different from the South-South approach. It appears that China was pushed by developed countries to include provisions on national treatment, prohibition of performance requirements and others in these North–South BITs. In terms of mutual investment flows between China and Japan, South Korea, Canada and the US, China is not the net capital-export country, and so China was in a defensive position in these BIT negotiations. In light of the above, the author does not fully agree with Berger that China's evolution in BIT practice has been characterized as moving from a *restrictive model* (accentuating the regulation of inward FDIs) to a *legalized approach* emphasizing the encouragement of outward Chinese FDIs.[83] While China's BITs practice can be characterized as adopting a more *legalized* approach, it cannot be said that China initiated and actively pursued such a result, not to say that it was adopted for the purpose of encouraging China's OFDI. From China's perspective, China would take a more balanced approach with important nuances. China's dual capacity as both major home and host country has meant that its policy to BITs is to keep a good balance between protecting host national interests and foreign investors' interests. As a host country, China seeks to maintain policy space to pursue its own legitimate public policy objectives. As a home country, China seeks to protect its investors and their outward FDI by asking for limited national treatment and strengthening investor-state dispute settlement. While China's recent practice certainly has been more "*legalized*", in fact, the emerging new BITs have afforded improved legal protection for both host and home country interests.

Since 2008, six China-Africa BITs have been concluded: China-Mali BIT (2009), China-Chad BIT (2010), China-Libya BIT (2010), China-Democratic Republic of Congo (2011), China-Tanzania BIT (2013) and China-Angola BIT (2023). Since the texts of China-Chad BIT, China-Democratic Republic of Congo, China-Tanzania BIT and China-Angola BIT are not available, the author compares the texts of China-Mali BIT and China-Libya BIT (these two BITs are almost exactly the same in both structure and specific provisions) with China's new BITs approaches. Upon closer scrutiny, it would appear that these recent Sino-African BITs followed the China-Africa BITs pattern (South-South BIT approach) in the second phase, and have not been influenced by China's recent BIT practice (North–South BIT approach). For example, the fair and equitable treatment remains to be a general statement as "Investments of investors of each Contracting Party shall all the time be accorded

81 For details, please refer to Karl P. Sauvant and Huiping Chen (2012).

82 China-US Strategic and Economic Dialogue promotes the substantial negotiations on the bilateral investment agreement, China News Net, July 12, 2013, available at http://www.chinanews.com/gn/2013/07-12/5035137.shtml.

83 Axel Berger (2011), p. 171.

fair and equitable treatment in the territory of the other Contracting Party"[84]; the provision on expropriation does not have any criteria for indirect expropriation or exception[85]; the investor-state dispute settlement mechanisms continue to be the "fork-in-the-road" model, and state consent to international arbitration remains to be *any* investor-state dispute with requirement of exhaustion of local administrative review procedure[86]; and the national treatment remains as limited post-establishment national treatment.[87] They do not cover those provisions contained in China's new BIT practice such as denial of benefits, performance requirements, labour standards or environmental standards. The latest Sino-African BITs did not show any evidence that China changed its position toward Africa.

Of the 37 Sino-African BITs (with 35 countries), most contain a range of investor-state dispute settlement mechanisms. Despite the fact that Chinese investors in Africa have suffered great losses arising from a range of political risks, such as Libya's civil war and Egypt riots, there are only two cases that Chinese investors have challenged the host governments on the basis of Sino-African BITs. One is Zhongshan Fucheng v. Nigeria,[88] and the other is Everyway Traffic and Lighting v. Ghana.[89] Both cases were submitted to ad hoc arbitration in accordance with the UNCITRAL arbitration rules. The two cases will be further discussed in the final part of this chapter. In contrast, African countries have been challenged by foreign investors from most developed countries. According to UNCTAD database, as of December 31, 2023, there are 171 cases that were brought to international arbitration against African countries on the basis of investment treaties. Among the 171 cases, 102 were initiated by European investors, and 16 were initiated by investors from North America.[90]

The above survey shows that China departed from the Western Hemisphere approach that focuses on market access, investment liberalization, abolition of performance requirements and strong investor-state dispute settlement mechanisms.[91] China differentiated its North–South BITs from the South-South BITs. The South-South Sino-African BITs signaled the friendly South-South investment cooperation, focused more on investment promotion and protection and left a lot of policy space for host state.

---

[84] Article 3 of both China-Mali BIT and China-Libya BIT.

[85] Article 4 of both China-Mali BIT and China-Libya BIT.

[86] Article 9 of both China-Mali BIT and China-Libya BIT.

[87] Article 3 of both China-Mali BIT and China-Libya BIT.

[88] Zhongshan Fucheng Industrial Investment Co. Ltd. v. Federal Republic of Nigeria https://jusmundi.com/en/document/decision/en-zhongshan-fucheng-industrial-investment-co-ltd-v-federal-republic-of-nigeria-final-award-monday-1st-march-2021.

[89] Everyway Traffic and Lighting Company Limited v. Ghana (PCA 2021-15) https://www.italaw.com/cases/10145.

[90] This result is got from the UNCTAD database through advanced search, https://investmentpolicy.unctad.org/investment-dispute-settlement/advanced-search.

[91] Ofodile shares this view. Uche Ewelukwa Ofodile (2013), p. 177.

## 3.5 Exploring the Prospect of Sino-African BITs

### *3.5.1 Assessing the Impact of China's Recent Approaches on Future Sino-African BITs*

Some scholars suggest that China's recent approaches to BITs will have a significant impact on China's future BITs practice with Africa. This paper presents a different view.

Firstly, we do not expect that China will conclude many more BITs with more African countries. Of the 35 countries that China has entered into BITs with, these cover all the major recipients of China's investment in Africa, including South Africa, Congo Democratic Republic, Nigeria, Algeria, Niger, Kenya, Sudan and Zambia.[92] China does not have significant investment with the remaining 21 African countries, and it is doubtful that China will conclude BIT with many of them. Even if China concludes BITs with these countries, it is expected that China will take its unique and consistent South-South BIT/cooperation model. In reality, China did not conclude more BITs with African countries for one decade. Only in December 2023 did China signed a BIT with Angola, almost ten years after China concluded a BIT with Tanzania in 2013.

Secondly, there is limited legal opportunity to change the existing Sino-African BITs. Among the 37 Sino-African BITs, 21 have entered into force, 14 are still pending, and two were terminated. For those BITs not yet in force, there is almost no space to modify them. The validity term of most of these is ten years with automatic renewal unless otherwise agreed. At present about 20 BITs have been in force for more than ten years. There are no signs that China will renegotiate these agreements so as to incorporate any new approaches. Even when China proposed the Belt and Road Initiative and Chinese investment in Africa has thus increased, no China-African BIT is updated in the recent ten years.

Thirdly, with international investment treaties under challenge around the world, it is unlikely that China will conclude aggressive BITs. The international community, especially developing countries including Africa, strongly opposes current investment agreements (especially those containing strong investor-state dispute settlement mechanisms). For example, some countries such as Ecuador withdrew from ICSID so that foreign investors cannot challenge it before ICSID. India and South Africa decided not to cover investor-state dispute settlement in their BITs. In 2010, the South African government concluded a three-year review of its BITs, assessing the role of foreign investment in South Africa, the levels of protection afforded to investment and the risks and benefits of BITs. It decided in July 2010 that South Africa would: refrain from entering into BITs unless there are compelling political or economic reasons to do so; terminate existing BITs and offer partners the possibility to renegotiate BITs on the basis of a new model; develop a new Foreign Investment Act that is aligned

[92] MOFCOM (2010), p. 10; MOFCOM (2011), p. 10.

with the constitution; and clarifies typical BIT provisions under South African law.[93] Indonesia is planning to terminate more than 60 bilateral investment treaties that allow disgruntled foreign investors to bypass local courts and seek compensation in international tribunals, amid a growing global backlash against such provisions.[94] Some international institutions also propose new models for international investment agreements. The International Institute for Sustainable Development (IISD) proposed the Model International Agreement on Investment for Sustainable Development in 2005,[95] the 15-member Southern African Development Community (SADC) drafted SADC Model Bilateral Investment Treaty Template with Commentary in 2012,[96] and UNCTAD is advocating a new generation of investment policies, "Investment Policy Framework for Sustainable Development", in 2012.[97] The common message from all of these is a clarion call for a better balance between the interests of foreign investors and host states, and a stronger commitment to promote sustainable development. In light of this, it is likely that China will adapt its Sino-African BITs practice to a more comprehensive approach. The most latest concluded China-Angola BIT is declared to be a high-standard BIT, but no text is available so far.

### 3.5.2 Suggesting an Emerging Paradigm of Sino-African BITs as an Enhanced South-South Model

In the future, the total amount of China's investment in Africa will continue to increase, while the relative percentage will remain about the same. China, a capital-export country vis-à-vis African countries, will receive growing investment from African countries. In recent years, as the economic strength of African countries has increased and China-Africa relations have grown, more African companies have started to invest in China. By the end of 2012, the volume of African countries' direct investment in China totaled US$14.242 billion, increasing by 44% over 2009 levels.[98] Investing countries included Mauritius, Seychelles, South Africa and Nigeria, and their investments covered petrochemical industries, manufacturing and processing,

---

[93] Xavier Carim (2013).

[94] Ben Bland, Indonesia to terminate more than 60 bilateral investment treaties, available at http://www.ft.com.

[95] IISD Model International Agreement on Investment for Sustainable Development, available at http://www.iisd.org/pdf/2005/investment_model_int_agreement.pdf.

[96] Southern African Development Community, SADC Model Bilateral Investment Treaty Template with Commentary, available at http://www.iisd.org/itn/wp-content/uploads/2012/10/SADC-Model-BIT-Template-Final.pdf.

[97] UNCTAD (2012).

[98] China-Africa Economic and Trade Cooperation (2013), a white paper published by the Information Office of the State Council of China, in August 2013 in Beijing. It is available at http://www.scio.gov.cn/zfbps/ndhf/2013/Document/1344914/1344914.htm.

and wholesale and retail, among other fields.[99] The mutual investment flows require the China-Africa BITs to adopt a balanced approach with regard to the interests of foreign investors and host states, which is what China is seeking. The mutual investment flows show that the South-South cooperation between China and Africa is increasing and being enhanced, reflecting the spirits of South-South cooperation.

Further, future China-Africa BITs will adapt to meet changing circumstances and practice and, in particular, seek to address developing countries concerns in this area. UNCTAD, embracing the notion of sustainable development, advocates an approach that balances between pursuing purely economic growth objectives through investment liberalization and promotion, and the need to protect people and the environment. The SADC Model BIT Template introduces some new ideas: it balances the rights and obligations of both investors and state parties, by granting post-establishment national treatment to foreign investors, on the one hand, and imposing obligations against corruption and on environment and labor standards, on the other hand. While an investor-state dispute settlement mechanism is included, it is optional for SADC countries. China and Africa can learn from these proposals in their future BITs.

Given the fact that the current Sino-African BITs have already shown salient features of South-South model, the author suggests future Sino-African BITs will maintain these key provisions, which include: limited national treatment, the "fork-in-the-road" approach for investor-state dispute settlement mechanisms and the exhaustion of local administrative review procedure before submitting a dispute for international arbitration, some friendly provisions to leave policy space for the host state, and the institutional framework of "consultation" (consultation can be developed into a more institutionalized contracting party committee). The performance requirements issue would be not covered.

In addition, the author suggests the incorporation of the following new notions to enhance the Sino-African South-South BIT/cooperation model.

(i) In responding to the development concerns of developing countries (including the African countries), the new South-South approach may include a development objective in the investment treaty. A statement like "realizing the sustainable economic growth and development goals on the basis of equality and mutual benefits so as to achieve a win–win outcome" is a good choice.[100]

(ii) Since the 56 African countries are at different stages of development, some are even the least developed countries, while China is a comparatively more developed developing country, the future BITs may provide special and differential treatment for those less developed countries. Special and differential treatment means that contracting parties at different stages may bear different treaty

[99] China-Africa Economic and Trade Cooperation (2013), a white paper published by the Information Office of the State Council of China, in August 2013 in Beijing. It is available at http://www.scio.gov.cn/zfbps/ndhf/2013/Document/1344914/1344914.htm.

[100] China-ASEAN Investment Agreement has such a statement in its Preamble.

obligations. UNCTAD suggested two ways to address special and differential treatment, i.e., asymmetrical obligations and additional tools.[101]

(iii) To leave more policy space to the host state, the BIT may include some general exceptions to the overall agreement, in addition to the exceptions to some specific provisions. The first is an essential security exception that allows the host state to take actions contrary to their BIT obligations if that is necessary for the protection of its essential security interests. The second is an environmental exception that allows the host state to adopt or maintain measures necessary to protect human, animal or plant life or health. The third is a financial prudential measure exception that allows the host state to adopt or maintain reasonable measures for prudential reasons. The first two exceptions actually have been embodied in some Sino-African BITs in the first phase, such as the China-Mauritius BIT.[102]

To realize a new paradigm of China-Africa BITs reflecting South-South cooperation, capacity-building is also important for both China and Africa. In this regard, China, with more experience and expertise in BITs, could do more to provide training to African officials and negotiators.

China's increasing investments in Africa account for small share of both China's outward investments and Africa's inward investments, and thus Africa is not central to China's investment strategy. No positive correlation is found between the number of Sino-African BITs and the total amount of China's investment in Africa. China concludes BITs with Africa to provide a stable, transparent and predictable investment environment, and to deepen friendly bilateral relations as a cornerstone of Sino-African cooperation. This is a distinct feature of the China's South-South BITs, revealing the nested nature of these engagements. The evolution and substantive contents of the existing Sino-African BITs show clear characteristics of South-South BITs, which is different from the North–South BITs. The author suggests that a new legal paradigm of enhanced South-South BITs will emerge in future Sino-African BITs. These will include several existing key provisions (i.e., limited national treatment, restrictive investor-state dispute settlement mechanism and institutional framework), and also incorporate new provisions on development objectives, special and differential treatment, and general exceptions. Concerns expressed by some scholars in this field appear to be unwarranted. China's future BIT practice with Africa is infused with the potential to address contemporary development concerns in a more comprehensive way.

[101] UNCTAD (2012), pp. 47–48.

[102] China-Mauritius BIT, Art. 11.1.

## 3.6 The China-African BITs Practice Regarding Investor-State Dispute Settlement

As mentioned above, there are two cases that Chinese investors brought to international arbitration against African countries, that is Zhongshan Fucheng v. Nigeria and Everyway Traffic and Lighting v. Ghana. In the former case, the tribunal decided in favor of Chinese investor while in the latter case, the tribunal decided that it had no jurisdiction and thus in favor of Ghana. The following will briefly discuss the two cases.

### *3.6.1 Zhongshan Fucheng V. Nigeria*

The Claimant is Zhongshan Fucheng Industrial Investment Co. Ltd ("Zhongshan" or "Claimant"), a Chinese registered company. It instituted an ad hoc arbitral proceeding against the Federal Republic of Nigeria ("Nigeria" or "Respondent") under the China-Nigeria BIT on August 30, 2018. The place of arbitration is in London, United Kingdom. The China-Nigeria BIT was signed on August 27, 2001, and came into force as of February 18, 2010. This BIT allows any investment dispute to be submitted to an ad hoc arbitral tribunal.[103] It also has a provision on fork-in-the-road, which means, if the investor has resorted to local remedies by submitting the dispute to the competent court of the host state, he could not submit it to international arbitration.[104]

Zhongshan's claim relates to rights in the Ogun Guangdong Free Trade Zone ("the Zone"), a substantial area of land in Ogun State in Nigeria, which is owned by the Ogun State Government ("Ogun State"). The Zone was the subject of a Joint Venture Agreement entered into on June 28, 2007, ("the 2007 JVA") between the Ogun State and Guangdong Xinguang International China-Africa Investment Ltd (hereinafter "CAI"), and CCNC Group Ltd ("CCNC"). The arrangement envisaged by the 2007 JVA involved CAI effectively carrying out the development, marketing and management of the Zone, albeit through Ogun Guangdong Free Trade Zone Company (OGFTZ). By 2010, only limited development had been carried out and CAI was running short of funds, and that, as a result, Zhuhai Zhongfu Industrial Group Co Ltd ("Zhuhai"), another Chinese registered company, was introduced. On June 29, 2010, Zhuhai and OGFTZ entered into the 2010 Framework Agreement (to which CAI was not a party) authorizing Zhuhai the right to develop and operate Fucheng Industrial Park ("Fucheng Park"). Another document dated October 10, 2010, ("the 2010 Deed") was entered into by Zhuhai, OGFTZ and Zhongshan (a subsidiary of Zhuhai, also the parent company of Zhongfu), being treated by Zhongshan and Zhuhai as having the practical effect of transferring Zhuhai's rights and obligations under the 2010 Framework Agreement to Zhongshan. On January 15,

[103] China-Nigeria BIT, Article 9.3.

[104] China-Nigeria BIT, Article 9.2 and 9.3.

2013, by a document ("the 2013 document"), Zhuhai assigned its interest in the 2010 Framework Agreement to Zhongfu. On September 28, 2013, Ogun State, Zhongfu and Zenith Global Merchant Limited ("Zenith") entered into a "Joint Venture Agreement for the Development, Management and Operation" of the Zone ("the 2013 JVA"), which mainly stated that (1) the participation of CAI in the Zone had been terminated and that (2) Zhongfu had been appointed as the new manager of the Zone. However, the relationship between the parties was shattered in 2016, after the Economic and Commercial Section of the Consulate of the PRC in Lagos sent a Note Verbale to the Ogun State authorities, asking for transferring Shareholding interests of CAI in the OFGTZ to the New South Group. In a letter dated April 12, 2016, Mr Adeoluwa (who was then the Secretary to the Ogun State) claimed that "the implication" could be that the "agreement between [Ogun State] and Zhongfu was premised upon misrepresentation and concealment of facts, and, therefore cannot be allowed to stand". Zhongfu was invited to "clarify the position and respond to the demand of" the PRC government. In July 2016, the Ogun State and Nigerian police proceeded to remove Zhongfu personnel from the Zone, allegedly by threatening and mistreating them; all individuals affiliated with the Claimant eventually left the country.

The Claimant contended that Nigeria deprived it of a substantial investment contrary to the provisions of articles 2, 3 and/or 4 of the China-Nigeria BIT. Article 2(3) of the BIT provides that "......neither Contracting Party shall take any unreasonable or discriminatory measures against the management, maintenance, use, enjoyment and disposal of the investments by the investors of the other Contracting Party". Article 3(1) provides that "Investments of investors of each Contracting party shall all the time be accorded fair and equitable treatment in the territory of the other Contracting Party". Article 4(1) provides that "Neither Contracting Party shall expropriate, nationalize or take similar measures (hereinafter referred to as "expropriation") against the investments of investors of the other Contracting Party in its territory, unless ......".

Nigeria raised various jurisdictional and preliminary arguments. In the March 26, 2021, award, the Tribunal decided in favor of the investor, dismissing all of Nigeria's jurisdictional objections, including contentions that the claims were barred by a fork-in-the-road clause and that the dispute with the Ogun State was not attributable to the Federal Republic. The Tribunal first rejected the argument that Zhongshan had no valid claim against Nigeria as the federal entities' actions complained of could and should not be attributed to Nigeria. The Tribunal then rejected the argument that Zhongshan did not hold an investment. It also dealt with a range of issues such as fork-in-the-road clause, exhaustion of domestic remedies and alleged misrepresentations. In the end, the Tribunal decided that Zhongshan had locus to pursue a claim for compensation under the BIT in respect of its rights under the 2010 Framework Agreement and the 2013 JVA and that Nigeria is in breach of its obligations under articles 2(3), 3(1) and 4(1) of the Treaty. Thus, the Tribunal ordered Nigeria to pay to Zhongshan and the sum of compensation for the expropriation is USD 55.6 million.[105]

---

[105] Zhongshan Fucheng v. Nigeria, Final Award (2021).

Nigeria opposed to the Award and made a remedy claim to the High Court of Justice of England and Wales on April 23, 2021, seeking an order declaring that the Award on the merits is of no effect in whole (or in such part as the Court thinks fit) because the tribunal did not have substantive jurisdiction. Alternatively, Nigeria sought an order setting aside or varying the Award of the tribunal as to its substantive jurisdiction in such terms as the Court thinks fit.[106] On October 8, 2021, Nigeria notified the Court to discontinue its claim.[107]

However, Nigeria did not comply with the Award and pay the compensation to Zhongshan. On December 8, 2021, Zhongshan commenced enforcement proceedings in the United Kingdom, and the English court issued an order that recognized the Award. Then on January 25, 2023, Zhongshan lodged a petition to recognize and enforce this Award in the United States District Court for the District Of Columbia under the Convention on the Recognition and Enforcement of Foreign Arbitral Awards (the "New York Convention"), which was confirmed by the Court. On the same date, the Superior Court Commercial Division of Canada Province of Quebec District of Montreal granted Zhongshan's request for the issuance of an order to seize property in the hands of a third person before judgment, and authorized it to seize before judgment the property described in the judgment.[108]

### *3.6.2 Everyway Traffic and Lighting V. Ghana*

On February 10, 2021, Beijing Everyway Traffic & Lighting Tech. Co., Ltd (the "Claimant" or "Everyway") commenced ad hoc arbitration proceedings against the Government of the Republic of Ghana (the "Respondent" or "Ghana") under the China-Ghana BIT (the Treaty) concluded on October 12, 1989, and came into force as of November 22, 1990. The BIT only allows the investor-state investment concerning the amount of compensation for expropriation be submitted to an arbitral tribunal. On January 30, 2023, the Tribunal issued a Final Award on Jurisdiction in favor of the state deciding that it lacked jurisdiction to decide the Claimant's claims in this arbitration.

The dispute arose out of the underlying contract between the Claimant and the Respondent, which is an Engineering, Procurement, Installation and Commissioning Contract signed on September 17, 2012 (the "EPIC Contract"). Under the EPIC Contract, the Claimant agreed to supply equipment and provide technical services to the Respondent for the planning, design, construction, supervision, operation and training for the "Accra Metropolitan Area Traffic Management Project" (the "AITMS

---

[106] Remedy Claimed in the High Court of Justice of England and Wales, Witness Statement Made in Support of the Claimant's Application, available at https://italaw.com/sites/default/files/case-documents/180224.pdf.

[107] Notice of Discontinuance of Claim in the High Court of England and Wales, available at https://italaw.com/sites/default/files/case-documents/180226.pdf.

[108] Zhongshan Fucheng v. Nigeria, available at https://italaw.com/cases/9287#.

Project" or the "Project"). During the execution of the EPIC Contract, the Claimant issued two Interim Payment Certificates, which to date remain unpaid. On November 19, 2020, the Parliament of Ghana rescinded the EPIC Contract with the Claimant. According to the Claimant, the Respondent had decided to rescind the EPIC Contract and award the works for the AITMS Project to two third-party companies already from June 2019. On December 30, 2021, the Claimant served the Respondent with a notice purporting to terminate the EPIC Contract.

In this arbitration, the Claimant sought a declaration that the Tribunal had jurisdiction over the Claimant's claims under Article 10(1) and Article 3(2) of the Treaty. As regards the merits of the dispute, the Claimant sought a declaration that the Respondent's arbitrary decision to rescind the EPIC Contract with the Claimant and award the project to third parties as well as the Respondent's failure to pay the Claimant for work performed under the EPIC Contract amount to: a. a direct or indirect expropriation of the Claimant's investment which constitutes a breach of Article 4 of the Treaty; b. a failure on the part of Ghana to provide equitable treatment and protection to the Claimant's investment that constitutes a breach of Article 3(1) of the Treaty; c. a breach on the part of Ghana of its contractual obligations under the EPIC Contract which amounts to a breach of Ghana's duty under the Treaty to observe any obligation it has entered into with regard to investments made by Chinese investors ("Umbrella Clause"), especially under Article 3(2) of the Treaty which contains a most-favored-nation treatment clause ("MFN"). Also, the Claimant sought an order awarding Everyway the damages which it has incurred as a result of the above-mentioned breaches of the Treaty.

On June 30, 2021, the Respondent filed its Response to the Notice of Arbitration, in which it raised a jurisdictional objection, claiming that the Claimant's claims fell out of the scope of the China-Ghana BIT. The Respondent contended that the provision of Article 10(1) of the Treaty limits the jurisdiction of the Tribunal to the determination of the quantum of compensation for expropriation and does not include the question of the entitlement of expropriation. As regards Article 10(1) of the Treaty, after having considered the width of the ordinary meaning of the terms "any dispute", "concerning" and "amount of compensation for expropriation" stipulated in that article, the Tribunal adopted a narrow interpretation and decided that the ordinary meaning of Article 10(1) could not be read as meaning to include the question of entitlement of expropriation. As regards Article 3(2) of the Treaty, the Tribunal considered that the terms "treatment and protection" in Article 3(2) must be given a narrow meaning according to which the MFN clause applies to substantive treatment and protection only and dispute resolution is not included in the scope of Article 3(2). Thus, it is difficult to see how investor-state arbitration can be a significant aspect of the purpose and object of the Treaty which would accord Article 3(2) of the Treaty a broad meaning to extend to investor-state arbitration provisions contained in other treaties.

Finally, the Tribunal upheld the Respondent's objections to the Tribunal's jurisdiction and found that it had no jurisdiction to decide the Claimant's claims in this arbitration.[109]

## Annex: List of China-Africa BITs (in Chronological Order)

| No | African country | Date of signature | Date of entry into force | Remarks |
|---|---|---|---|---|
| 1 | Ghana | 12-Oct-89 | 22-Nov-90 | |
| 2 | Egypt | 21-Apr-94 | 1-Apr-96 | |
| 3 | Morocco | 27-Mar-95 | 27-Nov-99 | |
| 4 | Mauritius | 4-May-96 | 8-Jun-97 | Terminated |
| 5 | Zimbabwe | 21-May-96 | 1-Mar-98 | |
| 6 | Zambia | 21-Jun-96 | 01-Feb-14 | |
| 7 | Algeria | 17-Oct-96 | 28-Jan-03 | |
| 8 | Gabon | 9-May-97 | 16-Feb-09 | |
| 9 | Cameroon | 10-May-97 | 24-Jul-14 | |
| 10 | Nigeria | 12-May-97 | – | Terminated |
| 11 | Sudan | 30-May-97 | 1-Jul-98 | |
| 12 | DR Congo | 18-Dec-97 | 18-Dec-97 | Terminated |
| 13 | South Africa | 30-Dec-97 | 1-Apr-98 | |
| 14 | Cape Verde | 21-Apr-98 | 1-Jan-01 | |
| 15 | Ethiopia | 11-May-98 | 1-May-00 | |
| 16 | Congo | 20-Mar-00 | 01-Jul-15 | |
| 17 | Botswana | 12-Jun-00 | – | |
| 18 | Sierra Leone | 16-May-01 | – | |
| 19 | Mozambique | 10-Jul-01 | 26-Feb-02 | |
| 20 | Kenya | 16-Jul-01 | – | |
| 21 | Nigeria | 27-Aug-01 | 18-Feb-10 | The second one |
| 22 | Côte d'Ivoire | 30-Sep-02 | – | |
| 23 | Djibouti | 18-Aug-03 | – | |
| 24 | Benin | 18-Feb-04 | – | |
| 25 | Uganda | 27-May-04 | – | |
| 26 | Tunisia | 21-Jun-04 | 1-Jul-06 | |
| 27 | Equatorial Guinea | 20-Oct-05 | 15-Nov-06 | |
| 28 | Namibia | 17-Nov-05 | – | |
| 29 | Guinea | 18-Nov-05 | – | |
| 30 | Madagascar | 21-Nov-05 | 1-Jul-07 | |
| 31 | Seychelles | 10-Feb-07 | – | |
| 32 | Mali | 12-Feb-09 | 16-Jul-09 | |

(continued)

109 Beijing Everyway Traffic and Lighting v. Ghana, Final Award (2023).

(continued)

| No | African country | Date of signature | Date of entry into force | Remarks |
|---|---|---|---|---|
| 33 | Chad | 26-Apr-10 | – | |
| 34 | Libya | 04-Aug-10 | – | |
| 35 | DR Congo | 11-Aug-11 | 17-Nov-16 | The second one |
| 36 | Tanzania | 24-Mar-13 | 17-Apr-14 | |
| 37 | Angola | 06-Dec-23 | – | |

*Sources* Own compilation based on MOFCOM, UNCTAD database and other sources

## References


Axel Berger (2008) China's new bilateral investment treaty programme: substance, rational and implications for international investment law making, the politics of international economic law: the next four years. Available at http://www.asil.org/files/ielconferencepapers/berger.pdf

Axel Berger (2011) The politics of China's investment treaty-making program, in The politics of international economic law, edited by T. Broude, M. Busch, A. Porges, Cambridge University Press

Beijing Everyway Traffic and Lighting Company Limited v. Ghana, Final Award on Jurisdiction (Save As To Costs) (2023)

Congyan Cai (2009) China-US BIT negotiations and the future of investment treaty regime: a grand bilateral bargain with multilateral implications. J Intern Econ Law, Oxford University Press

Deborah Brautigam (2009) The Dragon's gift: the real story of China in Africa, Oxford University Press

Karl P. Sauvant, Huiping Chen (2012) A China—US bilateral investment treaty: a template for a multilateral framework for investment?, Columbia FDI Perspectives, No. 85, December 17, 2012

Ken Davies (2011) While global FDI falls, China's outward FDI doubles, in Inward and Outward FDI Country Profiles, edited by Karl P. Sauvant, Thomas Jost, Ken Davies, Ana-Maria Poveda Garcés, Vale Columbia Center, January 2011

MOFCOM (2010) Statistical Bulletin of China's Outward Foreign Direct Investment. Available at http://images.mofcom.gov.cn/hzs/accessory/201109/1316069604368.pdf

MOFCOM (2011) Statistical Bulletin of China's Outward Foreign Direct Investment, China Statistics Press

MOFCOM (2012) Statistical Bulletin of China's outward Foreign Direct Investment, China Statistics Press

MOFCOM (2013) Statistical Bulletin of China's outward Foreign Direct Investment, China Statistics Press

MOFCOM (2014) Statistical Bulletin of China's Outward Foreign Direct Investment, China Statistics Press

MOFCOM (2021) Statistical Bulletin of China's Outward Foreign Direct Investment, China Statistics Press

MOFCOM (2022) Statistical Bulletin of China's Outward Foreign Direct Investment, China Statistics Press

Norah Gallagher, Wenhua Shan (2008) Chinese investment treaties: policies and practice, Oxford University Press

Uche Ewelukwa Ofodile (2013) Africa-China bilateral investment treaties: a critique. 35 Michigan J Intern Law 131–211

UNCTAD (2005) South-South Cooperation in International Investment Arrangements, UNCTAD Series on International Investment Policies for Development
UNCTAD (2012), Investment Policy Framework for Sustainable Development. Available at http://unctad.org/en/PublicationsLibrary/webdiaepcb2012d6_en.pdf
Valentina Vadi (2011–2012) Converging divergences: the rise of China's outward foreign investment and its implications for international (Investment) law, Yearbook on International Investment Law & Policy
Xavier Carim (2013) Lessons from South Africa's BITs review, Columbia FDI Perspectives, No. 109, November 25, 2013
Yingji Piao (2006) The evolution and future trend of Chinese investment in Africa, Overseas Investments and Export Credits, vol. 5
Zhongshan Fucheng Industrial Investment Co. Ltd. v. Federal Republic of Nigeria, Final Award (2021)

# Chapter 4
# China–US Bilateral Investment Treaty Negotiations

## 4.1 Introduction

China—the largest developing country—and the US—the largest developed country—launched their negotiations on a bilateral investment treaty (BIT) for the promotion and protection of foreign investment in 2008. Unfortunately, the negotiations were later suspended until 2012 due to the fact that the US was trying to update it model BIT. When the negotiations were resumed in the year of 2012, the international background of international investment agreements has been changed, and it seemed benefitable for the success of BIT negotiations between China and the US. It was once presumed that if the agreement were reached between both, it would provide a template for future international investment agreements. However, when the negotiations almost reached consensus on all major articles of the agreement, it was left in the air until now due to the then newly-elected President Donald Trump came to office.

However, the convergence and divergence of the two countries during the negotiations were deserved to be revisited for future possible reset of the negotiations, and also for China to reflect when it updates its BITs with other countries in implementing the Belt and Road Initiative.

---

A summary of this chapter was published in the title of A China-US bilateral investment treaty: A template for a multilateral framework for investment?, in: Transnational Corporations Review, Volume 5, Number 1, March 2013. The summary was co-authored by Karl P. Sauvant and the author.

 
H. Chen, *China's Practice in International Investment Law*, Modern China and International Economic Law, https://doi.org/10.1007/978-981-96-5016-3_4

## 4.2 The Progress of the China-US BIT Negotiations

The launch of the China-US BIT negotiations was officially declared at the conclusion of the fourth China-US Strategic Economic Dialogue (SED) on June 18, 2008.[1] Actually, informal contacts and talks commenced earlier than the declaration, according to a Chinese official. The two parties exchanged their respective template texts (the US side used the 2004 Model BIT as the template) as basis for the negotiations and discussed each article one by one in detail focusing on the two sides' respective negotiating positions on the main BIT text.[2] Six rounds of US-China BIT negotiations have taken place before they were ended in September 2009.

In November 2009, President Hu Jintao of China and President Obama of the US declared that both countries would "expedite negotiation on a bilateral investment treaty" in a joint announcement of the US and China.[3] This signaled the second stage of the negotiations that intended to touch upon the substantive issues of the BIT. Unfortunately, the intended substantive negotiation was terminated in 2010. The reason was guessed that the US 2004 Model was put to review and update in 2009 and would be replaced by a new one in 2010, but the new one could not come out in 2010 as expected. This guess proved to be true in February 2012 when the US-China Business Council Board of Directors appealed that "The US should finalize its internal review of the US Model BIT and resume negotiations with China as soon as possible" in its Statement of Priorities in the US-China Commercial Relationship.[4]

The new US Model BIT was eventually released in April 2012.[5] Shortly before the release, a cabinet-level agreement between the two governments was reached *at the fourth US China Strategic and Economic Dialogue on May 4, 2012,* to schedule *a* seventh and subsequent negotiating rounds, and to intensify investment negotiations.[6] Discussions resumed in Beijing in mid-October 2012 while the two sides were still in the "discussion phase".[7] The US and Chinese officials met in Washington on December 19, 2012, in the 23rd China-US Joint Commission on Commerce and Trade and will discuss the BIT again.

Ever since, the negotiations came to a substantial stage and great progress was made. In July 2013, China accepted the "pre-establishment national treatment plus negative list approach". In March 2015, the text of the agreement was almost

---

[1] Congyan Cai (2009), pp. 457–506.

[2] Market Access Is Key Area In U.S.-China BIT Talks, But Outcome Uncertain, Inside U.S. Trade, October 19, 2012.

[3] The White House (2009).

[4] U.S.-China Business Council (2012) .

[5] United States Concludes Review of Model Bilateral Investment Treaty, available at http://www.state.gov/r/pa/prs/ps/2012/04/188198.htm, last visited on December 18, 2012. The text of the 2012 US Model BIT can be viewed at: http://www.state.gov/e/eb/ifd/bit/index.htm.

[6] Joint U.S.-China Economic Track Fact Sheet, U.S. China Strategic and Economic Dialogue, available at http://www.cfr.org/china/joint-us-china-economic-track-fact-sheet-us-china-strategic-economic-dialogue/p28196, last visited on December 19, 2012.

[7] Hormats Says BIT Talks With China May Not Lead To Comprehensive Deal, Inside U.S. Trade, December 7, 2012.

completed. Later on, the two countries focused on negotiations on the negative lists of both countries. Unfortunately, when President Trump came to office in January 2017, the BIT negotiations were left in the air until now.

## 4.3 International Background for the Resuming of Negotiations in 2012

The US, representing the developed countries as both the largest foreign-direct-investment (FDI) host and home country, updated its 2004 model BIT and released the new Model BIT in April 2012,[8] to revert from excessive liberalization to gentle liberalization. China is also changing its BITs due to its new identity as the largest FDI host and home country among emerging markets, as a result of its Going Out Policy, Belt and Road Initiative and its rich foreign currency reserves. Some of China's recent BIT articles were quite "Americanized" such as articles on expropriation, the denial of benefits, general exceptions including prudential measures, and taxation. The typical practice in this regard was the signing of the China-Japan-Korea Trilateral Investment Agreement on May 13, 2012,[9] and the China-Canada Promotion and Reciprocal Protection of Investments on September 9, 2012.[10] As host countries, both US and China seek to maintain policy space to pursue their own legitimate public policy objectives; as home countries, both seek to protect their investors' outward FDI. The development of their bilateral investment treaties (BITs) over the past decade reflects this: Chinese BITs have become more protective of investors, US ones more respectful of host country interests.

International investment agreements were also in a crossroad ever since the early twenty-first century. Hot discussions lied on the reform of the standards of protection and investor-state dispute settlement laid down in investment agreements. Due to the expansion of the EU's Common Commercial Policy to include FDI, it is EU instead of its member states that has the competence to negotiate and sign investment treaties

[8] U.S. Department of State, Model Bilateral Investment Treaty, Fact Sheet, available at http://www.state.gov/r/pa/prs/ps/2012/04/188199.htm, last visited December 17, 2012. The text of the 2012 Model BIT can be viewed at: http://www.state.gov/e/eb/ifd/bit/index.htm.

[9] Ministry of Foreign Affairs of Japan, Signing of the Japan–China-Korea Trilateral Investment Agreement, available at http://www.mofa.go.jp/announce/announce/2012/5/0513_01.html, last visited on December 17, 2012. The text of the Agreement among the Government of Japan, the Government of the Republic of Korea and the Government of the People's Republic of China for the Promotion, Facilitation and Protection of Investment can be views at: http://www.mofa.go.jp/announce/announce/2012/5/pdfs/0513_01_01.pdf.

[10] Foreign Affairs and International Trade Canada, Canada-China Foreign Investment Promotion and Protection Agreement (FIPA) Negotiations, available at http://www.international.gc.ca/trade-agreements-accords-commerciaux/agr-acc/fipa-apie/china-chine.aspx?lang=eng&view=d, last visited on December 17, 2012. The text of the Agreement Between the Government of Canada and the Government of the People's Republic of China for the Promotion and Reciprocal Protection of Investments can be viewed at http://www.international.gc.ca/trade-agreements-accords-commerciaux/agr-acc/fipa-apie/china-text-chine.aspx?lang=eng&view=d.

with other countries.[11] Scholars suggest EU to strike a better balance in investment agreements between the private interests of investors and the interests of the public.[12] The developing countries also changed their attitude toward BITs from conservative before 1990s to comparatively open and free in late 1990s and early twenty-first century, but later they had the tendency to return to the traditional and conservative attitude.[13]

This background imposed significant impact on the resuming of the China-US BIT negotiations in 2012 and on the shaping of the text of the BIT.

## 4.4 The Convergence and Divergence Between the Two Countries

Based on publicly available documents, it appears likely that the two parties share similar general purpose and aims of concluding the BIT due to the fact that both of them act as both capital-import and capital-export countries. They also have some commons and convergences as to some articles in the BIT since they have almost reached to consensus as to protecting host country's interest and limiting the power and discretion of international tribunal as a result of the past practice by international investment treaty arbitration.

They agreed basically that all investors (including state-controlled entities) are covered, that the MFN clause only applies to substantive clauses rather than applying to both substantive and procedural issues. For the heatedly disputed fair and equitable treatment that was broadly interpreted by international investment arbitration tribunals in many cases, the US government made substantial amendment to this article in its 2004 Model BIT (and the 2012 Model BIT remains the same) to correspond to the customary international law minimum standard of treatment, which is basically agreed with by China. For the article of expropriation, the US 2004 Model BIT (and the 2012 Model BIT remains the same) added Annex B "Expropriation" to clarify the rules on expropriation and the criteria for indirect expropriation, which is almost accepted by China. For the article of denial of interest, China did not have one in its past BITs, but now it adopted a similar one as that in the US 2004 Model BIT (and the 2012 Model BIT) in its BITs such as BITs with New Zealand, Mexico,

[11] Article 207 of the Treaty on the Functioning of the European Union, especially Article 207.1 that reads "The common commercial policy shall be based on uniform principles, particularly with regard to changes in tariff rates, the conclusion of tariff and trade agreements relating to trade in goods and services, and the commercial aspects of intellectual property, foreign direct investment, the achievement of uniformity in measures of liberalisation, export policy and measures to protect trade such as those to be taken in the event of dumping or subsidies. The common commercial policy shall be conducted in the context of the principles and objectives of the Union's external action".

[12] Axel Berger (2012).

[13] Huiping Chen (2008).

Canada and the trilateral investment agreement with Japan and Korea, for the purpose of avoiding abuse of the BIT benefits by unqualified foreign investors.

However, many differences existed between the two parties. In general, the US insists on high-standard treatment of and protection to private investors, while China hopes to balance the interests of both host state and private investor. Differences are more pronounced regarding performance requirements, labor and environment standards, and investor-state dispute settlement.

For performance requirements, the US seeks to expand the TRIMs list and has a long list of prohibited performance requirements in its 2012 Model BIT, while China does not want to cover it in any BIT. This matter might be solved by reaffirming China's WTO accession commitments to leave the use of certain requirements to the parties to a given investment. China's concession in the China-Canada BIT is incorporating by reference the obligations under the WTO *Agreement on Trade-Related Investment Measures* (TRIMs) and its annex. Such incorporation is more than merely a symbolic statement.[14] Reading it together with the investor-state dispute settlement mechanism embodied in the investment treaty, foreign investor might rely on it to sue host government for its violations of its TRIMs commitments, which is impossible within the WTO.

For labor and environment standards, the US desires strong language like the one in its 2012 Model BIT. However, China could follow the approach of side agreements of the China-New Zealand free trade agreement which reaffirms commitments already made in other fora and provides for purposeful cooperation between the parties in these areas.

For investor-state dispute settlement, the 2012 US Model BIT has many detailed articles while China only agrees with some general articles. The key difference lies in the transparency of arbitral proceedings. China could follow the approach of 2012 Canada-China BIT regarding transparency that requires that arbitral awards are public by default. Whether arbitral hearings and documents submitted to the Tribunal are public is a determination ultimately left to the state that is party to the investor-state dispute.[15]

## 4.5 The Most Difficult Issue—National Treatment

Not surprisingly, the most difficult issue concerned the phase of investment to which national treatment applies: host countries typically want to maintain flexibility relating to when and where they allow FDI into their economies (including given industrial policy considerations), while the US business community seeks

---

[14] Saulino JJ (2012).

[15] Saulino JJ (2012).

strong market access commitments.[16] Accordingly, the US government seeks pre-establishment national treatment with a "negative list" approach which lists sectors to which national treatment does not apply. As a USTR official stated, including a market access component and negotiating it on a "negative list" basis, in the US-China BIT, are "core elements".[17] However, China had limited its agreements for a long time to post-establishment national treatment with carve-outs for existing non-conforming measures. This key architectural question had profound implications for market access.

Given their different views on key topics, the US and China might not be able to conclude a BIT.[18] Therefore, compromise was the approach to solution. At the beginning, concerning national treatment, some compromises were suggested including a negative list approach for national treatment regarding post-establishment and a positive list approach which lists sectors to which national treatment applies regarding pre-establishment. China's Guidance Catalogue and the US exceptions in BITs may constitute starting points as they identify sectors. In a hybrid approach, the two governments would (1) list the broad sectors to which *national treatment applies pre-establishment* (positive list) and (2), within each broad sector, list all sub-sectors to which *national treatment does not apply pre-establishment* (negative list).

Either approach would be a major concession by the parties and would require a political decision. This could be facilitated (and hence limit the concession) by grandfathering existing non-conforming measures (including a narrowly defined national security review); agreeing a standstill on new restrictions (to provide transparency, predictability and stability, but perhaps with the flexibility that new restrictions for future investments need to be offset by negotiated new openings) and a commitment to remove non-conforming measures progressively. One could also carve out particularly important sectors and agree on a tailored approach for them. Or one could grant pre-establishment MFN but not pre-establishment national treatment, as per the Canada-China BIT. There are many approaches to protect the essential interests of both sides.

US concerns as a host country seem to become more pronounced, reflected in the more active screening of certain incoming investments (see, e.g., President Obama's September 2012 veto, on national security grounds, of a Chinese investment, the first such veto in 22 years), while China has introduced its own FDI national security review (which includes economic security and conceivably also industrial policy)—making investment entry less predictable. Moreover, China's outward FDI is rising rapidly and, with it, the desire to protect it. Hence, both countries should be interested in concluding their BIT negotiations, to put their bilateral investment relationship on a predictable footing. In particular, a BIT would increase the protection that investors

[16] Market Access Is Key Area In U.S.-China BIT Talks, But Outcome Uncertain, Inside U.S. Trade, October 19, 2012.

[17] Market Access Is Key Area In U.S.-China BIT Talks, But Outcome Uncertain, Inside U.S. Trade, October 19, 2012.

[18] Hormats Says BIT Talks With China May Not Lead To Comprehensive Deal, Inside U.S. Trade, December 7, 2012.

from both countries would receive in each other's territory, provide a mechanism for dispute resolution and likely improve market access.

Things have been changed in July 2013 when China decided to accept pre-establishment national treatment with a negative list approach. This change is partly because of the US insistence, but mostly is because China's domestic economic situation has changed and required such a national treatment. China has become the third state of overseas investment in the world in 2013, making China both the major capital-import country and major capital-export country. The time for China to accept pre-establishment national treatment with negative list is ripe and would benefit China. Further, in 2019 when China adopted its totally new national Foreign Investment Law, it unilaterally offers the pre-establishment national treatment with negative list to any foreign investor, regardless the fact that China did not accept it in almost all of the BITs it concluded with other countries. With the promotion of the Belt and Road Initiative which would have and actually has greatly promoted Chinese overseas investment in the Belt and Road countries, the pre-establishment national treatment, if adopted in the investment agreements that China concludes with other countries, would also benefit Chinese investors.

## 4.6 Conclusion

If the China-US BIT could be concluded, it would provide a solution to the challenge of balancing the interests of a given country in its capacity as a (capital-importing) *host* country with its interests in its capacity of a (capital-exporting) *home* country. Meeting this challenge would represent a historic compromise between the traditionally quite diverging host and home country positions and (together with other important negotiations, e.g., involving the European Union, Japan, India and a Trans-Pacific Partnership Agreement) might well become a platform on which, sooner or later, a multilateral framework could be built. These negotiations were therefore of crucial importance not only for the economic relations of the world's two largest economies, but also for the evolution of the international investment law regime. Unfortunately, this became an impossible dream.

## References

Axel Berger (2012) Recognising the signs of the times—investment protection in the 21st century, The Current Column of 22 October 2012.

Congyan Cai (2009) China-Us BIT Negotiations and the Future of Investment Treaty Regime: A Grand Bilateral Bargain with Multilateral Implications. J Intern Econ Law 12(2).

Hormats Says BIT Talks With China May Not Lead To Comprehensive Deal, Inside U.S. Trade, December 7, 2012.

Huiping Chen (2008) Investor-State Dispute Settlement Mechanism: Where to go in the 21st Century? J World Invest Trade 9(6).

Saulino JJ (2012) The Canada-China Investment Treaty - Lessons for a U.S.-China BIT? Transnational Dispute Management.

Market Access Is Key Area In U.S.-China BIT Talks, But Outcome Uncertain, Inside U.S. Trade, October 19, 2012.

The White House (2009), Office of the Press Secretary, U.S.-China Joint Statement. Available at http://www.whitehouse.gov/the-press-office/us-china-joint-statement

U.S.-China Business Council (2012) Board of Directors Statement of Priorities in the U.S.-China Commercial Relationship, U.S.-China Business Council, February 10.

# Chapter 5
# The Impacts and Implications of China's "Belt & Road" Initiative on China's International Investment Law Practice

## 5.1 Introduction

The "Belt & Road" Initiative (BRI) was first proposed by China's President Xi Jinping in 2013 in his first term in office. To strengthen and deepen the BRI, the Chinese Communist Party incorporated the BRI into its Constitution in late 2017 in President Xi's second term. The major target and spirit enshrined in the Initiative is "building a human community with shared destiny" which was also incorporated into a UN resolution in late 2017.[1] In March 2018, during the national meeting of the Chinese National People's Congress, it was decided to add this spirit to China's Constitution as a guiding principle for China.

The BRI is generally an international economic cooperation initiative through the building of mutual connectivity targeting on mutual benefits and win–win. It hopes to create more opportunities for global economic growth and the common development of different countries. The Initiative intends to promote infrastructure construction, trade and investment, among other activities, between China and those countries and regions in the Belt and Road domain. One of the focuses is to promote China's outward investment. As a result, China's outward investment has been greatly increased. Currently, China has become the second largest country of both capital-import and capital-export in the world. Since 2016, the total amount of China's outward investment has exceeded the amount of its inward investment.

The Initiative and the resulted change of the outward foreign investment structure have great impacts on China's outward foreign investment law and policy including on both the national level and international level, as well as China's attitude toward investor-state dispute settlement (ISDS). Moreover, China is trying to innovate its own ISDS to respond to the problems it faces in the BRI practice and to respond to

[1] For example, the Resolution 2344 (2017) adopted by the Security Council at its 7902nd meeting, on 17 March 2017, available at https://documents-dds-ny.un.org/doc/UNDOC/GEN/N17/069/96/PDF/N1706996.pdf?OpenElement, last visited on October 18, 2023.

 
H. Chen, *China's Practice in International Investment Law*, Modern China and International Economic Law, https://doi.org/10.1007/978-981-96-5016-3_5

the ISDS reform in the international community.Lastly, the BRI has significance and implications for Sino-African investment relations.

## 5.2 Overview of the Belt and Road Initiative

Since 2000, China carried out the "Going Global Strategy" to encourage outward investment. Now it is one of the world's major capital-export countries and has concluded many bilateral investment treaties (BITs) with most of the countries in the world. The Belt and Road Initiative is the continuing and deepening of the "Going Global Strategy". The "Belt" means the "Silk Road Economic Belt", which is land-based routes focusing on bringing together China, Asia, Russia and Europe. The "Road" means the "21st-Century Maritime Silk Road", which is an ocean-based route designed to go from China's coast to Europe through the South China Sea, the Indian Ocean and the South Pacific.[2]

The "Silk Road Economic Belt" and "21st Century Maritime Silk Road" are initiatives first introduced by President Xi Jinping in the fall of 2013 during his visits to Kazakhstan and Indonesia, respectively. In the December of 2015, the Belt and Road Initiative was featured prominently in China's 13th Five-Year Plan, which runs from 2016 to 2020 and guides national investment strategy throughout that period.

According to the Vision and Actions on Jointly Building Belt and Road, issued by the National Development and Reform Commission, Ministry of Foreign Affairs and Ministry of Commerce of the People's Republic of China in 2016, "The Belt and Road run through the continents of Asia, Europe and Africa, connecting the vibrant East Asia economic circle at one end and developed European economic circle at the other, and encompassing countries with huge potential for economic development. The Silk Road Economic Belt focuses on bringing together China, Central Asia, Russia and Europe (the Baltic); linking China with the Persian Gulf and the Mediterranean Sea through Central Asia and West Asia; and connecting China with Southeast Asia, South Asia and the Indian Ocean. The 21st-Century Maritime Silk Road is designed to go from China's coast to Europe through the South China Sea and the Indian Ocean in one route, and from China's coast through the South China Sea to the South Pacific in the other".[3]

More than 70 countries in various regions and economic groupings are located in the Belt and Road domain. However, the BRI does not define a geographic limit since it is an initiative for international cooperation and thus open to any country

[2] For details of the Belt and Road Initiatives, please refer to the official website https://www.yidaiyilu.gov.cn/.

[3] The National Development and Reform Commission et al. (2016), Vision and Actions on Jointly Building Belt and Road, available at http://english.cri.cn/12394/2015/03/29/2941s872030.htm, June 30.

which echoes with it. Such states as Argentina, Panama and Chile in South America are also covered by the Belt and Road Initiative.[4]

To partially complement and support the Initiative, two financial institutions have been established: Silk Road Fund (SRF)[5] and Asian Infrastructure Investment Bank (AIIB).[6] SRF was established in 2014 as a liability limited Fund Corporation, for the purpose of providing service for the construction of Belt and Road. By the end of 2022, SRF has made investment in over 60 countries and regions for the total amount of about 20 billion of USD.[7] AIIB was established in 2015 as a multilateral development bank focusing on developing Asia, but with members from all over the world. Its investments in infrastructure and other productive sectors seek to foster sustainable economic development, create wealth and improve infrastructure connectivity.[8] Until October 2023, it has approved 230 projects, and 65 projects have been proposed.[9] All those projects have been located in the countries and regions in the Belt and Road domain. However, it does not mean that AIIB only invests in the Belt and Road domain.

## 5.3 Impacts of BRI on China's Outward Foreign Investment

The BRI aims to further integrate China into the global economy through trade, investment, infrastructure construction, connectivity and other development projects. One of the major tasks of jointly building the Belt and Road is to increase investment and trade cooperation. Thus, the Initiative could help to enhance regional economic growth, development and integration. The Initiative is a win–win cooperation policy. Investment and trade cooperation is a major task in building the Belt and Road.

In terms of investment, the Belt and Road Initiative has promoted and will continue to greatly promote Chinese outward foreign direct investment majorly in developing countries. As a result, investment dynamism has built up rapidly ever since. Chinese outward FDI surged. In 2016, it rose 44 percent to $183 billion, and made China to the position of second largest home country for FDI flow for the first time. China became a net outward direct investor in this year.[10] In 2017, China was the third largest home country for FDI flows next to the US and Japan, but the second largest

[4] For a list of the Belt and Road Countries, please refer to https://www.yidaiyilu.gov.cn/country.

[5] For details of SRF, please refer to its official website: http://www.silkroadfund.com.cn/.

[6] For details of AIIB, please refer to it official website: https://www.aiib.org/en/about-aiib/index.html.

[7] This figure comes from the SRF website of http://www.silkroadfund.com.cn/cnweb/tzdt/tzgl/index.html, last visited on October 18, 2023.

[8] Please refer to https://www.aiib.org/en/about-aiib/index.html, last visited on October 18, 2023.

[9] This figure comes from the AIIB website https://www.aiib.org/en/index.html.

[10] UNCTAD (2017), p. 14.

home country for FDI stock next to the US.[11] China's total outward FDI flows to the 63 countries along the Belt and Road in 2017 is more than 20 billion of USD.[12] A number of countries located in the Belt and Road domain such as Singapore, Kazakhstan, Malaysia and Indonesia, have started to attract a significant amount of FDI flows from China as a result of their active participation in the BRI.[13] By the year of 2023, the Belt and Road has been in implementation for ten years. The ten years has produced significant progress in China's outward investment, especially in the Belt and Road domain. For example, in the year of 2022, China's outward FDI reached the amount of 163.12 billion of USD, being the second in the world. The accumulated amount of China's outward FDI by the end of 2022 has reached 2750 billion of USD, being the third in the world.[14]

The countries and regions in the Belt and Road domain are majorly developing countries that are in shortage of capital for economic development. They welcome Chinese investment very much. It is a win–win policy since foreign countries receive the capital they need and Chinese enterprises receive projects. China has been the largest home economy investing in LDCs for years.[15]

## 5.4 Impacts of BRI on China's Outward Foreign Investment Law and Policy[16]

The Belt and Road Initiative and the change of the investment structure in China have great impacts on China's foreign investment law and policy on both national and international levels, which will be elaborated as follows.

On the national level, the Initiative requires China to adopt new national investment law and policy so as to carry out the Initiative and promote Chinese outward investment, on the one hand, and regulate and protect ODI, on the other hand.

Before 2000, China did not encourage, or even restricted its outward investment (ODI). As a result, the relevant law and policy reflected such a restriction. Since 2000, the "Going Abroad" strategy was proposed, and then new or updated laws and policies were adopted to support this strategy. To carry out the Belt and Road Initiative, China's Ministry of Commerce (MOFCOM), China's National Development and Reform Commission (NDRC), State Administration of Foreign Exchange (SAFE)

[11] China's Ministry of Commerce et al. (2017), pp. 83–85.

[12] China's Ministry of Commerce et al. (2017), p. 153.

[13] UNCTAD (2017), p. 19; China's Ministry of Commerce et al. (2017), p.153.

[14] The figures comes from the website of China's Ministry of Commerce, http://file.mofcom.gov.cn/article/zwgk/gkbnjg/202309/20230903443704.shtml, last visited on October 18, 2023.

[15] UNCTAD (2017), p. 80.

[16] The part is excerpt and updated based on my article published in the title of The Belt & Road Initiative and the New Landscape of China's ISDS Policy and Practice, in: The BRICS in the New International Legal Order on Investment: Reformers or Disrupters, Published by Brill Nijhoff, 2020.

and other governmental organs have issued some new regulations and policies to promote China's outward investment majorly in 2013 and 2014.

Since 2017, MOFCOM, NDRC and other organs abolished and terminated several out-of-date regulations and rules. They are active in making new regulations and rules not only for promoting outward investment, but also for supervising Chinese ODI. In December 2017, NDRC issued China's new Administrative Measures for Overseas Investment by Enterprises, to replace the Administrative Measures for Verification and Filing of Overseas Investment Projects issued in 2014. This new document cancels and relaxes many restraints on outward investment but strengthens supervision over ODI not only in the ex ante event but also in the interim and ex post event. In early 2018, NDRC also issued the Measures for the Interim and Ex Post Supervision of Enterprise Investment Projects. In early 2018, MOFCOM and SAFE together with other organs jointly issued the Interim Measures for the Filing (Verification) and Reporting of Overseas Investment.

NDRC, MOFCOM and other organs issued Guidance on Further Directing and Regulating Overseas Investment Direction in 2017, listing the sectors for encouragement, restriction and prohibition. NDRC updated a List of Sensitive Sectors for Outbound Investment in 2018 deleting telecoms and electricity and adding the arms industry, transboundary water resources and several high-profile sectors. Investment in the sectors on the list is subject to additional regulation. More new and detailed regulations and rules on Chinese outward investment are expected.

BRI is not unilateral actions but a jointly built project. On the international level, there will be the following five major impacts since BRI proposes jointly building the Belt and Road with countries in the Belt and Road domain.

Firstly, jointly building the Belt and Road means more international economic cooperation through general governmental agreements or treaties. The first Belt and Road Forum for International Cooperation was held in Beijing in May 2017, attracting leaders from over 60 countries and international organizations to attend. More than 50 agreements have been signed between China and its partners, covering six major international economic corridors.[17] Until the end of 2018, more than 120 countries concluded various agreements including joint statements with China concerning the joint building of BRI.[18] The second Belt and Road Forum for International Cooperation was held in Beijing in April 2019, which attracted participants from more than 150 countries and 90 international organizations to attend the event.[19] The third Belt and Road Forum for International Cooperation was held in Beijing in October 2023, which attracted representatives from more than 150 countries and

[17] UNCTAD (2017), p. 19.

[18] For the list of countries in the BRI domain and the various agreements, please refer to the BRI website: https://www.yidaiyilu.gov.cn/, last visited December 5, 2018.

[19] Xi Focus: Xi opens up new horizons for high-quality B&R cooperation, available at http://www.xinhuanet.com/english/2019-04/26/c_138013041.htm, last visited on July 25, 2019.

over 40 international organizations.[20] The Forum produced a lot of new economic cooperations.[21]

Secondly, the Initiative and the increase of Chinese outward investment require China to update its BITs. Concluding bilateral investment treaties (BIT) is a good way to protect foreign investment. So far China has concluded 152 IIAs including 123 BITs (among which 107 are in force) and 29 treaty with investment provisions (TIPs) (among which 24 are in force).[22] China has concluded BITs with most of the countries and regions in the Belt and Road domain. However, after careful review of these BITs, we find that most of them were concluded before 2000 and the contents are simple and general. The defensive BITs could not provide strong protection to the increasing amount of China's overseas investment. The current IIA reform in the whole world is to provide a high standard but more balanced protection to foreign investment. Recently, China also concluded some new generation of BITs including China-Canada BIT and the China-Japan-Korean Trilateral Investment Agreements. The high-standard China-EU BIT negotiation is underway while the China-USA BIT is suspended. It is easy to predict that China would review and update the existing BITs with the BRI countries and regions, to indicate China's shift from a host country to both host and home country, and thus to strengthen protection to its overseas investment. For example, China is negotiating a new BIT with Kazakhstan recently to replace the old one concluded in 1992.

Thirdly, the Initiative and the growing outward FDI would drive China to take the initiative to propose investment rules and set investment standards in both regional and global levels. The first try was in 2014 when they reached "A BRICS Perspective on International Investment Agreements", as they think it important to "continue to build common approach" to investment treaties.[23] Then the G20 Guiding Principles for Global Investment Policymaking, proposed by China and agreed on by the G20 in 2016 during the group's Shanghai Ministerial Meeting and at the Hangzhou Summit. This is the first time that multilateral consensus on an investment matter has been reached between a varied group of developed, developing and transition economies.[24] Currently, the Chinese Government majorly works to set up rules on investment facilitation and promotion. Based on the G20 Guiding Principles, China proposed the investment facilitation issue in WTO in 2016, which received common support. A joint ministerial declaration on investment facilitation was announced

---

[20] Hongzhen liu, Xiaoping Xu (2023), The Third Belt and Road Forum for International Cooperation was successfully held in Beijing, available at https://news.qq.com/rain/a/20231019A03OUL00, last visited on November 30, 2023.

[21] Please refer to the list of cooperation achievements, available at http://www.beltandroadforum.org/134/index.html, last visited on November 30, 2023.

[22] The data is searched through UNCTAD International Investment Agreements Navigator, available at http://investmentpolicyhub.unctad.org/IIA/CountryBits/42#iiaInnerMenu, last visited Novermber 30, 2023.

[23] Brics Perspective On International Investment Agreement (2014), available at https://www.tralac.org/documents/resources/external-relations/brics/1595-brics-perspective-on-international-investment-agreements-2014/file.html.

[24] UNCTAD (2017), pxii.

in December 2017 during the WTO Ministerial Meeting. In August 2017, before the BRICS Summit was held in Xiamen, China, the Outline for BRICS Investment Facilitation proposed by China was concluded. China's effort in setting up standard rules on investment facilitation coincides with and supports UNCTAD's Investment Facilitation Action Menu. Eventually, the negotiations on Investment Facilitation for Development within WTO were finally concluded in July 2023. The Investment Facilitation for Development will improve the investment and business climate, and make it easier for investors in all sectors of the economy to invest, conduct their day-to-day business and expand their operations. Facilitating greater participation of developing and least developed members in global investment flows also constitutes a core objective of the future Agreement. The initiative does not cover market access, investment protection and investor-state dispute settlement.[25]

Fourthly, the principles and spirits of the Belt and Road Initiative would be incorporated and inspire the contents of BITs and regional and global investment rules. The essential spirit of the Belt and Road is to promote win–win cooperation, common development and prosperity, peace and cooperation, openness and inclusiveness, and mutual understanding and trust. This conforms to the purposes and principles of the UN Charter as well as the values of the UN 2030 Agenda. The three-in-one target of the Initiative is to build a community of shared interests, destiny and responsibility featuring mutual political trust, economic integration and cultural inclusiveness. The Chinese concept of "building a human community with shared destiny" incorporated into a UN resolution in 2017 mirroring the global recognition of the concept and manifesting huge Chinese contribution to global governance. In almost all events including the establishment of AIIB, the establishment of new international commercial tribunals, China emphasizes again and again the principle of achieving shared growth through discussion and collaboration.

Based on the above spirits and values, China hopes to formulate a more equitable, reasonable and balanced global governance regime. All these would be reflected in the future BITs and regional and global investment rules.

## 5.5 China's Innovative ISDS Mechanisms and Its Implications[26]

The huge volume of outbound investment in the BRI domain is a source of special concern to the Chinese Government. As the BRI advances, the number of investor-state disputes between Chinese investors and the host governments could very well increase. Most of the countries in the BRI domain are developing or least developed

[25] WTOIFD, available at https://www.wto.org/english/tratop_e/invfac_public_e/invfac_e.htm, last visited on November 30, 2023.

[26] This part was updated based on my article published in the title of China's Innovative ISDS Mechanisms and Their Implications, AJIL Unbound (American Journal of International Law Unbound), Vol. 112, 2018.

countries whose domestic laws and regulations are inadequate. In addition, other dispute settlement mechanisms that are currently available to Chinese investors are quite limited: some of the international investment agreements (IIAs) that China concluded with the BRI countries have not entered into force, or do not include a dispute settlement provision, or provide for investor-state settlement only for disputes over the amount of an expropriation. And in the near future, China is unlikely to be able to update its IIAs to allow for broader and stronger ISDS options for Chinese investors. In these scenarios, Chinese foreign investors could face substantial and even excessive risk.

The new ISDS mechanisms could help to mitigate this problem. Take the China-Africa Joint Arbitration Centre (CAJAC) as an example. Since the beginning of the twenty-first century, China has invested extensively in African countries. In 2016 alone, Chinese total investment in Africa reached US$2.4 billion.[27] However, national laws and judicial systems in African countries have proven to be inefficient, uncertain and highly restrictive on matters involving foreign parties.[28] China has concluded thirty-four BITs with African countries, but the standard of protection is low and international arbitration available for investor-state claims is very limited.[29] Moreover, some countries, like South Africa, have adopted policies that permit the resolution of foreign investment disputes only in their domestic courts. CAJAC helps to resolve these difficulties by offering a mutually agreed forum as an alternative.

Second, and in a more general way, the new mechanisms enable China to amplify its voice in the international discourse on the IIA-making. Mostly because of the BRI, China has become the second largest economy in terms of both capital importing and exporting, and is already a net capital-exporting state.[30] Consequently, since 2014 China has sought to "[v]igorously participate in the formulation of international norms,… strengthen [its] discourse power and influence in international legal affairs, [and] use legal methods to safeguard [its] sovereignty, security, and development interests".[31]

With this ambition in mind, China enjoyed some success in pursuing the adoption of the G20 Guiding Principles for Global Investment Policymaking in 2016,[32] the proposal to include the issue of investment facilitation on the WTO's agenda in

[27] China's Ministry of Commerce (2016).

[28] Francis Kariuki, 'The Vision of Co-building China-Africa Joint Arbitration Centres in Different Legal Systems', available at http://kmco.co.ke/wp-content/uploads/2018/08/Co-building-China-Africa-Joint-Arbitration-Centres-in-Different-Legal-Systems.pdf, last visited November 14, 2018.

[29] Huiping Chen (2012).

[30] UNCTAD (2017), p. 14.

[31] CCP Central Committee Decision Concerning Some Major Questions in Comprehensively Moving Governing the Country According to the Law Forward, para. 7 (Oct. 23, 2014), China Copyright & Media Blog, available at https://chinacopyrightandmedia.wordpress.com/2014/10/28/ccp-central-committee-decision-concerning-some-major-questions-in-comprehensively-moving-governing-the-country-according-to-the-law-forward/. updated Oct. 30, 2014.

[32] G20 Guiding Principles for Global Investment Policymaking, G20 Trade Ministers Meeting Statement, Shanghai, Ann. III (July 9–10, 2016), available at http://www.g20.utoronto.ca/2016/160710-trade-annex3.html. Last visited Sep 05 2018.

2017[33] and the conclusion of the Outlines for BRICS Investment Facilitation in 2017.[34] China has also been involved in the ongoing global reform of investor-state dispute settlement; when UNCITRAL proposes reform options, China has actively participated in the negotiations.[35] But China's influence in the multilateral setting may not yet match its economic status.

In this context, the new ISDS mechanisms benefit China in a couple of ways. For one, they operate as trial runs for potential global reforms in the future. Once these mechanisms prove successful, China could incorporate institutions such as the SCIA and CIETAC in future Chinese IIAs as options for the investor-state dispute settlement, or propose its international commercial courts to resolve contract-based international investment dispute. In addition, as China pursues innovative models for the ISDS, such as "arbitration + mediation", it will accumulate experience and human resources, both of which will empower China to offer new perspectives on reforming the ISDS system.

Third and finally, China's reform help to break the monopoly of existing Western-initiated institutions. Although the SCIA and CIETAC expanded their jurisdiction just recently, they will conceivably play a significant role in the resolution of future investment disputes. For IIAs to which China is a party, Chinese investors may refer their treaty-based claims to the SCIA or CIETAC for resolution if the UNCITRAL rules are applicable or ad hoc arbitration is available. Contractual claims could also be referred to these China-based institutions for resolution. For infrastructure investments that require a concession agreement between the host state and the Chinese investors, the latter may insist that any dispute arising under the agreement be referred to Chinese arbitral institutions. Similarly, China could establish the jurisdiction of China's international commercial courts through bilateral memorandums of understanding with some seventy individual nations along the Belt and Road routes. Together these changes would shift the locus of China-related dispute resolution from ICSID or other Western institutions to China, where Chinese parties will encounter a system that is more familiar to them.

Other states are helping to facilitate this shift. The creation of CAJAC, for example, reflects not only Chinese interests, as discussed above, but also the desire of African countries, many of which are dissatisfied with the established international tribunals whose rulings have mostly gone against them.[36] In this sense, the new mechanisms reflect a win–win strategy against the hegemony of the West.

---

[33] WTO (2017).

[34] BRICS (2017).

[35] For example, China expresses its opinion to the ISDS reform through the statements made by Group 77 and China. Statement on Behalf of the Group Of 77 and China by H.E. Mr. Mohamed Edrees, Permanent Representative of Egypt to the United Nations, at UNCITRAL Working Group III Meeting on the Investor-State Dispute Settlement Reform (New York, 23 April 2018), http://www.g77.org/statement/getstatement.php?id=180423, last visited January3, 2019.

[36] Francis Kariuki, 'The Vision of Co-building China-Africa Joint Arbitration Centres in Different Legal Systems', available at http://kmco.co.ke/wp-content/uploads/2018/08/Co-building-China-Africa-Joint-Arbitration-Centres-in-Different-Legal-Systems.pdf, last visited on November 14, 2018.

Ultimately, the new institutions may compete with and exist next to the ICSID and other established arbitral tribunals, just as the Asian Infrastructure Investment Bank and the BRICS New Development Bank operating next to the International Monetary Fund and the World Bank. And they will have certain advantages in this competition. Although the Chinese institutions have not yet heard any investor-state investment cases, their high efficiency and low cost in handling general commercial arbitration disputes will surely be maintained in their future handling investor-state disputes. For instance, the SCIA in 2016 used the "arbitration + mediation" model and successfully handled an investment case between two equal parties from the US and China within only thirteen days and at a much lower cost.[37] This is distinct and in contrast to the investor-state dispute settlement before established international institutions typically entailing high costs and lengthy delays. Over time, the efficiency of the SCIA is likely to attract more and more investors from both China and other countries to resolve their disputes. The "arbitration + mediation" model is also likely to prove attractive to investors, as it is more flexible and efficient than traditional arbitration.

In summary, China has created innovative mechanisms to deal with investor-state claims stemming from its Belt and Road Initiative, but the significance of these mechanisms extends well beyond the BRI. The aim is not to replace one hegemony with another but to create alternatives that protect Chinese investors, amplify China's voice and break the existing monopoly of the West. In the long run, these new reforms could very well succeed.

## 5.6 The Implications of BRI for Sino-African Investment Relations[38]

Originally, Africa is not one of the major regions along the Belt and Road. Chinese investments in Africa have increased rapidly; however, it has not been proportionate to the increase in pace and volume of Chinese outward investment. African States neither attract much FDI from China, nor do they benefit enough from China's Belt and Road Initiative. There is still room for Africa to promote its economic development by increasing connections with China. African states should take action in order to grasp the opportunities to benefit from China's Belt and Road Initiative.

If Africa could be included in the initiative, it would create more jobs, improve the economic well-being of locals and boost the industrial development of Africa. In this sense, the initiative could provide additional momentum to enhance the scope and

[37] Ruolin Wang, Xuezhong Wan (2015), The Latest Development of the Arbitration Innovation in the Special Zone Reported by Shenzhen Special Zone Daily and Legal Daily) (in Chinese), Shenzhen Court of International Arbitration, available at http://www.sccietac.org/web/news/detail/1724.html. last visited on Nov. 13, 2018.

[38] This part was excerpted and updated based on my article published in the title of China's 'Belt and Road' initiative and its implications for Sino-African investment relations, in: Transnational Corporations Review, 8:3 in 2016.

depth of China's economic initiatives in Africa. In February 2015, Justin Yifu Lin, former chief economist of the World Bank, made the first call to insert Africa into the Belt and Road Initiative. He argues that through infrastructure development, China could both foster the growth of African countries and transfer its labor-intensive industries to Africa.[39] African countries welcome the initiative. The joining of the AIIB by South Africa and Egypt demonstrates their responding to the Initiative. The call for inclusion was adopted by the Chinese Government. In the Vision and Actions on Jointly Building Silk Road Economic Belt and 21st-Century Maritime Silk Road published in March 2015, it is clear that Africa would be the major region for the implementation of the initiative.

The African region and states should take action at various levels to benefit from the initiative. It is suggested that Africa takes advantage of this opportunity to cooperate with China in various ways, and renew the BITs with China so as to improve the promotion and protection of Chinese investment in Africa.

As a first step, the African Union signed with China a Memorandum of Understanding (MoU) regarding cooperation on infrastructure construction on January 27, 2015. According to the MoU, it will connect all 54 African countries through transportation infrastructure projects, including modern highways, airports and high-speed railways. The MoU is within the framework of the African Union's Agenda 2063, which aims to accelerate the continental integration of Africa. African countries may take advantage of China's Belt and Road Initiative to strengthen the economic cooperation with China, so as to benefit from the Initiative. Africa's infrastructure lags behind, which seriously restricts its economic progress. In 2015, Chinese enterprises have already started some projects on railroad, airport, ports, etc., in countries such as Ethiopia, Djibouti, Kenya and Nigeria. Ever since, the Forum on China-Africa Cooperation has become a major platform for Africa to cooperate with China regarding the implementation of the Belt and Road Initiative in Africa. So far, China has signed joint statements of cooperation with many African countries, and many infrastructure projects have been or are being implemented in Africa. Now African countries are the major economic partners of China and substantially benefit from China's Belt and Road Initiative.

The major aim of concluding BITs is to promote and protect foreign investment. Until 2024, China has concluded 37 BITs 35 with various African countries (two BITs were replaced by new ones), among which one concluded in 1980s, 16 in 1990s and 21 in the twenty-first century. 22 of them are currently in force, while 13 are pending, and 2 were terminated. 20 out of the 22 in force have been in force for over 10 years, and could be renewed any time.[40] The Sino-African BITs belong to the "South-South" BITs which were signed between developing countries, in contrast to the "North- South" BITs which were originally concluded between developed

[39] Yun Sun, Inserting Africa into China's One Belt, One Road strategy: A new opportunity for jobs and infrastructure?, available at http://www.brookings.edu/blogs/africa-in-focus/posts/2015/03/02-africa-china-jobs-infrastructure-sun, last visited on March 2, 2015.

[40] For details of Sino-African BITs, please refer to my article Huiping Chen (2012), pp. 59–98.

countries and developing countries. The contents of the existing Sino-African BITs are often simplistic and out of date.

Both China and African countries are reforming and improving their BITs. As such, it is possible for them to renew/renegotiate some expiring/not in force BITs, so as to promote and protect more Chinese investment in Africa. In December of 2023, China concluded a BIT with Angola, which is the latest one that China concluded with African country.

## 5.7 Conclusion

The "Belt & Road" Initiative proposed by China has produced great impacts on China's outward foreign investment law and policy on both national level and international level, and will continue to generate more impacts in the near future. Moreover, to respond to the limited access to investor-state dispute settlement for Chinese investors in the BRI countries, China is innovating its own ISDS. African countries are in the BRI domain and could benefit from China's BRI to attract more Chinese investment. Improving Sino-African BITs is a necessary and effective step for African countries to take, among others so as to benefit from the BRI.

## References

BRICS (2017), *Outlines for BRICS Investment Facilitation*, available at https://www.brics2017.org/wdfj/201708/t20170831_1829.html

China's Ministry of Commerce (2016), Statistical Bulletin of China's Outward Foreign Direct Investment (in Chinese)

China's Ministry of Commerce, National Bureau of Statistics & State Administration of Foreign Exchange (2017), Statistical Bulletin of China's Outward Foreign Direct Investment, China Statistics Press

Francis Kariuki, 'The Vision of Co-building China-Africa Joint Arbitration Centres in Different Legal Systems'. Available at http://kmco.co.ke/wp-content/uploads/2018/08/Co-building-China-Africa-Joint-Arbitration-Centres-in-Different-Legal-Systems.pdf

Huiping Chen (2012) Sino-African BITs practice: a new legal paradigm? Soochow Law J 9(2)

National Development and Reform Commission, Ministry of Foreign Affairs, and Ministry of Commerce of the People's Republic of China (2016), Vision and Actions on Jointly Building Belt and Road. Available at http://english.cri.cn/12394/2015/03/29/2941s872030.htm

UNCTAD (2017) World Investment Report

WTO (2017) Joint Ministerial Statement on Investment Facilitation for Development (WT/MIN(17)/59

Yun Sun, Inserting Africa into China's one belt, one road strategy: a new opportunity for jobs and infrastructure? http://www.brookings.edu/blogs/africa-in-focus/posts/2015/03/02-africa-china-jobs-infrastructure-sun

# Chapter 6
# The Legitimacy Crisis of International Investment Arbitration: The Expansion of Jurisdiction by Tribunal

## 6.1 Introduction

In recent years, the investor-state dispute settlement mechanism (sometimes it is referred to as international investment arbitration) has received extensive critique from developing countries, scholars and civil society. Its legitimacy is challenged or questioned due to various reasons including the inconsistency of arbitral awards, lack of transparency, etc.[1] In my opinion, the practice of expansion of jurisdiction by some ICSID tribunals also contributes to the critiques and challenges, because some cases which did not fall into the jurisdiction of arbitral tribunals were improperly or wrongfully arbitrated by the tribunals. This chapter examines the various approaches used by ICSID tribunals in practice to expand their jurisdiction, the possible reasons for such expansion and the potential damages caused thereby.

## 6.2 The Legal Basis for ICSID Tribunal's Jurisdiction

If a tribunal has jurisdiction over a dispute, this is the premise and condition for the tribunal to hear and decide the case. In other words, only after the tribunal determines that it has jurisdiction over a dispute can it hear and decide the merits of the dispute. Therefore, the respondent of a case will normally challenge the tribunal's jurisdiction as a first step and a procedural issue before it defends for the merits of the case.

[1] There are several articles and books discussing the legitimacy crisis of the investor-state dispute settlement mechanism. For example, Susan D. Franck (2005); HHA Van Harten (2007).

This chapter was updated based on my previously published article in the title of The Expansion of Jurisdiction by ICSID Tribunal: Approaches, Reasons and Damages in The Journal of World Investment & Trade, Vol. 12, Issue 5, October, 2011.

 
H. Chen, *China's Practice in International Investment Law*, Modern China and International Economic Law, https://doi.org/10.1007/978-981-96-5016-3_6

According to Article 25 of the Convention on the Settlement of Investment Disputes between States and Nationals of Other States (the "Washington convention" or "ICSID convention" or "Convention"), for a dispute to fall into the jurisdiction of an ICSID tribunal, it has to meet three requirements.[2] Firstly, the dispute must be a "legal" one, arising "directly out of an investment". Secondly, the parties to the dispute must be, on the one side, a contracting state or a designated constituent subdivision or agency thereof and, on the other side, the national of another contracting state. Thirdly, the parties to the dispute must have "consent in writing" to ICSID jurisdiction over their dispute.

For a dispute to be submitted to ICSID for resolution, the party to the dispute wishing to institute arbitration proceedings shall address a request to that effect in writing to the Secretary-General of ICSID. The Secretary-General has the power of preliminary examination to decide whether the dispute falls within the jurisdiction of ICSID. He shall register the request unless he finds that the dispute is manifestly outside the jurisdiction of the Centre.[3] However, the registration by the Secretary-General in itself does not demonstrate that ICSID has definite jurisdiction over the relevant case. The other party to the dispute at issue may still challenge the ICSID jurisdiction.

It is the tribunal who has final say as to the jurisdiction since the Convention confers the authority to the tribunal to judge its own competence and determine whether it has jurisdiction over a specific dispute.[4]

Since the tribunal has discretion to determine the jurisdiction, this leaves space for it to expand its jurisdiction, intentionally or unintentionally.

## 6.3 The Approaches the Tribunal Uses to Expand Its Jurisdiction in Practice

Since there are three requirements in Article 25 of the ICSID Convention for the tribunal to have jurisdiction over a specific dispute to expand its jurisdiction, the tribunal will have to expand the interpretation or the scope of application of Article 25 to fit the above requirements, or to expand the interpretation or scope of application of relevant articles in a related bilateral investment agreement (BIT) that addresses

[2] Article 25 of the Convention provides that "The jurisdiction of the Centre shall extend to any legal dispute arising directly out of an investment, between a Contracting State (or any constituent subdivision or agency of a Contracting State designated to the Centre by that State) and a national of another Contracting State, which the parties to the dispute consent in writing to submit to the Centre".

[3] Article 36(3) of the ICSID Convention.

[4] Article 41 of the ICSID Convention provides that "(1) The Tribunal shall be the judge of its own competence. (2) Any objection by a party to the dispute that that dispute is not within the jurisdiction of the Centre, or for other reasons is not within the competence of the Tribunal, shall be considered by the Tribunal which shall determine whether to deal with it as a preliminary question or to join it to the merits of the dispute".

the elements of the three requirements. The following will elaborate the approaches of expansion from the perspectives of both Article 25 and BITs.

### *6.3.1 Expanding Jurisdiction by Broadening Interpretation of Article 25 of the ICSID Convention*

As mentioned above, under Article 25 of the ICSID Convention, three requirements must be satisfied for the ICSID to have jurisdiction. For the purpose of acquiring jurisdiction, the tribunal spares no effort to broaden the interpretation and application of such three criteria.

#### 6.3.1.1 Expanding the Interpretation and Scope of Application of "Any Legal Dispute Arising Directly Out of an Investment"

The first requirement of ICSID jurisdiction is that the dispute must be a legal dispute directly arising out of an investment. Since the Convention itself does not define either "legal dispute" or "investment", it leaves this to the tribunal. The tribunal often broadly interprets these two terms.

For example, in Alcoa v. Jamaica,[5] the dispute arose out of an agreement between Alcoa and the Government of Jamaica entered into in 1968. Alcoa undertook to construct at its own expense an aluminum refining plant in Jamaica; in return, the Jamaican Government was to confer tax concessions upon Alcoa and grant it long-term bauxite mining leases. The agreement contained an ICSID arbitration clause. In 1974, Jamaica imposed a new tax on bauxite mining; Alcoa considered these a violation of the 1968 agreement and, therefore, initiated ICSID arbitration. Jamaica argued that the dispute was in connection with violations of the agreement, not "directly arising out of investment", so the tribunal should not have jurisdiction. The tribunal initially acknowledged that the dispute was a legal dispute arising from the agreement, but it later added that the mining company had invested substantial amounts in Jamaica in reliance upon the agreement, and moreover, consent to ICSID arbitration in the agreement itself indicated that the parties viewed their contract as investment-related. For these reasons the tribunal found that the claim arose from an investment and thus asserted its jurisdiction.

Some people commented that this case demonstrated that the subject matter jurisdiction requirement was liberally construed, and the ICSID practice of accepting a wide range of disputes confirmed the laxity of the requirement.[6]

---

[5] Alcoa Minerals of Jamaica, Inc. v. Jamaica (ICSID Case No. ARB/74/2).

[6] William Rand et al. (1986–1987), pp. 37–38; Schmidt (1976), p.90.

#### 6.3.1.2 Expanding the Interpretation and Scope of Application of "a National of Another Contracting State"

The second requirement of ICSID jurisdiction is that one of the parties to the dispute must be a national of another contracting state. National of another contracting state covers natural person and juridical person with the nationality of another contracting state, and the juridical person that owns the nationality of one contracting state but the two parties have **agreed to treat** it as a national of another contracting state because of foreign control.[7] The tribunal often interprets "national of another state" broadly in practice.

For example, in the case of SOABI v. Senegal,[8] SOABI is a Senegalese company. All of the shares of SOABI were owned by Flexa, a Panamanian company. At that time, Panama had not signed the ICSID Convention and therefore it was not a Contracting State. The Government of Senegal challenged SOABI's identity as "a national of another Contracting State". Since Flexa was controlled by Belgian nationals and Belgium is a Contracting State, the Tribunal held that indirect control by nationals of Contracting States of the company established under local law was sufficient to satisfy the nationality requirement of Article 25 of the Convention, and thus obtained jurisdiction over the dispute.

Another example is the case of Holiday Inns v. Morocco.[9] In this case, the Government of Morocco executed an agreement in 1966 (hereinafter 1966 Agreement) with Holiday Inns SA (a Swiss subsidiary of Holiday Inns Inc., a US company), and an unnamed subsidiary of Occidental Petroleum Corporation (hereinafter OPC, a US company). Under that agreement, the Holiday Inns group undertook to build four hotels in Morocco, which were to become Holiday Inns' local subsidiaries' property. The agreement contained an ICSID arbitration clause. As a result of disputes that arose during the construction period in 1972, Holiday Inns SA and OPC filed jointly for ICSID arbitration. The two companies stated that besides acting in their own names, they were acting on behalf of Holiday Inns Inc. and the four of its Moroccan subsidiaries as well as the unnamed subsidiary of OPC. Morocco argued that Holiday Inns Inc. and OPC did not sign the agreement containing ICSID clause, therefore, they had no right to be parties to the arbitration. The fact is that on the same day that the 1966 Agreement was signed, Holiday Inns Inc. and OPC undertook to assume all responsibilities of Guarantors to warrant all commitments and liabilities and the true and complete fulfillment of all obligations their subsidiaries have entered into pursuant to the Agreement. Based on this fact, the tribunal concluded that, "any party on whom rights and obligations under the agreement have devolved, is entitled to the benefits and subject to the burdens of the arbitration clause". In this way, even though both Holiday Inns Inc. and OPC were not signatories to the agreement, the tribunal decided that they had right to be parties to the arbitration, and thus broaden the scope of applicants from two to four.

---

[7] Article 25(2) of the ICSID Convention.

[8] Société Ouest Africaine des Bétons Industriels (SOABI) v. Senegal (ICSID Case No. ARB/82/1).

[9] Holiday Inns v. Morocco (ICSID Case ARB/72/1).

Another case is Amco Asia v. Indonesia.[10] Amco Asia (a US Corporation) and Wisma Kartika (hereinafter Wisma, an Indonesian company), signed an agreement in 1968, under which Amco Asia undertook to build a hotel on Wisma's land. In the same year, Amco Asia formed a local company, P.T. Amco, and transferred its rights arising from the contract with Wisma to P.T. Amco. In 1972, Amco Asia transferred 90% of its shares in P.T. Amco to Pan American Development Limited (hereinafter Pan American). The Indonesian Government approved this transaction. When the disputes arose, Amco Asia, P.T. Amco and Pan American jointly filed a request for ICSID arbitration. Indonesia argued that the tribunal lacked jurisdiction over P.T. Amco—an Indonesian company, since the parties had not expressly agreed to treat P.T. Amco as a foreign national. However, the tribunal concluded that "Since the Indonesian Government knew perfectly that P.T. Amco would be under foreign control, therefore, it is crystal clear that it agreed to treat P.T. Amco as a national of another contracting state". The tribunal found that no language in Article 25 required an expressed statement that the parties have to agree to treat locally incorporated company as a foreign control. The author disagrees with the tribunal because, when a government recognizes a local company under foreign control, it doesn't necessarily mean that it agrees to treat it as a national of another contracting state. Moreover, the parties' agreement to treat a local company as a national of another contracting state should at least be supported by some kind of evidence, if not an expressed statement. From this case, we can see that the tribunal intended to expand its interpretation of the term "**treated** as a national of another contracting state", for the purpose of expanding its jurisdiction.

In contrast, in the case of Vacuum Salt Products v. Ghana[11] which has similar facts of the case of Amco Asia v. Indonesia, the tribunal gave a completely different decision. Vacuum is a Ghanaian company, the majority shareholder of which was a national of Greece. In 1988, Ghana signed a lease agreement with Vacuum. This agreement had an ICSID arbitration clause. When the dispute arose, Vacuum filed a request for ICSID arbitration. Ghana objected to the jurisdiction on the ground that Vacuum was a Ghanaian company and they never agreed to treat Vacuum as "a national of another Contracting State". The tribunal upheld Ghana's argument and concluded that the existence of ICSID arbitration clause in an investment agreement was not enough to prove the nationality of the subsidiary.

#### 6.3.1.3 Expanding the Interpretation and Application Scope of "Consent in Writing"

The third requirement for ICSID jurisdiction is that the parties to the dispute consent in writing should submit disputes to the ICSID for resolution. The Convention does not stipulate the specific ways to express the consent in writing. In practice, consent in writing can be found in the ICSID arbitration clause in the investment agreement

[10] Amco Asia v. Indonesia (ICSID Case No. ARB/81/1).

[11] Vacuum Salt Products Ltd. v. Republic of Ghana (ICSID Case No. ARB/92/1).

between the two parties, in relevant provisions of domestic investment law of the host state, and the articles of ICSID arbitration in the bilateral investment treaty (BIT). Furthermore, prior to the 1990s, consent was mainly expressed in the investment agreement and domestic investment law, while since 1990s, it is mainly found in BITs. So far, consent in the BITs has been the most important way, which will be further elaborated in Sect. 6.3.2.

ICSID tribunal has the practice to expand the interpretation and application scope of "consent in writing" in cases so as to expand its jurisdiction. A typical case is the above-mentioned case of Amco Asia v. Indonesia.

The agreement signed between Amco and Wisma did not contain an ICSID arbitration clause in itself. However, when Amco Asia applied to the Indonesian Government for a foreign investment license, this application mentioned ICSID arbitration for disputes. The dispute arose in 1980. Amco filed a request for ICSID arbitration. One of the objections Indonesia made to the jurisdiction of ICSID was that the ICSID arbitration clause was in the foreign investment license application. Indonesia alleged that the approval of the investment license application did not constitute "consent" under the Convention. However, the tribunal held that "consent in the convention is to be construed in a way, which leads to find out, and to respect common will of parties". It also added that there is no need to express consent "in a solemn, ritual and unique formulation". Such an argument is not persuasive because Article 25 requires that "the parties to the dispute consent in writing" which by definition is an expressed and solemn formulation. Thus, it is clear that the tribunal has the intention to broaden its jurisdiction by expanding the interpretation of "consent in writing" requirement.

ICSID tribunals' practice of expanding its jurisdiction by way of expanding interpretation of relevant articles of the ICSID Convention was recognized by some people. After the Klockner v. Cameroon and Amco v. Indonesia cases have been decided, the counsels of the two cases wrote an article claiming that ICSID tribunals have interpreted the three criteria of ICSID jurisdiction "broadly and flexibly", and "ICSID's jurisdiction has been liberally asserted in questions regarding all three areas".[12]

### 6.3.2 *Expanding Interpretation and Application Scope of Relevant Articles in BITs*

Ever since 1990s, almost all BITs agree to submit investor-state investment disputes to international arbitration. However, the extent of "consent" to arbitration varies in different BITs. Practice shows that it is always the foreign investor who brings the dispute to international arbitration. According to the BITs, for a dispute to be submitted to arbitration, three requirements should be met: firstly, the disputing

[12] William Rand et al. (1986–1987), p. 33. The three authors were counsels of the cases of Klockner v. Cameroon and Amco v. Indonesia.

investor should be the qualified investor defined in the BITs; secondly, the disputing investor has qualified investment defined in the BITs in the host state; and thirdly, the dispute at issue falls into the scope of disputes that the parties to the dispute consent to arbitration. Moreover, the disputing investor should make a prima facie case to prove that the host state has violated the BIT. The host state sued by foreign investor usually objects to the tribunal's jurisdiction by challenging the above four aspects. The tribunals, on the other hand, try their best to broaden their jurisdiction by expanding interpretation or application scope of relevant BIT articles concerning the above aspects.

#### 6.3.2.1 Expanding the Interpretation and Application Scope of "Investment"

Every BIT will define covered investment in its text and the definition of investment varies in different BITs. Whether the investment in question falls into the scope of investment defined in the BIT has to be decided by the tribunal established for the dispute. Practice shows that tribunals have the tendency to broadly interpret the investment at issue so as to acquire jurisdiction over the case.

A case in this regard is the case of Fedax v. Venezuela.[13] Fedax, a company of Netherlands, acquired by way of endorsement promissory notes issued by Venezuela for service rendered by itself. After Venezuela failed to pay the sum due under the notes, Fedax instituted ICSID proceedings under Netherlands-Venezuela BIT which was signed in 1991. Venezuela raised objection to jurisdiction and argued that Fedax's holding of the above-mentioned promissory notes did not qualify as an "investment" defined in both Article 25 of the ICSID Convention and the Netherlands-Venezuela BIT. The definition of investment was set forth in Article 1 (a) of Netherlands-Venezuela BIT that "the terms investment shall comprise every kinds of asset and more particular though not exclusively:...(ii) rights derived from shares, bonds, and other kinds of interests in companies and joint ventures; (iii) titles to money, to other assets or to any performance having an economic value..." The tribunal asserted that "this definition evidences that the contracting parties to the Agreement intended a very broad meaning for the term investment".[14] Therefore, the tribunal defined "investment" in broad terms to cover promissory notes and decided that the dispute was within its jurisdiction.[15]

In general, BIT requires the asset is invested within the territory of the host state to constitute foreign investment. However, if the asset arises from a debt or contractual right, it is hard to decide whether the foreign investor has invested the said asset into the territory of the host state so as to be protected by relevant BIT. For such cases, tribunals often decide that there is qualified investment. For instance, in SGS

[13] Fedax v. Veneruela, Decision (1997).

[14] Fedax v. Veneruela, Decision (1997), p. 32.

[15] Fedax v. Veneruela, Decision (1997), pp. 25–43.

v. Pakistan[16] and SGS v. Philippines,[17] SGS, a Swiss company, entered into the Pre-Shipment Inspection Agreement (PSI Agreement) with Pakistan and Philippines, respectively. Then the host countries broke the agreements and there arose disputes. SGS instituted ICSID arbitration under SGS-Pakistan BIT and SGS-Philippines BIT, respectively. Both host countries argued that the agreement with SGS was a service agreement and the services were not made in the territory of the host country as required in the BIT. The tribunal decided that SGS had certain expenditures and they involved the injection of funds into the territory of the host country for the carrying out of SGS's engagements under the PSI Agreement. Accordingly, the tribunals decided that they constituted an investment within the meaning of the BIT.[18] In other cases such as Salini v. Morocco, LESI v. Algeria and Bayindir v. Pakistan, the tribunals also broadly interpreted the definition of investment and thus expanded their jurisdiction.

#### 6.3.2.2 Broadening or Distorting the Interpretation of the Articles Concerning the Disputes that the Parties Consent to Arbitration, or the Scope of Consent for Arbitration

Many BITs set restrictive conditions or impose qualifications for ICSID arbitration. These conditions and qualifications include, for instance, only the disputes on the amount of expropriation or only the disputes that directly arise from the enforcement of the BIT. These disputes can be submitted for arbitration only after local remedies have been exhausted, or, once foreign investor resorts on domestic courts, they cannot rely on international arbitration (the so-called fork-in-the-road). Moreover, some BITs do not contain any articles for ICSID arbitration. Nevertheless, tribunals can find ways to interpret the above articles to the result that consent exists and they have jurisdiction over the disputes. These ways will be further elaborated as follows.

##### Expanding the Scope of Disputes Agreed for ICSID Arbitration so as to Broaden Jurisdiction

In BITs or the investment chapter of FTAs, the disputes that contracting state parties agree for international arbitration vary. Some BITs agree to submit investment disputes for international arbitration, while others only agree to those disputes concerning expropriation or the amount of compensation for expropriation or others. Some tribunals tried to expand the scope of disputes that the parties agree to submit to ICSID for arbitration. In Saipem v. Bangladesh[19]—Saipem, an Italian company, entered into a contract to build a pipeline, providing that any dispute would be referred to the ICC arbitration. The dispute was indeed addressed to ICC arbitration.

---

16 SGS v. Pakistan, Decision (2003).

17 SGS v. Philippines, Decision (2004).

18 SGS v. Pakistan, Decision (2003), p. 136; SGS v. Philippines, Decision (2004), p. 111.

19 Saipem v. Bangladesh, Decision (2007).

Article 9 of Saipem-Bangladesh BIT provides that "Any disputes arising between a Contracting Party and the investors of the other, relating to compensation for expropriation, ..., the investor in question may submit the dispute, at his discretion for settlement to the court of the host country, UNCITRAL or ICSID". Moreover, Article 5 whose heading is "Nationalization or Expropriation", which speaks of expropriation of "investments", provides that "The investments to which this Agreement relates shall not be subject to any measure which might limit permanently or temporarily their joined rights of ownership, possession, control or enjoyment, save where specifically provided by law and by judgments or orders issued by Courts or Tribunals having jurisdiction". According to the above articles, Saipem could not bring the dispute again to ICSID. However, Saipem argued that the domestic court interfered with the ICC arbitration and de facto annulled the ICC award. These acts allegedly deprived Saipem of the sums awarded to it by the ICC Award, and thus amount to an illegal expropriation. Saipem brought a claim for expropriation to ICSID under Article 9. Bangladesh raised objections to ICSID jurisdiction as follows: the dispute was not a legal one arising directly out of investment; the Claimant has not discharged its prima facie burden of proof; most important of all, Bangladesh's consent to arbitration does not cover disputes arising out of the acts of its courts pursuant to Article 5.[20] Unfortunately, the tribunal holds that the dispute is within the jurisdiction of ICSID and the competence of the Tribunal.[21]

### Expanding Jurisdiction by Applying the MFN Clause

Most-Favored-Nation clause is one of the main articles in almost all BITs or other investment treaties. It functions to ensure that investors from different countries can enjoy the same investment treatment in the same host state. Traditionally, MFN only applies to the substantive treatment instead of procedural provisions such as the articles on dispute settlement. However, some tribunals, for the purpose of acquiring jurisdiction, try to apply MFN clause to procedural provisions so as to cover those disputes which do not meet the arbitration requirements in the BIT or to cover those BITs which do not agree to ICSID arbitration.

The case of Maffezini v. Spain[22] is an example. The 1991 Argentina-Spain BIT Article 10 is about the investor-state dispute resolution. Paragraph 2 provides that if a dispute cannot be resolved amicably within a period of six months, it shall be submitted to the competent tribunals of the home state. Paragraph 3 stipulates that the dispute may be submitted to an international arbitral tribunal, if no decision was rendered by the competent tribunal on the merits after the expiration of a period of eighteen months, or, if such decision has been rendered, but the dispute between the parties continues; or, if both parties to the dispute agree thereto. When the instant dispute between Maffezini and Argentinean Government arose, Mr Maffezini did not

[20] Saipem v. Bangladesh, Decision (2007), p. 76.

[21] Saipem v. Bangladesh, Decision (2007), p. 161.

[22] Emilio Agustin Maffezini v. The Kingdom of Spain (ICSID CASE No. ABR/97/7).

submit the case to Spanish courts as required by the BIT, but immediately turned to ICSID arbitration. The tribunal acknowledged that "had this been the Claimant's sole argument on the issue, the Tribunal would have had to conclude that the Centre lacked jurisdiction and the Tribunal lacked competence to hear the case".[23] However, the tribunal turned to the Argentina-Chile BIT which did not require the submission to domestic tribunal—or the lapse of eighteen months before resorting to international arbitration, relying instead on the MFN clause in the Argentina-Spain BIT. The tribunal uses eleven pages in the Decision of the Tribunal on the Objections to Jurisdiction to argue that MFN clause could be applied to procedural issues. In this way, it decides that it has jurisdiction over the case.

The Maffezini case is the first case in ICSID that applies MFN clause to procedural issues so as to broaden jurisdiction. This is followed by some other cases such as the Siemens v. Argentina, Camuzzi v. Argentina, Tecmed v. Mexico, Interaguas v. Argentina, Grid v. Argentina and Suez Vivendi v. Argentina. However, not all tribunals, such as the tribunals in Plama v. Bulgaria and Telenor v. Hungary, recognize that MFN clause should be applied to procedural issues.

#### Expanding Jurisdiction by Distorting the Fork-In-The-Road Clause in the BIT

Many BITs provide options to foreign investors to settle disputes in either domestic courts or international tribunals. The fork-in-the-road clause requires foreign investors to choose only one forum when a dispute arises, and the choice is final to the exclusion of the other. However, some tribunals would find various reasons to give foreign investors another opportunity to resort to international arbitration, if they choose domestic court at the beginning.

The case of Desert Line Projects (DLP) v. Yemen[24] is an example. DLP entered into a contract with Yemen to build roads in Yemen. Article 11(2) contains a fork-in-the-road provision requiring the investor to submit its dispute to one of the following forums:(1) the competent court of the host party; (2) a special arbitral committee, in accordance with the arbitration law of the host state; (3) the Arab Investment Court; or (4) ICSID arbitration. When the dispute arose, DLP submitted the dispute to local arbitration, with the arbitral committee making a final and binding award.[25] However, DLP re-submitted the case to ICSID later. Yemen asserted that the fork-in-the-road clause barred the DLP from attempting to re-litigate the same underlying dispute before ICSID. The tribunal noted that the economic essence of the claims in both the local and the international arbitration was to seek compensation for construction works performed under the contracts, and compensation for damages incurred during and after the execution of the contracts. However, it argues that the Yemen Arbitration and the present arbitral proceedings were brought pursuant to fundamental different causes of action. The claims before ICSID were not said to

[23] Emilio Agustin Maffezini v. The Kingdom of Spain, Decision (2000), pp. 36–37.

[24] Desert Line Projects LLC v. The Republic of Yemen (ICSID Case No. ARB/05/17).

[25] Desert Line Projects LLC v. The Republic of Yemen, Award (2008), p. 124.

arise under the terms of the contracts. The claimant alleged that it had been deprived of procedural rights by the respondent's interference with the proper conduct of the Yemen Arbitration, the subsequent aborted correction and enforcement phases, and the allegedly coercive negotiation and signature of the Settlement Agreement; this amounted to the deprivation of its fundamental rights under the BIT. Therefore, the settlement of the claimant's contractual claims in the Yemen Arbitration did not bar the ICSID tribunal from having jurisdiction in the present case, since the claims formulated by the claimant here were capable of constituting violations of the BIT if they are upheld. The tribunal finally took over the case. However, the application of fork-in-the-road article is highly disputed.

#### Expanding Jurisdiction by Applying the Umbrella Clause in the BIT

Many BITs provide that the dispute settlement provisions apply to those disputes concerning whether the host state violates the obligations under the investment treaty. The dispute concerning whether the host state violates the investment contract with individual investor is generally not covered since contract claim is different from treaty claim. Host state's breach of investment contract with foreign investor does not necessarily mean the violation of the BIT. However, some tribunals believe that breach of the contract is a violation of treaty and thus foreign investors may initiate an international arbitration according to the BIT.

The above-mentioned case of SGS v. Philippines is an example. Philippines did not pay SGS under the CISS agreement. SGS alleged that, in refusing to pay the amount claimed, the Philippines was in breach of the CISS agreement. According to Article 12 of the CISS Agreement, any dispute in connection with the obligations of either party shall be filed at the Regional Trial Courts of Makati or Manila. However, SGS submitted the dispute to ICSID relying on Article 8 of the Swiss-Philippines BIT which provides that "For the purpose of solving disputes with respect to investments between a Contracting Party and an investor of the other Contracting Party, ... the investor may submit the dispute ... to international arbitration" including ICSID. SGS argued that Philippines violated Article 10 of the BIT which provides that "Each Contracting Party shall observe any obligation it has assumed with regard to specific investments in its territory by investors of the other Contracting Party". Article 10 is an umbrella clause. Philippines stressed that the CISS Agreement is not an investment agreement but rather a service agreement, and moreover, breaches of contract did not constitute breaches of treaty, so that SGS could not bring a claim under the BIT. However, the tribunal held that the term "any obligation" in the umbrella clause was capable of applying to obligations arising from a contract.[26] The tribunal also held that the object and purpose of the BIT supported such an effective interpretation of that Article.[27] By this way, the tribunal decided that it had jurisdiction over the

[26] SGS v. Pakistan, Decision (2003), p. 136; SGS v. Philippines, Decision (2004), p. 115.
[27] SGS v. Pakistan, Decision (2003), p. 136; SGS v. Philippines, Decision (2004), p. 116.

dispute. Such an interpretation of the umbrella clause is deemed as inappropriate by some scholars.[28]

In contrast, in a similar case, the case of SGS v. Pakistan, the tribunal held completely different opinion with regard to the umbrella clause. Article 11 of the Swiss-Pakistan BIT is an umbrella clause saying that "Either Contracting Party shall constantly guarantee the observance of commitments it has entered into with respect to the investments of the investors of the other Contracting Party". SGS argued that the inclusion of an "umbrella clause" has the effect of elevating a simple breach of contract claim to a treaty claim under international law.[29] However, the tribunal believed that BIT claims and contract claims appear reasonably distinct in principle,[30] and the breach of contract does not constitute or amount to breaches of the substantive standards of the BIT.[31] Therefore, the tribunal decided that it had no jurisdiction with respect to SGS's claims based on alleged breaches of the PSI Agreement.

### *6.3.3 Expanding Jurisdiction by Lowering the Standard of Proving a* **Prima Facie** *Case*

In general, the foreign investor should prove the *prima facie* case when bringing the dispute before ICSID. Otherwise, it would be easy for investor to abuse the arbitration or raise frivolous claims. However, in practice, some tribunals try to lower the standard of proving a *prima facie* case and thus acquire jurisdiction.

The case of Salini v. Jordan[32] is an example. Salini, an Italy company, after having presented the contractual claims in detail, quoted only some articles of the BIT, which, in their opinion, had been violated. But they explained nowhere how the alleged facts could constitute a breach of the BIT. They presented no argument, and no evidence whatsoever, to sustain their treaty claim and they did not show that the alleged facts were capable of falling within the provisions of BIT.[33] Jordan argued that the tribunal has no jurisdiction to consider relevant treaty claim. The Tribunal observed that the file submitted by the Claimants was lacking in terms of both the facts and the law, however, it "did not believe that it must rule out from the outset that the alleged facts, if established, might constitute breaches of … the BIT".[34] Thus, the tribunal rejected Jordan's objection to jurisdiction.

---

[28] For instance, Prof. Chongli Xu from Xiamen University holds such an opinion. Chongli Xu (2008), p. 53.

[29] SGS v. Pakistan, Decision (2003), p. 136; SGS v. Philippines, Decision (2004), p. 98.

[30] SGS v. Pakistan, Decision (2003), p. 136; SGS v. Philippines, Decision (2004), p. 148.

[31] SGS v. Pakistan, Decision (2003), p. 136; SGS v. Philippines, Decision (2004), p. 162.

[32] Salini v. Jordan (ICSID Case No. ARB/02/13).

[33] Salini v. Jordan, Decision (2004), p. 163.

[34] Salini v. Jordan, Decision (2040), p. 166.

Another example is the case of Impregilo S.p.A. v. Pakistan.[35] The claimant did not present detailed factual information, but only argued that Pakistan had violated Italy-Pakistan BIT. The Tribunal admitted that it was not presently in a position to decide whether or not these could be considered as breaches of the BIT, but held that it "had no choice but to decide upon its jurisdiction with respect to these alleged breaches when considering the merits".[36]

In contrast, the tribunal in the case of Telenor v. Hungary[37] held different opinions. It believed that onus was on the claimant to show what was alleged to constitute expropriation was at least capable of so doing. In other words, there must be a *prima facie* case that the BIT applies.[38] Since Telenor had failed to make out a *prima facie* case of expropriation, the tribunal concluded that it had no jurisdiction over claims for expropriation.[39]

## 6.4 Analysis of the Possible Reasons for ICSID Tribunals to Broaden Jurisdiction and the Negative Impacts Arising Therefrom

Practice shows that some ICSID tribunals have the tendency to broaden their jurisdiction. People will have to doubt the reasons behind this practice, and consider the possible negative effects that will arise therefrom.

### *6.4.1 Possible Reasons for the Expansion*

In theory, arbitrators should be independent, neutral and impartial in deciding cases. However, some arbitrators are prone to expand interpretations to investment treaty provisions and show keenness to acquire jurisdiction over some cases. The possible reasons could be as follows.

#### 6.4.1.1 Arbitrators Could Have Individual Interests in the Expansion

The arbitration system has become monopolized by a group of lawyers and professors, either from or trained in the developed countries. They show support to investment liberalization advocated by the Western developed countries. Moreover, the

[35] Impregilo S.p.A. v. Pakistan, ICSID Case No. ARB/03/3.

[36] Impregilo S.p.A. v. Pakistan, Decision (2005), p. 271.

[37] Telenor Mobile Communications A.S. v. The Republic of Hungary (ICSID Case No. ARB/05/15).

[38] Telenor Mobile Communications A.S. v. The Republic of Hungary, Award (2006), p. 68.

[39] Telenor Mobile Communications A.S. v. The Republic of Hungary, Award (2006), p. 80.

arbitrators could have a conflict of interest that weighs in favor of interpreting investment protected provisions as widely as possible to promote future investment arbitrations and thus further employment and other business opportunities.[40] Further, nowadays, more and more BITs provide more options to foreign investors including ICSID, ICC, UNCITRAL and other ad hoc tribunals. Therefore, ICSID is facing competition from other institutional tribunals or ad hoc tribunals. ICSID tribunals would thus be driven by such a competition to expand jurisdiction.

#### 6.4.1.2 The Tribunal Would Pay More Attention to Private Investor's Interests

Due to the advocated theory of investment liberalization, many developing countries opened their domestic markets and adopted various preferential measures to encourage and attract foreign investment. The foreign investors mainly come from developed countries. During the dispute between the government of developing countries and foreign investors from developed countries, the arbitrators who are from or educated in developed countries would naturally cast more weight on the people from their own culture or show sympathy to the investors who are aliens in the host countries. Therefore, when deciding the jurisdiction, they would show preference to foreign investors. They adopted the investor-centered interpretative approach and explained their duties from the perspective of investors rather than the contracting parties.[41]

#### 6.4.1.3 The Tribunal Would not Care Much About Developing Countries' Interests

Until 2009, in all cases to the ICSID, all of them except for one are the cases that host countries are challenged by foreign investors.[42] Among almost all the ICSID cases that the jurisdiction is expanded, the respondents are developing countries. The tribunals tend to opine that developing countries' willingness to sign the ICSID Convention and the BITs shows their willingness to provide higher international protection so as to attract foreign investors. Therefore, developing countries have the "intention" to widen the protection of investors' interest. What the tribunals do is to find and help achieve the "intention". They claim that their determination to have jurisdiction is not to frustrate the reasonable expectations of the parties (actually, in the author's opinion, it is for the investor's reasonable expectations rather than the host countries'). The Amco case and the Klockner case are echoed with each other

---

[40] Sornarajah (2006), p. 348. It is cited by Paul Michael Blyschak (2009), p. 121.

[41] Sornarajah (2006), p. 348. It is cited by Paul Michael Blyschak (2009), p. 136.

[42] The only case that foreign investor is respondent is Gabon v. Société Serete S.A. (ICSID Case No. ARB/76/1).

in this respect.[43] However, this is what exactly distorts the intention and expectations of developing countries and ignores the interest of developing countries.

### *6.4.2 Potential Negative Impacts*

The ICSID tribunal had earlier stated that its interpretation of an arbitration clause should be neither restrictive nor expansive, but actually they tried to broaden the jurisdiction by acknowledging that arbitration benefits both sides.[44] Some attorneys of investors also claimed that ICSID's emerging jurisprudence on (expanding) the scope of its own jurisdiction enhances the possibility that ICSID will fulfill its purpose of encouraging international investment to the mutual benefit of investors and host states.[45] Is it true? Not really. The expansion of jurisdiction will only benefit investors since they are the claimant who initiates the arbitration and thus surely hopes the ICSID to have jurisdiction. But for host countries who are respondents, what benefits do they have?

In the author's opinion, the tribunal's practice in broadly interpreting the treaties so as to expand its jurisdiction will cause far-reaching negative effects including the following four aspects.

#### 6.4.2.1 It Will Affect the Interpreting Principles of Treaties and the Seriousness of Treaties

The principles of fairness and justice are fundamental principles of international law in interpreting legal instruments or legal relations. The practice to "guess" the intention of one party or "infer" the agreement of one party for the benefit of another party, as what some ICSID tribunals do, should not be the correct interpreting approach.

Although more and more countries agree in the BITs to submit investment disputes to international arbitration for resolution, the premise of arbitration is the consent to arbitration of both parties. The established rule in domestic law or international law is that such consent should be clear and unambiguous. Just as the Plama tribunal stated, doubts as to the parties' clear and unambiguous intention could arise if the agreement to arbitrate was to be reached by incorporation or by reference.[46] Moreover, dispute resolution provisions in a specific treaty have been negotiated with a view to resolving disputes under that treaty. Contracting States cannot be presumed to have agreed that those provisions can be enlarged by incorporating dispute resolution provisions from other treaties negotiated in an entirely different context,[47] under the MFN clause.

---

43 William Rand, et al. (1986–1987), p. 50.

44 William Rand, et al. (1986–1987), p. 58.

45 William Rand, et al. (1986–1987), p. 61.

46 Plama Consortium Limited v. Republic of Bulgaria, Decision (2005), pp. 198–199.

47 Plama Consortium Limited v. Republic of Bulgaria, Decision (2005), p. 207.

If the tribunal enlarges its jurisdiction by relying on the umbrella clause, it will tremendously damage the seriousness of treaty. The reason being that, by applying the umbrella clause in the BITs, any alleged violation of those contracts and other instruments would be treated as a breach of the BIT. There would be no real need to demonstrate a violation of those substantive treaty standards. An investor may, at will, nullify any freely negotiated dispute settlement clause in a State contract.[48]

#### 6.4.2.2 It Will Create False "Precedent" and Mislead Other Tribunals

Some people consider that ICSID's jurisdiction has been evolved (i.e., enlarged) through the interpretation and application of the ICSID Convention by ICSID arbitral tribunals, and these jurisdictional decisions reflect an emerging ICSID jurisprudence and a significant contribution to general principles of international commercial law.[49] They thought that by doing so, these ICSID tribunals may have set a non-binding but nevertheless persuasive precedent of wider application, facilitating recognition of the ICSID's power to settle disputes even in the absence of an express ICSID arbitration clause.[50] Many tribunals also put such assertions into practice and create more "precedents" to expand jurisdiction through misusing or distorting the MFN clause, umbrella clause and the fork-in-the-road clause.

However, these "precedents" are not correct precedents. They misled some other tribunals to expand jurisdiction and thus ICSID has more and more cases whose jurisdiction is enlarged.

#### 6.4.2.3 It Will Damage ICSID's Impartiality and Credibility

The original intention of the establishment of ICSID is to benefit both developing countries and foreign investors. The arbitrary expansion of its jurisdiction will surely damage ICSID's intention to balance the interests of developing countries and foreign investors and damage the confidence of contracting parties in ICSID. The expansion of jurisdiction will easily lead to the uncertainty of jurisdiction and will possibly cause the following negative impacts: It may restrict further acceptance of the ICSID arbitration by new states; may result in enforcement problems; and may impair the efficiency of arbitration process by lengthening the procedure.[51] More seriously, some ICSID contracting states would as a result cancel their consent to ICSID arbitration or even withdraw from ICSID. Therefore, some scholars appeal that arbitration tribunal needs to be consistent in its decisions on jurisdiction to provide clear

---

48 SGS v. Pakistan, Decision (2003), p. 136; SGS v. Philippines, Decision (2004), p. 168.

49 William Rand, et al. (1986–1987), p. 34.

50 William Rand, et al. (1986–1987), p. 61.

51 Sule Akyuz (2003), p. 336.

guidance, to avoid uncertainty and to be continuously chosen by the parties to a dispute.[52]

#### 6.4.2.4 It Will Damage Host Country's State Sovereignty and State Interest

The accession to ICSID Convention or the consent to ICSID arbitration in BITs themselves is the reflections of a country to exercise its state sovereignty. Moreover, the consent to ICSID arbitration itself is a restriction to one country's sovereignty. Therefore, the interpretation of consent should be clear and unambiguous, and only thus is a respect to sovereignty. However, the tribunal broadly interprets the consent through the purpose of the BIT in the preamble, or "guesses" the host country's intention to protect foreign investor through its accession to ICSID or conclusion of BITs, or take away the real intention of contracting country through the application of MFN clause, for the final purpose of expanding jurisdiction. This is to infringe upon sovereign prerogatives and to protect investor rights at the expense of sovereign rights of the host countries.[53] Long before there were scholars who asserted that investment tribunals were overly eager to adopt broad interpretations of investment provisions that illegitimately expanded their application in favor of investors and at the expense of host states.[54] ICSID seemed to enlarge its jurisdiction by further delimiting the sovereignty of member states.[55] However, the lawyers of the investors boasted that expansion of ICSID arbitration consistent with the reasonable expectations of the parties should not be resisted as an affront to the sovereignty of the host state.[56]

Due to the arbitrary expansion of jurisdiction, many host countries are forced to be in a disadvantageous position to have to bear not only the arbitration cost and the tribunal's cost in the jurisdictional procedure, but also huge amount of compensation awarded to foreign investors in the merits award. This may greatly damage the host country's state interest.

## 6.5 Conclusion

Some ICSID tribunals, with the discretion to determine their own competence and jurisdiction, have employed various approaches to broaden their jurisdiction over investment disputes—whether intentionally or not. However, despite the various possible reasons, such expansion has caused or will cause various damages to international law principles, ICSID or host states. More importantly, the expansion of

[52] Sule Akyuz (2003), p. 336.

[53] Sornarajah (2006), p. 348. It is cited by Paul Michael Blyschak (2009), p. 137.

[54] Sornarajah (2006), p. 348. It is cited by Paul Michael Blyschak (2009), p. 119.

[55] Sule Akyuz (2003), p. 336.

[56] William Rand, et al. (1986–1987), p. 61.

jurisdiction and the damages caused intensifies the legitimacy crisis of international investment arbitration. This in turn has led the international community to question the effectiveness of investor-state dispute settlement mechanisms, in redressing legitimacy problems. Thus, in the author's opinion, implementing a more effective mechanism to limit the tribunals' discretion to expand jurisdiction is simply necessary.

## References

Chongli Xu (2008) Controversies over the Applicable Scope of Umbrella Clause and China's Countermeasures, Journal of The East China University of Politics Science and Law (Chinese), vol 4

Desert Line Projects LLC v. The Republic of Yemen (ICSID Case No. ARB/05/17), Award (2008)

Emilio Agustin Maffezini v. The Kingdom of Spain (ICSID CASE No. ABR/97/7), Decision of the Tribunal on Objections to Jurisdiction (2000)

Fedax v. Veneruela (ICSID Case No. ARB/96/3), Decision of the Tribunal on the Objections to Jurisdiction (1997)

HHA Van Harten (2007) Investment treaty arbitration and public law, Oxford University Press

Impregilo S.p.A. v. Pakistan (ICSID Case No. ARB/03/3), Decision on Jurisdiction (2005)

Paul Michael Blyschak (2009) State Consent, Investor Interests and the Future of Investment Arbitration: Reanalyzing the Jurisdiction of Investor-State Tribunals in Hard Cases, Asper Review of International Business and Trade Law, vol 9

Plama Consortium Limited v. Republic of Bulgaria (ICSID Case No. ARB/03/24), Decision on Jurisdiction (2005)

Saipem v. Bangladesh (ICSID case No. ARB/05/07), Decision on Jurisdiction and Recommendation on Provisional Measures (2007)

Salini v. Jordan (ICSID Case No. ARB/02/13), Decision on Jurisdiction (2004)

Schmidt (1976) , Arbitration Under the Auspices of the International Centre for Settlement of Investment Disputes (ICSID): Implications of the Decision on Jurisdiction in Alcoa Minerals of Jamaica, Inc. v. Government of Jamaica, Harvard International Law Journal, vol 17

SGS v. Philippines (ICSID Case No. ARB/02/6), Decision of the Tribunal on Objections To Jurisdiction (2004)

Sornarajah M (2006) A law for need or a law for greed?: Restoring the lost law in the international law of foreign investment. International Environmental Agreements, vol 6

Sule Akyuz A (2003) The Jurisdiction of ICSID: The Application of the Article 25 of Convention on the Settlement of Investment Dispute Between States and Nationals of Other States, C.52 Sa.3

Susan D Franck (2005) The Legitimacy Crisis in Investment Treaty Arbitration: Privatizing Public International Law Through Inconsistent Decisions, Fordham Law Review, vol 73

Telenor Mobile Communications A.S. v. The Republic of Hungary (ICSID Case No. ARB/05/15), Award (2006)

William Rand, Robert N Hornick, Paul Friedland (1986), ICSID's Emerging Jurisprudence: The Scope of ICSID's Jurisdiction, N. Y. U. Journal of International Law and Politics, vol 19

# Chapter 7
# The Investor-State Dispute Settlement Mechanism: New Developments in the Early Twenty-First Century

## 7.1 Introduction

Traditionally, investment disputes between foreign investors and host countries were resolved in the local courts of host countries since many developing countries insisted on the Calvo Doctrine. However, developed countries tried to protect their overseas investors by resolving investor-state investment disputes in the international arena through diplomatic protection or international arbitration. They insisted that investor-state dispute settlement provisions, such as international arbitration by the International Centre for Settlement of Investment Disputes (ICSID), be inserted into investment treaties, including bilateral investment treaties (BITs) and free trade agreements (FTAs) signed with developing countries. Since the 1980s, more and more developing countries have deviated from their traditional conservative position and have increasingly accepted highly protective investor-state dispute settlement mechanisms (ISDSMs) in BITs or FTAs with both developed and developing countries.

The highest protective ISDSM in the 1990s is that of the North America Free Trade Agreement (NAFTA). As of the end of 1990s, some developing countries—such as Argentina and Mexico—were confronted by a number of investment lawsuits filed by foreign investors and thus realized the serious problems arising from highly protective ISDSMs. Therefore, developing countries began restricting or withdrawing from the jurisdiction of ICSID. At the same time, the US, the leading country of developed countries, after being challenged by several NAFTA investment cases, also changed its attitude toward NAFTA-style ISDSMs. The US made several improvements to some of its 1994 Model BIT provisions concerning ISDSMs and created a new indirect mechanism excluding ISDSMs in the Australia-US Free Trade Agreement (AUSFTA) in 2004. After a thorough review of these changes, the author concludes

This article is updated based on my previously published article in the title of The Investor-State Dispute Settlement Mechanism: Where to Go in the 21st Century? in the Journal of World Investment & Trade, Vol. 9, Issue 6, December 2008. It was updated in early 2024.

 
H. Chen, *China's Practice in International Investment Law*, Modern China and International Economic Law, https://doi.org/10.1007/978-981-96-5016-3_7

that both the improvements and the new mechanism echo the four "safety valves" once insisted on by many developing countries. The author opines that the new trends in both developed and developing countries reflect the emerging consensus between them and thus recommends that ISDSMs be improved and restricted in future investment rules in the twenty-first century.

## 7.2 New Trend in Developing Countries Toward Investor-State Dispute Settlement Mechanisms in the Early Twenty-First Century

The positions of developing countries regarding ISDSMs may be described in four stages. Before the 1960s, the traditional attitude was that investor-state disputes should be resolved by local remedies. From the 1960s through the 1980s, a conservative attitude insisted on four "safety valves" in ICSID arbitration. Almost full acceptance of ICSID jurisdiction and other arbitration occurred from the late 1980s to the early twenty-first century. The new trend in the early twenty-first century has reverted back to the traditional and conservative attitudes.

### *7.2.1 Developing Countries' Traditional Attitudes Toward ISDSMs*

In the twentieth century, transnational capital gradually started to flow to developing countries, in addition to flowing among developed countries. The flow was a "one-way street",[1] for there was almost no investment from developing countries to developed countries. The investment issue was touched upon in the Treaty of Friendship, Commerce, and Navigation (FNC Treaty) between developed and developing countries, without mentioning the resolution of investor-state disputes. This was because investment issues were not a key issue in the treaty, and Latin American countries, which were the main body of developing countries at that time, insisted on the Calvo Doctrine.

After World War II, many newly independent developing countries exercised economic sovereignty to nationalize some foreign investments in order to further develop their national economy. As a result, tensions between foreign investors and host countries were created and gradually intensified. Under such circumstances, developed countries—as home countries—started to sign new types of treaties with developing countries so as to protect the interests of their overseas investors. The new types of treaties included the Investment Guarantee Agreement (IGA) by the US with developing countries, and the Investment Protection Agreement (IPA) by

[1] James McIlroy (2004), p. 643.

Germany and other West European countries with developing countries. The focus of IGA is investment insurance and subrogation, while the focus of IPA is investment protection. Therefore, the IGA did not touch upon the settlement of investor-state disputes, while the IPA did.

The FCT Treaty, IPA and IGA are collectively called BIT, which from the very beginning was created as a treaty between developed and developing countries. Developed countries hoped to set the rights and obligations of developing countries toward foreign investors from developed countries through a binding international treaty. Therefore, when signing BIT, developed countries stood in the position of capital-exporting countries whose purpose was protecting their overseas investors and investments. The first IPA in the world was signed between Germany and Pakistan in 1959. The German-style BIT was a model for many developed countries, except for the US, for many years.

No ISDSM provision was contained in the German-style BITs or other BITs before the creation of ICSID (i.e., in the mid-1960s). The main reason was that the newly independent developing countries cherished very much their hard-won state sovereignty and thus insisted on the traditional Calvo Doctrine.[2] The Calvo Doctrine requested that disputes be resolved by domestic administrative tribunals or courts according to the domestic law of the host country.[3]

However, foreign investors regarded the domestic legal systems of developing countries as incomplete and lacking of just and unbiased experts who could fairly and effectively settle investor-state disputes.[4] Therefore, they did not want to be subject to the exclusive jurisdiction of the host country. Instead, they relied on their home country to exercise diplomatic protection. According to customary international law, the pre-requisite to a country exercising diplomatic protection is the exhaustion of available local remedies without a satisfactory result. This is to provide the host country a chance to redress foreign victims, to reduce the number of international claims, and to avoid involvement by the home country that might affect the political relations between the two countries. However, some developed countries started to exercise diplomatic protection before the exhaustion of local remedies by exerting political pressure, waging economic boycotts or even war. This changed the civil disputes between foreign investors and host countries to political disputes between the host and home countries and caused tense international relations.

[2] The Calvo Doctrine means that national law should govern the rights and privileges of aliens, and national courts should have exclusive jurisdiction over disputes. See Louis Henkin (1993), p. 685.

[3] Sornarajah (1994), pp. 270–271.

[4] UNCTAD (2003-1), p. 7.

### 7.2.2 *Developing Countries' Conservative Attitude Toward ISDSMs: The Creation of ICSID and the Four "Safety Valves"*

From the early 1960s, developed countries suggested the establishment of ICSID—a special institution to handle investment legal disputes between a host country and foreign investor by international arbitration or conciliation, instead of filing lawsuits in the courts of host countries. After several years of hard work in consultation, negotiation and compromise, an agreement was finally reached between developed and developing countries and the ICSID Convention was concluded in 1965.

When negotiating the ICSID Convention, developing countries agreed to a limited transfer of their sovereignty by submitting investor-state investment disputes to ICSID for resolution. However, they maintained the four "safety valves" including the exhaustion of local remedies, use of domestic law of the host country as one of the governing laws, consent for arbitration on a case-by-case basis and respect for national sovereignty and national security. The purpose of the four "safety valves" is to retain some control of the resolution of investment disputes. The following paragraphs give detailed analysis of the four "safety valves".

The first is the exhaustion of local remedies. To settle the contradiction between the Calvo Doctrine and arbitration by ICSID, the ICSID Convention allows contracting states to require the exhaustion of local administrative or judicial remedies by foreign investors as a condition of its consent to arbitration by ICSID.[5] Some developing countries take full advantage of this provision to protect themselves. For instance, in 1993, Costa Rica notified ICSID that "[t]here may only be recourse to arbitration pursuant to [the Convention] where all existing administrative or judicial remedies have been exhausted".[6] In this way, developing countries could reserve the right to resolve disputes in domestic courts according to its domestic law, and thus, preserve state sovereignty. This may also reduce the number of disputes submitted to ICSID. Exhaustion of local remedies was historically considered to be a necessary step prior to submitting a dispute to an international tribunal.[7]

The second is consent to arbitration on a case-by-case basis. Signing the ICSID Convention does not mean unconditional consent to arbitration by ICSID. On the contrary, whether a dispute will be submitted for arbitration is subject to consent by contracting states. According to the ICSID Convention, the parties to the dispute should give consent in writing to submit the dispute to ICSID.[8] This allows the host country to determine what types of disputes it would like to submit to ICSID. Thus,

---

[5] Article 26 of the ICSID Convention.

[6] ICSID (2020), Notifications Concerning Classes of Disputes Considered Suitable Or Unsuitable for Submission to the Centre, Footnote 5, in: Contracting States and Measures taken by them for the purpose of the Convention, available at https://icsid.worldbank.org/sites/default/files/2020_July_ICSID_8_ENG.pdf.

[7] UNCTAD (2007), p. 108.

[8] Article 25 (1) of the ICSID Convention.

the host country is still in a favorable position to control the types of disputes resolved by arbitration.

The third is domestic law of host country as one of the governing laws. Governing law is the legal basis for a court or arbitral tribunal to decide a case. Developing countries required that investment disputes be decided according to the domestic law of the host country, while developed countries contended international law governed. The ICSID Convention compromised by permitting both parties to choose the governing law by agreement. In the absence of such an agreement, the tribunal shall apply the law of the contracting state party to the dispute and such rules of international law as may be applicable.[9] The "law of the Contracting State party" is actually the law of the host country. Using the law of the host country as governing law is fair for both the host country and foreign investor since the foreign investor is doing business in the host country, and the result is predictable.

The fourth is State sovereignty and national security. The aforementioned requirements of exhaustion of local remedy, consent to arbitration on a case-by-case basis, as well as the requirement of domestic law as governing law are the manifestation of respect for state sovereignty and national security. In addition, the Convention provides that a contracting state may notify ICSID at any time of the class or classes of disputes that it will submit to the jurisdiction of ICSID.[10] This allows a host country, in consideration of its national security, to determine the disputes that will be submitted to ICSID even after it accedes to the ICSID Convention. Papua New Guinea notified ICSID in 1978 that it would only consider submitting those disputes to ICSID which are fundamental to the investment itself. Israel notified ICSID in 1983 that it would only submit disputes related to an approved investment under one of the Israeli Laws for the Encouragement of Capital Investments. China notified ICSID in 1993 that it would only submit disputes over the amount of compensation resulting from expropriation and nationalization. In 1974 Jamaica notified ICSID that a legal dispute relating to minerals or other natural resources would not be subject to the jurisdiction of ICSID.[11]

Moreover, the Convention provides that if an investor and host state have consented to submit or have submitted a dispute to arbitration under ICSID, the contracting state of the investor cannot give diplomatic protection or bring an international claim, unless the other contracting state has failed to comply with the rendered award.[12] This provision also echoes the Calvo Doctrine.

The above four "safety valves" established in the ICSID Convention protected developing countries from being easily sued by foreign investors in an international arbitral tribunal. This was one of the main reasons why there were only 24 cases

---

[9] Article 42 (1) of the ICSID Convention.

[10] Article 25 (4) of the ICSID Convention.

[11] ICSID (2020), Notifications Concerning Classes of Disputes Considered Suitable Or Unsuitable for Submission to the Centre, in: Contracting States and Measures taken by them for the purpose of the Convention, available at https://icsid.worldbank.org/sites/default/files/2020_July_ICSID_8_ENG.pdf.

[12] Article 27 (1) of the ICSID Convention.

submitted to ICSID for the first 25 years of ICSID from 1966 to 1991, before a more highly protective ISDSM began to be accepted by developing countries.[13]

Nevertheless, during the beginning years of ICSID, since many developing countries, and Latin American countries in particular, still had serious concerns about submitting disputes to ICSID, they did not sign or accede to the ICSID Convention. Only a few developing countries, such as some African and Asian countries, signed or acceded to the ICSID Convention during the 1960s and 1970s. Most BITs signed during that period were between developed countries and the developing countries that were already ICSID contracting states. Although these BITs contained ISDSM provisions regarding ICSID, the four "safety valves" were also maintained. A good example of this is Article 11 of the Netherlands-Singapore BIT signed in 1972.[14]

### 7.2.3 *Developing Countries' Almost Full Acceptance of Highly Protective ISDSMs and the Risks Arising Therefrom*

Developing countries have changed dramatically their position toward ISDSMs since the end of the 1980s. They deviated from the Calvo Doctrine, gave up the four "safety valves" and almost fully accepted highly protective ISDSMs in their BITs. There are three reasons for this dramatic change. One is that it came to be accepted that accession to the ICSID Convention could promote an atmosphere of mutual confidence, and thus stimulate a larger flow of private international capital into those countries desiring it.[15] The second is that from the 1980s, the US started to sign IPAs instead of IGAs with developing countries based on its newly adopted Model BIT. Since the US is very adamant about keeping its Model BIT, those developing countries who would like to sign BITs with the US have no choice but to accept its high standard. This US practice has been gradually followed by other developed countries, such as Canada. This echoes an ancient Chinese saying that "when the river rises, the boat floats high". Third, developing countries considered signing high-standard BITs with developed countries as an important means to improve the domestic legal environment for foreign investment.[16] In order to attract more foreign investment to develop domestic economies, many developing countries began competing to sign

[13] ICSID (1991).

[14] This article stipulates that "[T]he Contracting Party in the territory of which nationals of the other Contracting Party make or intend to make investments, shall after the exhaustion of all local administrative and judicial remedies, agree to any demand on the part of such nationals to submit, for arbitration or conciliation, to the Centre established by the Convention of Washington of 18 March 1965 on the settlement of investment disputes between States and nationals of other States, any disputes that may arise in connection with the investments". ICSID (1972).

[15] International Bank for Reconstruction and Development (1965), pp. 524–525.

[16] UNCTAD (2003-1), p. 6.

high-standard BITs containing highly protective ISDSMs with developed countries without considering the negative consequences.

As a result, more and more developing countries acceded to ICSID from the late 1980s to the 1990s as a gesture of protecting foreign investors and their investments. Currently, there are 155 signatory States to the ICSID Convention, and almost all developing countries joined the Convention.[17] Moreover, developing countries have signed various international investment treaties including BITs, bilateral tax agreements and other agreements such as FTAs with investment clauses. Many Latin American countries started to move away from the Calvo Doctrine when signing investment treaties, especially with the US. Mexico is a typical example. In the 1980s, there were only 211 BITs, however, in the 1990s, there were 2392 BITs.[18] As for the end of 2005, there were over 5000 various investment agreements altogether.[19]

Most of the investment agreements signed by developing countries during the 1990s to the early 2000s contained clauses of high-standard protective ISDSMs. NAFTA and other investment agreements, based on the US 1994 Model BIT, have the highest standards with regard to ISDSMs. However, the above four "safety valves" contained in the ICSID Convention were almost completely eliminated.

First, the forum for ISDSMs is not limited to ICSID, but extends to other forums. For example, NAFTA provides that investors can submit their claims for arbitration according to the ICSID Convention, the ICSID Additional Facility Rules, the UNCITRAL Arbitration Rules or any other arbitration rules.[20] Fora other than ICSID do not have any "safety valves" for host states. The number of arbitrations taking place under commercial arbitration rules (e.g., UNCITRAL, International Chamber of Commerce, Stockholm Chamber of Commerce) appears to have eclipsed the volume of such cases at ICSID. For instance, at least 21 new investment treaty arbitrations were initiated outside of ICSID in 2006, as compared with 15 such cases at ICSID in that same period.[21]

Second, the first "safety valve" of exhaustion of local remedy has almost disappeared. Even if the ICSID Convention allows for the "safety valve" of exhaustion of local remedies, some countries voluntarily gave it up. For instance, Israel required the exhaustion of local administrative or judicial remedies as a condition in 1983; however, it withdrew this requirement in 1991. Further, many investment agreements concluded during this period contained their own arbitration rules excluding the requirement of exhaustion of local remedies. For example, the 1994 US Model BIT regarded local remedy as an alternative to dispute settlement instead of as a

[17] For the developing countries that have signed the ICSID Convention, see ICSID: List of Contracting States and other Signatories of the Convention (as of November 4, 2007), available at http://icsid.worldbank.org/ICSID/FrontServlet?requestType=ICSIDDocRH&actionVal=ContractingStates&ReqFrom=Main.

[18] UNCTAD (2005), p. 13.

[19] UNCTAD (2005), p. 53.

[20] NAFTA, Article 1120.

[21] Editor's Note: ITN Year in Review for 2006 finds non-ICSID treaty arbitrations eclipse ICSID cases, Investment Treaty News (ITN), December 14, 2007, published by the International Institute for Sustainable Development, available at http://www.investmenttreatynews.com.

pre-requisite to international arbitration. If the investor does not resort to the host state's domestic court or administrative tribunals, he can submit the dispute to international arbitration.[22] Facing such a choice, most investors prefer arbitration. NAFTA requires investors to waive their rights to initiate or continue before any administrative tribunal or court under the domestic law if the investor would like to submit a claim to arbitration.[23] The US Government once proudly claimed that BITs give investors the right to submit an investment dispute to international arbitration and that there is no requirement to use that country's domestic courts.[24] Most BITs do not even mention exhaustion of local remedies. A number of BITs concluded since 1995 explicitly include an obligation for the parties not to request the exhaustion of local remedies if the investor has opted to submit the dispute to international arbitration.[25]

Third, the second "safety valve" of domestic law as governing law is also excluded by many investment treaties. For example, the governing law in NAFTA only includes the NAFTA Agreement and applicable rules of international law.[26] The host state's domestic law is obviously excluded.

Fourth, the third "safety valve" of consent to arbitration on a case-by-case basis has almost disappeared. Many investment treaties stipulate that signing the agreement itself constitutes unilateral and general consent to submit investment disputes to international arbitration. For instance, NAFTA provides that each party consents to the submission of a claim to arbitration in accordance with its provisions.[27] The US 1994 Model BIT provides that each contracting party consents to the submission of any investment dispute for settlement by binding arbitration.[28]

Fifth, the fourth "safety valve" of state sovereignty and national security has not been steadily and firmly maintained. Many countries have voluntarily given up the allowance by the ICSID Convention to determine what class or classes of disputes should be submitted to ICSID. For instance, Guyana notified ICSID in 1974 that it would not consider submitting legal disputes relating to its mineral and other natural resources to ICSID. However, that notification was withdrawn in 1987 in a communication stating that legal disputes arising directly out of an investment and which the parties consent in writing to submit to the Centre, could be referred.[29] In

---

[22] 1994 US Model BIT, Art. 9.2. The US 1994 Model BIT is used as a model when the US negotiates a BIT or FTA with investment chapter with other countries, thus most US BITs have the same articles.

[23] NAFTA, Art. 1121.1(b) & 2(b).

[24] Office of the USTR, Summary of U.S. Bilateral Investment Treaty (BIT) Program (02/24/2006), available at http://www.ustr.gov/Trade_Agreements/BIT/Summary_of_US_Bilateral_Investment_Treaty_(BIT)_Program.html.

[25] UNCTAD (2007), p. 108.

[26] NAFTA, Art. 1130.

[27] NAFTA, Art. 1122.

[28] 1994 US Model BIT, Art. 9.4.

[29] ICSID (2020), Notifications Concerning Classes of Disputes Considered Suitable Or Unsuitable for Submission to the Centre, in: Contracting States and Measures taken by them for the purpose of the Convention, available at https://icsid.worldbank.org/sites/default/files/2020_July_ICSID_8_ENG.pdf.

1991, Israel also withdrew its previous notification to ICSID limiting submission of disputes to ICSID.[30]

From the late 1990s, China also changed dramatically its attitude toward ISDSMs. Before China signed the ICSID Convention in 1992 and ratified it in 1993, the BITs signed between China and other countries provided that investor-state disputes should be submitted to local courts for resolution. Not long after China's ratification of the ICSID Convention, China was still cautious in accepting ICSID jurisdiction. For instance, from 1992 to 1998, China signed 89 BITs; 76 of them did not accept ICSID jurisdiction. The remaining 13 accepted partial ICSID jurisdiction by providing that only a dispute concerning the amount of compensation for expropriation may be referred to ICSID, and only if both parties could not settle the dispute by friendly consultation within six months.[31] Other disputes would be referred to the host state's domestic court for settlement, or to ICSID in accordance with the two parties' agreement. However, from the late 1990s, China almost fully accepted ICSID jurisdiction. For instance, from 1998 to 2006, China signed 26 BITs. Only eight of them did not accept ICSID jurisdiction, and 17 accepted full ICSID jurisdiction by providing that investors may refer any investment dispute to ICSID for arbitration.[32] Full acceptance could be extended to all BITs signed by China with the free-riding effect of the MFN clause.[33]

Most Latin American countries also changed their attitude from the Calvo Doctrine to accepting international arbitration by ICSID or other arbitration institutions in their BITs or other investment treaties. The first to do so was Mexico, which signed NAFTA in 1992. From then on, most Latin American countries signed BITs or FTAs with the US based on the US 1994 Model BIT or the newly updated 2004 Model BIT.[34] Some scholars have opined that the signing of BITs with the US by Latin American countries precipitated the abandonment or demise of the Calvo Doctrine.[35]

Thus developing countries accepted increased international protection for foreign investors and their investments, gave up the four "safety valves" and loosened protection of national security and state sovereignty. This resulted in numerous challenges and claims from foreign investors. Developing countries accepted ISDSMs from the late 1980s, and from the middle of the 1990s they started to be frequently challenged by investors, thus leading to an increase in ICSID cases. The number of cases filed

---

[30] ICSID (2020), Notifications Concerning Classes of Disputes Considered Suitable Or Unsuitable for Submission to the Centre, in: Contracting States and Measures taken by them for the purpose of the Convention, available at https://icsid.worldbank.org/sites/default/files/2020_July_ICSID_8_ENG.pdf.

[31] Yanru Wei (2006), p. 111. The 13 countries are: South Korea, Lithuania, Chile, Iceland, Peru, Morocco, Israel, Yugoslavia, Saudi Arabia, Gabon, Cameroon, Macedonia, Macedonia, and Yemen.

[32] Yanru Wei (2006), For example, Art. 9 (2) and (3) of the BIT between China and Germany has this provision.

[33] As for China's acceptance of ICSID jurisdiction, see Yanru Wei (2006), pp. 109-144.

[34] These countries include Peru, Colombia, Panama, Chile, Uruguay, the Dominican Republic, Costa Rica, El Salvador, Guatemala, Honduras and Nicaragua.

[35] Jessica S. Wiltse (2003), pp. 1172–1196.

with ICSID from 1994 to 1999 was more than double the number of cases filed with ICSID between 1965 and 1994.[36] Since then cases for international investment arbitration have rapidly increased; developing countries are the main targets and victims. Until November 2006, the total number of known treaty-based cases increased to a new peak of 255. At least 70 governments—44 of them in the developing world, 14 in developed countries and 12 in Southeast Europe and the Commonwealth of Independent States—have faced investment treaty arbitration.[37] Argentina is the most serious "disaster area" by topping the list with 42 claims lodged against it (39 of these disputes relate at least in part to that country's financial crisis).[38] Mexico has 17 claims and has the second highest number of known claims[39]; most of them arose from NAFTA. The US and the Czech Republic have the third highest number of claims filed against them with 11 each.[40] For developed countries, only the US and Canada faced many suits that arose from NAFTA. Nine countries faced arbitration proceedings for the first time in 2006, with one exception all were from the developing world.[41]

Thus, many more developing countries than developed countries are confronted by claims from foreign investors, even if they have the same BITs with the same ISDSM. The reason is that most investment treaties typically pair a developed country that is an exporter of capital with a developing country that imports capital but exports very little capital. In such circumstances, even though the treaty provisions are reciprocal, the litigation risk is not: there is little likelihood that the developed country will face a claim by an investor of the developing country.[42]

### *7.2.4 Developing Countries' New Trend Reverting to Traditional and Conservative Attitudes by Withdrawing from Highly Protective ISDSMs*

Due to the flood of cases against developing countries by foreign investors, and the great amount of compensation paid by host governments, many developing countries started to question, criticize and review the highly protective ISDSMs. South American governments have grown discontented with the system of international investment protection.[43] Venezuela, Argentina and Nicaragua have publicly criticized the

---

[36] ICSID (1999).

[37] UNCTAD (2006), p. 2.

[38] UNCTAD (2006), p. 2.

[39] UNCTAD (2006), p. 2–3.

[40] UNCTAD (2006), p. 2.

[41] UNCTAD (2006), p. 3.

[42] Barton Legum (2002), p. 537.

[43] Luke Eric Peterson (2008).

ICSID arbitration system.[44] Even developed countries, including the American and Canadian Governments have had second thoughts about the Investment Chapter of NAFTA due to the number of NAFTA cases.[45]

Highly protective ISDSMs receive criticism from many individuals and governments of developing countries. For example, many Koreans are opposed to the ISDSM provisions in the South Korea-US FTA, because they think these provisions could eventually undermine the capability of the government to adopt countercyclical macroeconomic policies as well as social policies that are necessary to supplement market failures.[46] Another example is the stagnancy of the Free Trade Area of the Americas (FTAA). FTAA was expected to be concluded by 2005, however, it is still currently under negotiation. One important reason is that the controversial investment chapter of NAFTA is incorporated into the draft text of the FTAA.[47] Brazil, the major player in the FTAA negotiations for Latin America, is not associated with ICSID or in a BIT with the US, and thus is less willing to abandon the Calvo Doctrine than some of its neighbors.[48] On the other hand, it is difficult to envision the US accepting the FTAA without an ISDSM. The ISDSM is a major stumbling block in the FTAA negotiations.[49] Moreover, the practice that the AUSFTA does not include an ISDSM provides a powerful precedential argument for those who have objected to the investment provisions in the FTAA agreement.[50]

Some developing countries started to take measures to change the highly protective ISDSMs to a more conservative position. The most aggrieved country is Argentina which has suffered greatly from ISDSMs. In October 2003, Argentina's government published a decree stating that the handing of an ISDSM case "presented a series of difficulties from the legal, political and economic point[s] of view". Argentina has tried to "renationalize" legal conflicts between the government and foreign investors, including disputes submitted to ICSID.[51] It is reported that the government's aim was to "recover the jurisdiction of national courts". Argentina attempted to make sure that foreign investors had first exhausted all legal channels in Argentina, and second, that the final decisions of international tribunals should undergo "analysis" by the local courts.[52] All this shows that Argentina would like to revert to the traditional Calvo Doctrine and require exhaustion of local remedies, and possibly withdraw from ICSID jurisdiction.

---

[44] Damon Vis-Dunbar (2008), Activists lobby in support of Bolivia's withdrawal from ICSID, Investment Treaty News (ITN), January 11, available at http://www.investmenttreatynews.com.

[45] Ann Capling and Kim Richard Nossal (2006), p. 157.

[46] South Korea-U.S. FTA deal would trigger unfair bilateral trade and investment agreement at the expense of the common interest of most developing countries, available at http://l.web.umkc.edu/leefs/htnf/htn43/Letter%20to%20President%20and%20National%20Assemblymen.pdf.

[47] Jessica S. Wiltse (2003), p. 1151.

[48] Jessica S. Wiltse (2003), p. 1177.

[49] Jessica S. Wiltse (2003), p. 1177.

[50] Ann Capling and Kim Richard Nossal (2006), p.166.

[51] Laurence Norman (2003).

[52] Laurence Norman (2003).

Other developing countries have reverted to the traditional conservative position and again apply the four "safety valves" allowed in the ICSID Convention to protect their interests. Guatemala notified ICSID that it would require the exhaustion of local administrative remedies as a condition of its consent to arbitration under ICSID in 2003.[53] On December 4, 2007, Ecuador notified ICSID that it withdrew its consent to submit certain types of disputes to ICSID for arbitration,[54] including disputes related to the exploitation of natural resources. Ecuador also withdrew all its previously expressed consent to ICSID as of the date of the notification, if the other party to the dispute had not yet given express and explicit consent.[55]

Some developing countries took even more dramatic measures including completely withdrawing from the ICSID Convention so that no foreign investor could sue them at ICSID. Bolivia notified the World Bank of its denunciation of the ICSID Convention on May 2, 2007.[56] This means that Bolivia withdrew from ICSID and is no longer a contracting state of ICSID. Sometime later, when Euro Telecom tried to register a claim against Bolivia at ICSID, Bolivia strongly opposed the registration. Bolivia held that both parties to an arbitration must give written consent to ICSID prior to a country's notice of withdrawal, in order to be eligible to arbitrate at ICSID. Although ICSID registered the case, Bolivia's position received great support from many in international circles.[57]

Some developing countries have also begun considering withdrawing from other existing investment agreements with ISDSM provisions. For instance, although Ecuador has withdrawn its consent for ICSID claims, this did not in itself preclude other arbitral claims because Ecuador has consented to UNCITRAL and other commercial arbitration in its BIT. Therefore, Ecuador has signaled that it plans to denounce treaties with El Salvador, Cuba, Guatemala, Honduras, Nicaragua, the Dominican Republic, Paraguay, Uruguay and Romania. It is also scrutinizing its

---

[53] ICSID (2020), Notifications Concerning Classes of Disputes Considered Suitable Or Unsuitable for Submission to the Centre, Footnote 6, in: Contracting States and Measures taken by them for the purpose of the Convention, available at https://icsid.worldbank.org/sites/default/files/2020_July_ICSID_8_ENG.pdf.

[54] ICSID News Release, Ecuador's Notification under Article 25(4) of the ICSID Convention, Dec. 5, 2007, available at http://icsid.worldbank.org/ICSID/FrontServlet?requestType=CasesRH&actionVal=OpenPage&PageType=AnnouncementsFrame&FromPage=Announcements&pageName=Announcement9. Pursuant to this article, a Contracting State may notify the Centre of the class or classes of disputes which the State would or would not consider submitting to the jurisdiction of the Centre. Such notification may be made at the time of ratification, acceptance or approval of the Convention or at any time thereafter.

[55] ICSID (2020), Notifications Concerning Classes of Disputes Considered Suitable Or Unsuitable for Submission to the Centre, Note, in: Contracting States and Measures taken by them for the purpose of the Convention, available at https://icsid.worldbank.org/sites/default/files/2020_July_ICSID_8_ENG.pdf.

[56] ICSID NEWS RELEASE, Bolivia Submits a Notice under Article 71 of the ICSID Convention, May 16, 2007, available at http://icsid.worldbank.org/ICSID/FrontServlet?requestType=CasesRH&actionVal=OpenPage&PageType=AnnouncementsFrame&FromPage=Announcements&pageName=Announcement3.

[57] Damon Vis-Dunbar (2008), Activists lobby in support of Bolivia's withdrawal from ICSID, Investment Treaty News (ITN), January 11, available at http://www.investmenttreatynews.com.

other investment treaties, including those with the US, Canada and various Western European Governments.[58]

As mentioned earlier, during the 1990s and early twenty-first century, China radically changed its attitude from the conservative position to almost complete acceptance of ICSID jurisdiction in many newly signed BITs. Although China has not yet been sued at ICSID, some Chinese scholars criticize this new practice and insist that China should return to only partial acceptance of ICSID jurisdiction.[59] In recent years, China has been negotiating a BIT with Canada, which insists on an ISDSM based on Canada's Model Foreign Investment Protection and Promotion Agreement (it is also called Canadian Model BIT). However, Chinese negotiators are reluctant to accept this.

The above recent and new practices indicate a trend among developing countries to tighten or narrow ICSID jurisdiction and to take conservative positions toward ISDSMs.

The reasons for the new trend are not limited to the flood of arbitration cases against developing countries. Another reason is that with the passing of time, the prevailing justifications for ICSID and protective ISDSMs have faded. One proposition offered that the creation of ICSID would stimulate a larger flow of private international capital into those countries desiring it.[60] Another proposition offered that signing a highly protective US-type BIT would lead to increased FDI flows.[61] However, the over 30-year practice does not see increased flows of investment to signatory developing countries.[62] Therefore, developing countries realize that little or no harm will occur to the flow of investment if they withdraw from ICSID or abolish the ISDSM provisions in investment treaties.

## 7.3 New Trend in Developed Countries Toward Investor-State Dispute Settlement Mechanism in the Early Twenty-First Century

In general, developed countries impose high protection obligations on developing countries when signing BITs or other investment treaties with them. Since developed countries are capital-exporting countries, as compared to developing countries, they

---

[58] Luke Eric Peterson (2008).

[59] Yanru Wei (2006), p. 144.

[60] International Bank for Reconstruction and Development (1965), pp. 524–525.

[61] Salacuse and Sullivan (2005), pp. 106–107.

[62] World Bank (2003), Global Economic Prospects and the Developing Countries, p. xvii, available at https://documents.worldbank.org/en/publication/documents-reports/documentdetail/867491468124755492/global-economic-prospects-and-the-developing-countries-2003-investing-to-unlock-global-opportunities.

have much less risk to be sued by foreign investors. When negotiating BITs, developed countries are concerned with effectively protecting their overseas investors by including highly protective ISDSMs.

Developed countries sign few BITs with each other since BITs were specifically designed for investments made in developing countries. Even if they sign BITs with each other, ISDSMs are not a part of their BITs. The NAFTA Investment Chapter signed in 1993 is the first investment treaty involving two developed countries (US and Canada). Later in 1998, the proposed Multilateral Agreement on Investment (MAI) among OECD countries included the NAFTA-style ISDSM. Both the US and Canada suffered from several investment lawsuits arising from NAFTA. Since learning lessons from these NAFTA cases, both countries have updated their model BITs to lower protection for foreign investors, including with respect to ISDSMs.

Modifications and improvements with regard to ISDSMs echo the four "safety valves" insisted on by developing countries at the ICSID Convention. More importantly, the 2005 AUSFTA completely abolished the ISDSM and created a new mechanism. Since the US has been the longtime leader in increasing high protection for foreign investors and their investments in both substantive and procedural rules in international investment treaties, the new US practice is also expected to create a trend in regard to ISDSMs, especially among developed countries. The following analysis takes the US as an example.

### *7.3.1 Evolution of US Attitudes Toward ISDSMs*

Before the 1990s, the US signed investment treaties only with developing countries, not with developed countries. There were no ISDSM provisions in either the FCN treaties or IGA treaties signed between the US and other developing countries. However, from the early 1980s, the US followed Germany and other European countries in signing investment promotion and protection treaties containing ISDSMs with developing countries. The first one was with Panama in 1982.

Subsequent to the Panama Treaty, the US formulated its first Model BIT in 1984. The 1984 Model BIT contains only one article with five paragraphs on ISDSMs.[63] This article provided that parties to the investment dispute should initially seek to resolve any disputes by consultation and negotiation. If the dispute could not be resolved, it should be submitted for settlement in accordance with previously agreed, applicable dispute settlement procedures. If after six months from the date upon which the dispute arose the dispute had not been submitted for resolution in accordance with any previously agreed applicable dispute settlement procedures, or the investor had not brought the dispute before the courts of justice or administrative tribunals or agencies of competent jurisdiction of the host state, the dispute could be submitted to ICSID for conciliation or arbitration. This article shows that, with regard to dispute settlement, the US respected the autonomy of the parties to the dispute as

---

[63] 1984 US Model BIT, Art. VI.

well as any local remedies. Submitting disputes to ICSID was not compulsory, but was a last resort, with the choosing right conferred to foreign investors.

In 1994, on the basis of NAFTA, the US updated its 1984 Model BIT to include a highly protective NAFTA-style ISDSM. However, ten years later, with the lessons learned from the NAFTA investment cases, the US modified its 1994 Model BIT again to be the 2004 Model BIT that has greatly lowered standards for ISDSMs.

### 7.3.2 NAFTA's ISDSM and Lessons Learned Therefrom

When the US signed BITs with developing countries with high standards and high protection, it was standing in the shoes of a capital-exporting country for the purpose of protecting the interests of its overseas investors. With little investment from developing countries, it never thought of itself being sued as a defendant.[64] When the US negotiated NAFTA with Canada and Mexico, it insisted on a highly protective ISDSM targeting Mexico. After NAFTA was concluded, the US Government claimed that "The NAFTA provides an historic investor-state dispute settlement mechanism, so that individual U.S. companies no longer face an unbalanced environment in an investment dispute with the Mexican government but can seek arbitration outside Mexico by an independent body".[65] The US certainly did not intend to encourage lawsuits against it by investors from Mexico or Canada.

Before the signing of NAFTA, most BITs had only a few paragraphs concerning investor-state dispute settlement procedures. The NAFTA Investment Chapter was the first investment treaty dedicating a whole section to the proceedings and thus provided the highest standard of ISDSM. The NAFTA-style ISDSM was followed by similar BITs in Austria, Canada, Mexico and the US.[66]

NAFTA has a specific Subchapter B—Settlement of Disputes between A Party and An Investor of Another Party—that contains 23 articles and numerous paragraphs. Compared to traditional or standard BITs, the NAFTA ISDSM represented a radical change in existing practices in at least two major respects. First, NAFTA was the first international investment and trade agreement to provide for investor-state arbitration between developed countries. Second, unlike BITs, which allowed only governments to seek arbitral relief on behalf of their nationals, NAFTA granted private investors the right to take a complaint against a government directly to binding international arbitration.[67] No exhaustion of local remedy is required. Investors from other contracting countries do not have to depend on the willingness of the host state to agree to arbitration since signing the investment agreement constitutes unilateral

[64] William S. Dodge (2006), p. 14.

[65] North American Free Trade Agreement, Text of Agreement, Implementation Bill, Statement of Administrative Action and Required Supporting Statements, H.R. Doc. No. 103–159, at 685 (1993).

[66] UNCTAD (2007), p. 119.

[67] Ann Capling and Kim Richard Nossal (2006).

unconditional consent to arbitration. Foreign investors could directly demand arbitration before ICSID, an Additional Facility of ICSID, UNCITRAL or other arbitration institution.

The officials who negotiated the NAFTA Investment Chapter in the early 1990s did not anticipate that lawyers would use the ISDSM provisions to launch claims that generated great opposition in the late 1990s.[68] Under NAFTA, the US and Canada acted as both capital-exporting countries and capital-importing countries. The ISDSM was taken advantage of by investors against the two developed countries. The role of the US in the investment arbitration was then greatly changed from the home country of complainants in arbitration to the host country respondent. Since 1998, when the first NAFTA claim was filed, the US has been sued 14 times by investors from Canada, three of whom sent out notices of intent for arbitration without actual arbitration proceedings.[69] In the four decided cases, the substantive issues were denied by the arbitration tribunal and the US was not held responsible.[70] However, the US Government was unhappy about the frequent lawsuits it faced in this international forum, and found itself under great pressure from the public media.

The challenges faced by the US from the NAFTA investment cases are the same problems faced by developing countries in the past. For instance, national sovereignty and regulatory competence of the host state was limited or even eroded. When the state exercises its legal power to regulate public health and environmental regulations, it is susceptible to challenges from foreign investors that such regulations have injured their investments and thus constitute expropriation.[71] In the game between foreign investor and host government, foreign investors are in an advantageous position as they can challenge the host government. Lack of transparency of the process and the relative lack of procedural safeguards is also a large problem.[72] Other criticisms are that the NAFTA Investment Chapter was characterized as "a Bill of Rights" conferring broad rights on multinational corporations without any corresponding international obligations,[73] and it forces governments to "pay polluters" to stop polluting.[74] In particular, for the US, foreign investors enjoy more rights than domestic American investors since domestic investors cannot sue the US before an international tribunal.[75]

---

[68] Ann Capling and Kim Richard Nossal (2006), p. 165.

[69] NAFTA Chapter 11 Investor-State Disputes (to March 1, 2007), Compiled by Scott Sinclair, available at http://policyalternatives.ca/documents/National_Office_Pubs/2007/NAFTA_Dispute_Table_March2007.pdf.

[70] NAFTA Chapter 11 Investor-State Disputes (to March 1, 2007), Compiled by Scott Sinclair, available at http://policyalternatives.ca/documents/National_Office_Pubs/2007/NAFTA_Dispute_Table_March2007.pdf.

[71] Ray C. Jones (2002).

[72] Ray C. Jones (2002).

[73] Ray C. Jones (2002).

[74] Ray C. Jones (2002).

[75] For critiques on NAFTA Investment Chapter, please refer to Jessica S. Wiltse (2003), pp. 1171–1172.

The original reason that developed countries insisted on ISDSMs is that they suspected the soundness of the legal systems of developing countries. In other words, the thought was that developed countries had sound legal systems and thus would not be challenged by foreign investors. The NAFTA investment cases, however, changed this. Corporate lawyers could be all pervasive and did seize opportunities to challenge the host state. The NAFTA cases gave developed countries, such as the US and Canada, the opportunity to experience the position of being a defendant. Learning from these NAFTA lessons, the US started to rethink ISDSM and realized the importance of keeping a balance of the rights and obligations between the host state and the foreign investor.

### *7.3.3 Modifications and Improvements Made by the US in Its 2004 Model BIT that Echo the Four "Safety Valves" by Developing Countries*

With more and more NAFTA claims from foreign investors, pressure from the public, and challenges to national sovereignty, the US began finding loopholes for future investment agreements since it was too late to directly amend the existing NAFTA investment articles. The US Government began improving the NAFTA-style ISDSMs in 1998, just after it was challenged by the first NAFTA claim. In 2002, the US Congress enacted the Bipartisan Trade Promotion Authority Act, which required the mechanism to be amended in a particular fashion.[76] In this Act, the US recognized that foreign investors are accorded greater rights (including the right to raise claims

---

[76] See 19 U.S.C. § 3802(b)(3)(F), (G) & (H), which states that.

"(F) providing meaningful procedures for resolving investment disputes;

(G) seeking to improve mechanisms used to resolve disputes between an investor and a government through—

(i) mechanisms to eliminate frivolous claims and to deter the filing of frivolous claims;

(ii) procedures to ensure the efficient selection of arbitrators and the expeditious disposition of claims;

(iii) procedures to enhance opportunities for public input into the formulation of government positions; and

(iv) providing for an appellate body or similar mechanism to provide coherence to the interpretations of investment provisions in trade agreements; and

(H) ensuring the fullest measure of transparency in the dispute settlement mechanism, to the extent consistent with the need to protect information that is classified or business confidential, by—

(i) ensuring that all requests for dispute settlement are promptly made public;

(ii) ensuring that—

(I) all proceedings, submissions, findings, and decisions are promptly made public; and

(II) all hearings are open to the public; and

(iii) establishing a mechanism for acceptance of amicus curiae submissions from businesses, unions, and nongovernmental organizations".

against the US in an international arbitral tribunal) than US investors.[77] The Act specifically sought to improve the procedures for resolving investment disputes (that is ISDSMs).

In accordance with the above Act, lessons from the NAFTA and Argentinean claims, other international arbitration rules and the WTO dispute settlement mechanism, the US updated and amended its 1994 BIT Model. Since the new BIT Model was enacted in November 2004, it was called the "2004 Model BIT". The new model will be used as a template for all future BIT or FTA negotiations.

With respect to ISDSMs, the 2004 Model BIT greatly weakened protection for foreign investors and strengthened protection for host countries, as compared to the 1994 Model BIT. Four measures of the Model BIT in this regard are worth mentioning and elaborating on as follows. The author opines that these four measures echo the four "safety valves" insisted on by developing countries in the past.

First, the 2004 Model BIT tried to deter frivolous claims by foreign investors. In the past, developed countries attempted this by requiring the exhaustion of local remedies. The 2004 Model BIT uses two methods for frivolous claims. One is allowing the tribunal to address and decide any objection by the respondent as a preliminary question.[78] The tribunal decides on an expedited basis an objection by the respondent and any objection that the dispute is not within the tribunal's competence.[79] In this way, the tribunal can reject frivolous claims as early as possible. This expedited procedure avoids spending time and resources on claims that lack a sound legal foundation[80] and according to the US, promote judicial economy.[81] The other method is that if the tribunal considers the claimant's claim or the respondent's objection as frivolous, it may award to the prevailing disputing party reasonable costs and attorney's fees incurred in submitting or opposing the objection.[82] This is the practice of US domestic courts. In this way, the losing party should bear arbitration and attorney costs, so that investors are deterred from raising frivolous claims.

Second, the 2004 Model BIT adds to the governing laws, domestic law, as well as the joint interpretation of an investment treaty by contracting parties. In the past, developing countries required that the domestic law of the host country be the governing law. This just requirement was rejected by the US. However, after the US experienced the costs associated with being a defendant country, it "borrowed"

---

[77] See the chapeau of 19 U.S.C. § 3802(b)(3) that states "Recognizing that United States law on the whole provides a high level of protection for investment, consistent with or greater than the level required by international law, the principal negotiating objectives of the United States regarding foreign investment are to reduce or eliminate artificial or trade-distorting barriers to foreign investment, while ensuring that foreign investors in the United States are not accorded greater substantive rights with respect to investment protections than United States investors in the United States, and to secure for investors important rights comparable to those that would be available under United States legal principles and practice, by—…".

[78] See Art. 28.4 of the 2004 Model BIT.

[79] See Art. 28.5 of the 2004 Model BIT.

[80] UNCTAD (2007), p. 122.

[81] UNCTAD (2007), p. 122.

[82] See Art. 28.6 of the 2004 Model BIT.

the above requirements and adopted a similar provision.[83] The 2004 Model BIT provided that, if the rules of law have not been specified or otherwise agreed, the governing law should be the law of the respondent.[84] This included the respondent's rules on the conflict of laws and such rules of international law as may be applicable.[85]

In addition, the US also added that the joint interpretation of treaty provisions by the parties should be governing law and binding on the tribunal. Specifically, the US 2004 Model BIT provided that the joint interpretation of BIT or FTA parties of a treaty provision was binding on a tribunal and awards must be consistent with that interpretation.[86] This is a lesson learned pursuant to NAFTA. NAFTA establishes a Free Trade Commission (Art. 2001) to interpret the provisions of the agreement as one if its functions. The interpretation made by the Commission shall be binding on a tribunal for investment disputes (Art. 1131 (2)). The Commission made its first interpretation of Art. 1105 (1) concerning fair and equitable treatment in July 2001 after the cases of Metalclad, S.D. Myers and Pope & Talbot. The Commission's interpretation was afforded some weight by the tribunals. But this interpretation was also criticized by some as being an amendment to the article, not an interpretation.[87] When updating the 1994 Model BIT, the US made it clear that the joint interpretation of such a commission should be binding on a tribunal by placing this provision under the general title of Article 30 "Governing Law" as Article 30.3. The placing of such a provision, as well as its strong language, indicate the absolute binding force of the interpretation on tribunals as governing law. This mechanism reserves the prerogative to interpret the content and scope of the annexes of non-conforming and future measures to the contracting parties, and not to arbitral tribunals. Only if the contracting parties cannot reach a joint decision is an arbitral tribunal allowed to give its own interpretation.[88]

Given that joint interpretations shall be used as governing law, and may be issued post-dispute, an interpretation may thus accord with the post-dispute interests of each contracting party. In this way, specialized authorities that interpret the agreements on behalf of the contracting parties become a control mechanism because their decisions are binding on the arbitration tribunal. Therefore, such interpretations can be uncertain and unexpected for foreign investors. It is clear that the adding of joint interpretations as governing law is more extensive than what developing countries

[83] The ICSID provision concerning governing law reflects the developing countries' requirement to apply the host state's national law as governing law. Art. 42 (1) of ICSID provides that "The Tribunal shall decide a dispute in accordance with such rules of law as may be agreed by the parties. In the absence of such agreement, the Tribunal shall apply the law of the Contracting State party to the dispute (including its rules on the conflict of laws) and such rules of international law as may be applicable".

[84] The "law of the respondent" means the law that a domestic court or tribunal of proper jurisdiction would apply in the same case.

[85] Art. 30.2(b) of the 2004 Model BIT.

[86] Art. 30.3 of the 2004 Model BIT.

[87] See Pope & Talbot v. Canada, Award in Respect of Damages (2002); Mondev v. USA, Award (2002); ADF v. USA, Award (2003).

[88] UNCTAD (2007), p. 121.

required in the 1960s—that national law should be one of the governing laws. This is understandable from the perspective of the host country. However, members who represent investors oppose such an article and claim that it effectively invites respondent governments to convert investor-state disputes, where the rule of law governs, into diplomatic negotiations between the parties to the BIT. As such, this provision runs contrary to one of the core purposes of BITs, that is, to de-politicize disputes between investors and host governments.[89]

Third, the 2004 Model BIT affords contracting parties (especially the host state) an opportunity to participate in and influence arbitral proceedings by oral or written submission, interim review, and appellate mechanism so as to limit the tribunal's discretion. The 2004 Model BIT allows the non-disputing treaty party to make oral and written submissions to the tribunal regarding the interpretation of the treaty,[90] because each treaty party is the stakeholder of all claims to the treaty for the reason that the interpretation by the tribunal will have direct impact on each contracting party. Submitting oral or written submissions is a way to participate in the arbitration proceedings and to express views on the interpretation of the treaty provision. In this way, the contracting parties can "assist" the tribunal to make a proper award. The real purpose is to allow contracting parties to influence the arbitrators' view on the claim and final award. In order to allow the non-disputing party to better participate in the proceedings, the new Model BIT adds an article on transparency,[91] providing that the respondent (that is the host country) should promptly transmit relevant arbitration documents to the non-disputing treaty party and make them available to the public.

Further, in order to limit the discretion of the tribunal, the US created an interim review system requiring the tribunal to make available its proposed award before issuing it as final. The interim review system is borrowed from the independent scrutiny system of the International Court of Arbitration[92] and the WTO's interim review system.[93] Art. 28.9(a) of the 2004 Model BIT allows a disputing party to request a tribunal, before issuing a decision or award on liability, to transmit its proposed decision or award to the disputing parties and to the non-disputing treaty

[89] Report of the Subcommittee on Investment Regarding the Draft Model Bilateral Investment Treaty (January 30, 2004), available at http://www.ciel.org/Publications/BIT_Subcmte_Jan3004.pdf, p. 18.

[90] Art. 28.2 of the 2004 Model BIT.

[91] Art. 29 of the 2004 Model BIT.

[92] The International Court of Arbitration (ICC) has a unique feature, i.e., the independent "scrutiny" of draft awards before they are final, so as to help assure the quality of awards. Article 27 of the ICC Rules reads: "Scrutiny of the Award by the Court; Before signing any Award, the Arbitral Tribunal shall submit it in draft form to the Court. The Court may lay down modifications as to the form of the Award and, without affecting the Arbitral Tribunal's liberty of decision, may also draw its attention to points of substance. No Award shall be rendered by the Arbitral Tribunal until it has been approved by the Court as to its form". Article 6 of Appendix II to the Rules reads: "Scrutiny of Arbitral Awards; When the Court scrutinizes draft Awards in accordance with Article 27 of the Rules, it considers, to the extent practicable, the requirements of mandatory law at the place of arbitration".

[93] WTO's interim review system is provided in Article 15 of the Understanding on Rules and Procedures Governing the Settlement of Disputes, which states that:

party. The parties may submit written comments to the tribunal concerning any aspect of its proposed decision or award. The tribunal shall consider any such comments and then issue its decision or award. This review system enables parties to the dispute, as well as other treaty parties, to know the arbitrators' views to the claim and the intended award, and to submit their comments on the award. Thus, a bridge can be built between the parties and the tribunal and increase the predictability of the arbitral result. This is also a legal chance for the host country to control the quality of the award or even to intervene in the arbitration result. This review of arbitral awards is designed to preserve the interests of the treaty parties.

An appeal system was not originally regarded as one of the advantages of an arbitration system since it would drive up costs when arbitration was hailed as a way to reduce costs and improve efficiency. However, it became more important as the NAFTA cases exposed a weakness in the inconsistency of arbitration decisions. Some scholars recommended long ago that an appeal system for arbitration be established.[94] The 2002 Bipartisan Act borrowed from the WTO's appeal mechanism to regard the establishment of an appeal system as one of its goals.[95] The reason for this is to subject investor-state awards to conspicuous, independent and apolitical review by a permanent institution. This should do much to promote heightened and concrete awareness of the rule of law as an influence affecting state actors.[96] Such appellate body or similar mechanism should be designed to provide coherence to the interpretation of investment provisions.

The 2004 Model BIT established an appeal system by two approaches. One is that if a separate, multilateral agreement establishes an appellate body to review investment dispute awards rendered by tribunals constituted pursuant to international trade or investment arrangements, such appellate body may review awards rendered according to the investment treaty.[97] The other is to establish a bilateral appellate body or similar mechanism to review awards rendered sometime after the concluding of the investment treaty.[98] For instance, the US-Dominican Republic-Central America FTA sets out that three months after the date of entry into force of this FTA, the Commission shall establish a Negotiating Group to develop an appellate body or

---

"1. Following the consideration of rebuttal submissions and oral arguments, the panel shall issue the descriptive (factual and argument) sections of its draft report to the parties to the dispute. Within a period of time set by the panel, the parties shall submit their comments in writing.

2. Following the expiration of the set period of time for receipt of comments from the parties to the dispute, the panel shall issue an interim report to the parties, including both the descriptive sections and the panel's findings and conclusions. Within a period of time set by the panel, a party may submit a written request for the panel to review precise aspects of the interim report prior to circulation of the final report to the Members. At the request of a party, the panel shall hold a further meeting with the parties on the issues identified in the written comments. If no comments are received from any party within the comment period, the interim report shall be considered the final panel report and circulated promptly to the Members".

[94] William H. Knull, III and Noah D. Rubins (2000), pp. 531, 533–534.

[95] 19 U.S.C. § 3802(b)(3)(G)(iv).

[96] Jack J. Coe, Jr. (2006), p. 1382.

[97] Art. 28 Para. 10 of the 2004 Model BIT.

[98] Annex D of the 2004 Model BIT, "Possibility of a Bilateral Appellate Mechanism".

similar mechanism to review awards rendered by tribunals.[99] The purpose of appellate mechanisms is, on the one hand, to promote consistent and sound jurisprudence on international investment law; and, on the other hand, to impose certain control of the tribunal and arbitral award by contracting parties.

The above interim review system and arbitration appeal system are regarded as the most important and frontier creation in this discussion.[100] The purpose is to constrain arbitral tribunals, to strengthen the state's intervention in the arbitration result, and to remedy the neglect of the state's administration power in the NAFTA practice.

Fourth, the 2004 Model BIT tried to strengthen protection of state sovereignty and national security by limiting or excluding some sensitive items from investor-state dispute settlement.[101] For example, the 2004 Model BIT generally excludes non-discriminatory public welfare policy measures taken by the host government to protect "[the public's] health, safety, and environment" from indirect expropriation and thus ISDSM.[102] In this way, the host country would not be challenged by foreign investors as before, for regulatory measures that protect the public's health, safety and environment. The US-Uruguay BIT also provides that certain public policy measures including a "negotiated restructuring of a debt instrument issued by Uruguay" are not subject to ISDSM.[103] The US–Korea FTA excludes "real estate price stabilization" policy measures from the scope of ISDSM.[104] Further, the 2004 Model BIT provides a special but more restrictive dispute settlement mechanism for disputes arising from financial services.[105] It also limits the application of arbitration to taxation measures involving an expropriation.[106] This provision allows the competent tax authorities of both contracting parties to decide whether a particular taxation measure is in fact an expropriation. If the authorities agree that this is not the case, the investor is prevented from submitting a claim under the investor-state dispute settlement provisions. This mechanism aims at ensuring that the decision as to whether a tax measure is an expropriation is primarily left to the competent tax authorities of the contracting

---

[99] Annex 10-F of the FTA.

[100] Gonzalo Biggs (2004), p. 84.

[101] Won-Mog Choi (2007), p. 740.

[102] The 2004 Model BIT, Annex B Expropriation, 4(b), "Except in rare circumstances, non-discriminatory regulatory actions by a Party that are designed and applied to protect legitimate public welfare objectives, such as public health, safety, and the environment, do not constitute indirect expropriations". In the Preamble of the 2004 Model BIT, it is also specifically stated that "Desiring to achieve these objectives in a manner consistent with the protection of health, safety, and the environment…".

[103] Annex G, Treaty between the United States of America and The Oriental Republic of Uruguay Concerning the Encouragement and Reciprocal Protection of Investment, available at http://www.ustr.gov/assets/Trade_Agreements/BIT/Uruguay/asset_upload_file748_9005.pdf.

[104] Annex 11-B, Negotiation Text of Free Trade Agreement between the Republic of Korea.
and the United States of America, available at http://www.mofat.go.kr/mofat/fta/eng/eng_list.htm.

[105] Art. 20 of the 2004 Model BIT.

[106] Art. 21 of the 2004 Model BIT.

parties, and not to arbitral tribunals.[107] This is also an example of the inclusion of a control mechanism. These exceptions or limitations are lessons from NAFTA and Argentina; they also reflect the past demand of developing countries for national security as an exception in the four "safety valves".

The above improvements and modifications of the ISDSM provisions by the US in the new model BIT seriously weaken protection to foreign investors, and in contrast, strengthen protection to host countries. They coincide with the demand of developing countries for the four "safety valves". Therefore, some US overseas investors criticize adopting the new model BIT for recent FTAs for providing less protection for US investors.[108]

The FTAs signed by the US with Chile, Singapore, Morocco and Uruguay incorporated the above modifications and improvements of the new 2004 Model BIT. The investment chapter of the FTA between the US and Korea is almost a copy of the new model.

Other developed countries such as Canada and Japan also absorbed or duplicated the US's newly modified Model BIT when updating their own model BITs or signing investment treaties with developing countries. For example, Canada followed the US in also modifying its Model BIT in 2004. The Agreement between Japan and the Republic of Chile for a Strategic Economic Partnership (March 2007) (Chapter 8 Investment) followed almost all the improvements made by the US. As a consequence, the general level of protection to foreign investors in the international arena has been lowered.

### *7.3.4 The New Indirect Mechanism Excluding ISDSM Created in the US-Australia Free Trade Agreement*

As mentioned earlier, there was no ISDSM in the investment treaties between developed countries until NAFTA in 1993. The US updated the 1994 Model BIT and the drafted Multilateral Agreement on Investment (MAI) in 1997 adopted the NAFTA-style highly protective ISDSM. However, such ISDSMs disappeared in the AUSFTA, and a new indirect mechanism excluding ISDSM was created therein.

#### 7.3.4.1 Background for the Birth of the New Mechanism

In the past, developed countries did not sign BITs with each other. Even if there was a BIT, it did not contain the investor-state dispute settlement provisions. The reason for this was that when the host country has a developed and generally respected

---

107 UNCTAD (2007), p. 120.

108 Report of the Subcommittee on Investment Regarding the Draft Model Bilateral Investment Treaty (January 30, 2004), available at http://www.ciel.org/Publications/BIT_Subcmte_Jan3004.pdf, p. 2.

internal legal order, a reference to dispute settlement in an international investment agreement was thought unnecessary. The internal laws and practices of a host country may be seen as sufficiently protective of the rights and obligations of both a private investor and a host state so that no further determination is needed in an international agreement.[109]

In the Canada-US Free Trade Agreement in 1989, there was no provision concerning investor-state dispute settlement. Although the title of Article 1608 of the FTA is "Dispute", this article does not clearly touch upon the investment dispute between a foreign investor and host state. Only Article 1608.4 states that, "4. In view of the special nature of investment disputes and the expertise required to resolve them, where the procedures of Chapter Eighteen (Institutional Provisions) are invoked, the Parties and the Commission shall give the fullest consideration, in any particular case, to settling any dispute regarding the interpretation or application of this Chapter by arbitration or panel procedures pursuant to Articles 1806 (Arbitration) or 1807 (Panel Procedures), and shall make every attempt to ensure that the panelists are individuals experienced and competent in the field of international investment. When deciding a dispute pursuant to Articles 1806 or 1807, the panel shall take into consideration how such disputes before it are normally dealt with by internationally recognized rules for commercial arbitration". Chapter Eighteen on Institutional Provisions includes only state-state dispute settlement mechanisms (arbitration and panel procedures). It could be deduced that the state-state dispute procedure in the FTA may be invoked to settle any investment dispute (including those between investor and state).

The Canada-US FTA was superseded by NAFTA in 1993 when Mexico joined, and a strong investor-state dispute settlement mechanism was incorporated therein. Then in the MAI negotiations in 1997, a NAFTA-style ISDSM was incorporated. However, criticism over the MAI's highly protective ISDSM contributed partly to the final abortion of the MAI.

In November 2002, when the US started to negotiate with Australia on the FTA, the US was strongly challenged by NAFTA investment cases and was eager to modify its 1994 Model BIT. The US expected to place the modified ISDSM in its 2004 Model BIT in AUSFTA. However, Australia strongly resisted the mechanism for at least two reasons. First, the numerous NAFTA investment cases suggested that if investor-state provisions were included in AUSFTA, the Australian Government could anticipate a comparable future of litigiousness by American investors. Second, and more importantly, the NAFTA cases had generated considerable public opposition to investor-state provisions.[110] Australian state governments also expressed to the federal government their opposition to the inclusion of investor rights and ISDSM in AUSFTA.[111] In the meantime, there were community campaigns in Australia using NAFTA examples to oppose ISDSM provisions.[112]

---

[109] UNCTAD (2003-2), p. 81.

[110] Ann Capling and Kim Richard Nossal (2006), pp. 157–158.

[111] Ann Capling and Kim Richard Nossal (2006), p. 158.

[112] Patricia Ranald (2006), pp 30–56. available at http://www.bilaterals.org/article.php3?id_article=6170.

The US finally had to give up the ISDSM but initiated a new indirect mechanism excluding ISDSM. The abandonment of NAFTA-style ISDSM in the AUSFTA is explained by Western scholars as associated with American security and intelligence policy—"blowback". "Blowback" is shorthand for saying that a nation reaps what it sows, even if it does not fully know or understand what it has sown.[113] The US pressed hard for a mechanism that rebounded, creating negative reactions not only abroad but also in domestic American politics.[114] This proposition also echoes the author's view that after the US was itself a defendant, it immediately found a way to extract itself from the ISDSM by modifying its 1994 Model BIT and abandoning the NAFTA-style ISDSM in AUSFTA.

The abandonment of the ISDSM in AUSFTA could prevent international arbitration cases between the two countries since mutual investments are plentiful. The US is the biggest source country for investment in Australia, while Australia is the eighth biggest source country for the US. Fifty percent of Australian overseas investment is directed to the US.[115]

#### 7.3.4.2 The New Indirect Mechanism Excluding ISDSM in AUSFTA

Chapter 11 of the AUSFTA is a specific chapter on investment. This chapter does not contain a provision directly on the settlement of investor-state disputes, in contrast to many American BITs with developing countries. However, compared with the Canada-US FTA, the AUSFTA contains a more detailed and complex provision related to the settlement of investor-state disputes, that is, Article 11.16 "Consultations on Investor-State Dispute Settlement". For a detailed elaboration of the new mechanism in the following paragraphs, it is necessary to quote Article 11.16 as follows:

> "1. If a Party considers that there has been a change in circumstances affecting the settlement of disputes on matters within the scope of this Chapter and that, in light of such change, the Parties should consider allowing an investor of a Party to submit to arbitration with the other Party a claim regarding a matter within the scope of this Chapter, the Party may request consultations with the other Party on the subject, including the development of procedures that may be appropriate. On such a request, the Parties shall promptly enter into consultations with a view towards allowing such a claim and establishing such procedures.
>
> 2. For greater certainty, nothing in this Article prevents a Party from raising any matter arising under this Chapter pursuant to the procedures set out in Chapter 21 (Institutional Arrangements and Dispute Settlement). Nor does anything in this Article prevent an investor of a Party from submitting to arbitration a claim against the other Party to the extent permitted under that Party's law".

---

[113] Ann Capling and Kim Richard Nossal (2006), p. 153.

[114] Ann Capling and Kim Richard Nossal (2006), p. 153..

[115] Ann Capling (2005) , All the Way with the USA: Australia, The US and Free Trade, UNSW Press, p. 71.

The US Trade Representative (USTR) Office's interpretation of why an investor-state dispute settlement was excluded is that "In recognition of the unique circumstances of this Agreement—including, for example, the longstanding economic ties between the United States and Australia, their shared legal traditions, and the confidence of their investors in operating in each other's markets—the two countries agreed not to adopt procedures in the Agreement that would allow investors to arbitrate disputes with governments. This issue will be revisited if circumstances change. Government-to-government dispute settlement procedures remain available to resolve investment-related disputes".[116]

The Australian Department of Foreign Affairs and Trade explains that "The dispute settlement mechanism established under the agreement only allows the Parties, that is, the two governments, to initiate dispute settlement procedures if they believe the other Party is not complying with its obligations under the Agreement. Unlike many FTAs and other agreements covering investment, AUSFTA does not include provision for 'Investor-State Dispute Settlement'. This outcome recognizes the fact that both countries have robust and sophisticated domestic legal systems that provide adequate scope for investors, both domestic and foreign, to pursue concerns about government actions".[117]

These interpretations once again express the view of developed countries that their common legal traditions and robust and sophisticated domestic legal systems allow foreign investors to seek local remedies; and thus, there is no need for international arbitration. In case there is any dispute that cannot be settled, the host state can employ diplomatic protection by the application of state-state dispute settlement mechanisms contained in the AUSFTA. Actually, local remedies and diplomatic protection to settle investor-state disputes were employed by the developed countries in the past.

If we combine the provisions of the AUSFTA as well as the interpretations of the two governments, the new indirect mechanism to settle investment disputes between host countries and foreign investors include the following:

First, if investors from one country believe that the other country has violated their obligations, they could seek redress through the other country's courts, rather than through international arbitration.[118] The claim by the US Government concerning "shared legal traditions, and the confidence of …investors in operating in each other's markets" **implies** that foreign investors can resort to local remedies, including national law and thus receive justice. In contrast, the claim by the Australian Government that "both countries have robust and sophisticated domestic legal systems that provide adequate scope for investors, both domestic and foreign, to pursue concerns about government actions" **explicitly** states that foreign investors should seek first local remedies as a domestic investor would.

---

[116] U.S.-Australia FTA Summary of the Agreement, 07/15/2004, available at http://www.ustr.gov/Trade_Agreements/Bilateral/Australia_FTA/US-Australia_FTA_Summary_of_the_Agreement.html.

[117] Australia Department of Foreign Affairs and Trade, AUSFTA Frequently Asked Questions, available at http://www.dfat.gov.au/trade/negotiations/us_fta/faqs.html.

[118] Ann Capling and Kim Richard Nossal (2006), p. 152.

Second, foreign investors can rely on general commercial arbitration to resolve disputes. Article 11.16.2 of the AUSFTA states, "[N]or does anything in this Article prevent an investor of a Party from submitting to arbitration a claim against the other Party to the extent permitted under that Party's law". This indicates that a foreign investor can submit the dispute for arbitration if the host country's law permits. "Arbitration" could have two meanings. One is general commercial arbitration in the host country; the other is international arbitration if the host country's domestic law permits it. The keyword in the article is "permitted under that Party's law". We can imagine that this emphasizes the importance of the host country's domestic law and thus is a respect to domestic law. This also echoes the demand by developing countries that investment disputes should be resolved according to domestic law.

Third, foreign investors can rely on their home country to apply state-state dispute settlement mechanisms as provided by AUSFTA to settle investor-state disputes. Article 11.16.2 provides that "nothing in this Article prevents a Party from raising any matter arising under this Chapter pursuant to the procedures set out in Chapter 21". The title of Chapter 21 is "Institutional Arrangements and Dispute Settlement" which provides for state-state dispute settlement. Therefore, once a dispute arises between foreign investors and host countries, any contracting party (whether it is the host country or the home country of the foreign investor) can resort to the state-state dispute settlement. This is the key point in dispute settlement according to the interpretations of the two governments. Some scholars opine that the created mechanism is a system for protecting foreign investors that depends entirely on diplomatic protection and resembles those in operation before the advent of ICSID and the BITs.[119] However, it is not certain that the investor's home state will act, for that state may prefer to forgive the breach in the interests of smooth diplomatic relations.[120]

Fourth, it is possible for foreign investors to bring an international arbitral claim against host governments, though the AUSFTA excludes NAFTA-style ISDSM. When negotiating the AUSFTA, the US Government did insist on a clause that leaves the door open for such a process to be requested for future particular claims, if conditions change, and the parties consult "with a view to allowing such a claim and establishing such procedures".[121] The Australian Government also admits that if there is certain change with regard to both parties' economic and legal environment, the parties could consider establishing a certain procedure (that is arbitration for investors) to hear claims from investors.[122] Article 11.16 requires that a number of conditions be fulfilled before any such claim can be made. First, "there has been a change in circumstances affecting the settlement of disputes on matters within the scope of this Chapter". In Australia's opinion, "circumstances change" means the

[119] William S. Dodge (2006), p. 27.

[120] William S. Dodge (2006), pp. 26–27.

[121] Patricia Ranald (2006), pp 30–56.

[122] Australian Government Department of Foreign Affairs and Trade, Australia-United States Free Trade Agreement: Guide to the Agreement, "Investment", available at http://www.dfat.gov.au/trade/negotiations/us_fta/guide/11.html.

economic and legal environments have changed.[123] However, the AUSFTA itself does not have such a restriction. Some commentators argue that such a change in circumstance is unlikely. If it does occur, through a change in policy by a future government, it is likely that the community debate that occurred during the negotiations would form the basis for further contestation.[124] Second, "in light of such change, the parties should consider allowing an investor of a party to submit to arbitration …". However, there are no objective criteria for why the parties should allow the arbitration. It is possible that one party would do so for political considerations or because an investor has strong economic power. Third, "On such a request, the Parties shall promptly enter into consultations with a view towards allowing such a claim and establishing such procedures". It is clear that whether to allow a claim and establish arbitration procedures is subject to the parties' discretion. Fourth, arbitration procedures should be established by both parties. However, Art. 11.16 does not specify what procedures are to be used in an arbitration.[125] We can see AUSFTA's Chapter 11 does provide for the possibility of arbitration for investors whose investments have been affected by government action. However, it specifies a much more indirect mechanism for the resolution of investor disputes.[126]

Though the FTA does not state the priority for these four approaches, according to the state's interest, seeking local remedies or arbitration is the first priority, the second is state-state dispute settlement, and international arbitration is a last resort.

It is obvious that this AUSFTA marks several important departures from NAFTA with regard to ISDSM. First, it ensures that investors are not the drivers of investment disputes. Instead, an aggrieved investor who has exhausted redress in the domestic courts of the other country must convince its own government to proceed further, for only a "party"—one of the governments—has the capacity to request a move to arbitration.[127] Second, arbitration can only occur when one of the governments considers that there has been "a change in circumstances affecting the settlement of disputes". However, these "circumstances" are highly unlikely to change, so this wording dramatically limits the scope and range of conditions under which it is likely that one of the governments will seek arbitration.[128]

---

[123] Australian Government Department of Foreign Affairs and Trade, Australia-United States Free Trade Agreement: Guide to the Agreement, "Investment", available at http://www.dfat.gov.au/trade/negotiations/us_fta/guide/11.html.

[124] Patricia Ranald, The Australia-US Free Trade Agreement: A Contest of Interests, Journal of Australian Political Economy, no. 57, June 2006, pp 30–56, available at http://www.bilaterals.org/article.php3?id_article=6170.

[125] Art. 11.16.1 of AUSFTA and Madelaine Cliam, Submission to the JSCOT (Joint Standing Committee on Treaties) Secretariat for Inquiry into the Australia-US FTA, http://www.aph.gov.au/house/committee/jsct/usafta/subs/SUB034.pdf.

[126] Ann Capling and Kim Richard Nossal (2006), p. 160.

[127] Ann Capling and Kim Richard Nossal (2006), p. 160.

[128] Ann Capling and Kim Richard Nossal (2006), p. 161.

Neither Australia nor the US have explained the absence of investor-state dispute resolution in terms of a desire not to be sued.[129] Actually, it is an important consideration and lesson from NAFTA. This system will undoubtedly protect the Australian and US Governments from having to defend themselves against direct claims from each other's investors.[130] The AUSFTA experience shows that developed countries are unlikely to repeat the mistake of NAFTA and allow themselves to be sued directly, at least without requiring exhaustion first. On the other hand, for the US, the new mechanism resolves the discrimination against domestic investors that was previously in place: foreign investors were allowed to submit a dispute for international arbitration while domestic investors were not. The new mechanism balances the rights of domestic and foreign investors, and thus weakens protection for foreign investors.

The new mechanism received completely different criticisms from the US and Australia. Many Australians consider the new mechanism "...a sleeper...that...is a springboard for...future action to bring investor-state disputes to life".[131] That is, it leaves the possibility for future challenges by a foreign investor against the host state. US business interests were the strongest advocates for including an investor-state provision. Industry representatives view this as a significant shortcoming of the agreement and an important step backward from previous FTAs and BITs concluded by the US.[132]

In the author's opinion, the new mechanism is not a setback as claimed by American investors; however, it is a return to what developing countries requested in the past. While the new mechanism is nevertheless new, its key point is still local remedies and diplomatic protection. This reflects the US awakening after it experienced the bitterness of being sued like a developing country.

The trend of US weakening of foreign investor protection and strengthening of state interest protection will continue in the near future. It could even grow, the reason being that the majority party in the US Congress—the Democrats—considers that trade agreements should give "no greater rights" to foreign investors than those enjoyed by US investors. Washington's standard model for FTAs has included investor protections so far-reaching that they have been accused of undermining the ability of governments to regulate in the public interest.[133] In March 2007, an agreement was concluded in the Congress between Democrats and Republicans that when signing free trade agreements, foreign investors in the US will not be accorded

---

[129] William S. Dodge (2006), p. 25.

[130] William S. Dodge (2006), p. 27.

[131] Joint Standing Committee on Treaties, Parliament of the Commonwealth of Australia, Report 61: The Australia-United States Free Trade Agreement, p. 53, available at http:// www.aph.gov.au/house/committee/jsct/usafta/report/fullreport.pdf.

[132] Joint Standing Committee on Treaties, Parliament of the Commonwealth of Australia, Report 61: The Australia-United States Free Trade Agreement, p. 53, available at http://www.aph.gov.au/house/committee/jsct/usafta/report/fullreport.pdf, p. 52.

[133] US Democrats Unveil Trade Policy, Days Before Key Deadline, Bridges Weekly Trade News Digest, Volume 11, Number 11, 28 March 2007.

greater substantive rights with respect to investment protections than US investors in the US.[134]

## 7.4 Investor-State Dispute Settlement: Where to Go in the Twenty-First Century for Future International Investment Treaties?

So far, international investment treaties mainly include BITs, FTAs with investment chapters, and taxation treaties. There is a lack of global comprehensive investment treaties like the WTO agreements. Some developed countries, such as the US, strongly advocated negotiating a global investment normative framework under the WTO but this was rejected by developing countries, mainly because of opposition to the highly protective ISDSM.

ISDSM is the most controversial issue for developing and developed countries concerning a possible multilateral comprehensive investment agreement. However, the new trends of ISDSMs in developing and developed countries, respectively, show two common points. One is that both try to increase state sovereignty and lower foreign investor protection; the other is that the state-state dispute settlement is intended to be used to complement the ISDSM. These common points will have a positive impact on future international investment treaties, especially a comprehensive multilateral investment treaty proposed by some developed countries in the WTO framework, or as suggested by some developing countries under the auspice of UNCTAD.

As to how to solve the disputed ISDSM problem, some scholars, as well as the UNCTAD, propose improving the current ISDSM—including the NAFTA provisions.[135] They argue that regardless of the merits of either argument, one thing seems certain—the investor-state dispute mechanism is here to stay. It is a feature of NAFTA, which has been in force for nearly a decade. The ICSID has been in existence since 1966. There are over 2000 Bilateral Investment Treaties in force worldwide, most of which provide for investor-state arbitration.[136]

However, NAFTA and AUSFTA show that the question of how to resolve investment disputes between developed countries is a vexing one.[137] This question is likely to arise again in the context of negotiations between Canada and the European Union on a Trade and Investment Enhancement Agreement. The early Framework

---

[134] The title of the agreement is "The New Trade Policy Template" consisting of six agreements, one of which concerns investment. See Office of the United States Trade Representative, Bipartisan Agreement on Trade Policy: Investment, May 2007, available at http://www.ustr.gov/assets/Document_Library/Fact_Sheets/2007/asset_upload_file146_11282.pdf.

[135] Jessica S. Wiltse (2003), p. 1184. See also UNCTAD (2005), pp. 54–55.

[136] Jessica S. Wiltse (2003), pp. 1183–1184.

[137] William S. Dodge (2006), p. 4.

for an agreement does not contain an ISDSM.[138] However, in the finally concluded Canada-European Union Comprehensive Economic and Trade Agreement (CETA), the establishment of an investment arbitration court is adopted.

Some scholars conclude that the abandonment of NAFTA-style protections in the AUSFTA will, on the one hand, effectively preclude the inclusion of such provisions in future trade agreements between developed countries,[139] and on the other hand, set important precedents for the future of international free trade agreements.[140] And therefore, the exclusion of a NAFTA-style Chapter 11 in AUSFTA received some opposition since it was argued that this omission would set a bad precedent for future US trade agreements, especially with developing countries.[141] Critics also argue that the AUSFTA precedent will make it more difficult for the US to insist on the inclusion of such mechanisms in future trade agreements with those developing countries that object to NAFTA-style protections, because such insistence could be viewed as a slight against their legal systems.[142]

The ISDSM is a hot issue for debate in the early twenty-first century. It will continue to receive a lot of attention in the coming decades. More improvements and restrictions of the ISDSM are expected.

## References

Ann Capling and Kim Richard Nossal (2006) Blowback: Investor–State Dispute Mechanisms in International Trade Agreements, Governance, vol 19

Barton Legum (2002) The Innovation of Investor-State Arbitration Under NAFTA, Harvard International Law Journal, vol 43

Damon Vis-Dunbar (2008) Activists lobby in support of Bolivia's withdrawal from ICSID, Investment Treaty News (ITN), January 11, available at http://www.investmenttreatynews.com

Gonzalo Biggs (2004) The Latin American Treatment of International Arbitration and Foreign Investments and the Chile-U.S. Free Trade Agreement, ICSID Review—Foreign Investment Law Journal, vol 19, no 1

ICSID (1972) Investment promotion and protection Treaties, Oceana Publications, Inc., Vol. 1, Booklet

ICSID (1991) ICSID Cases, November 15, 1991, Doc.ICSID/16/Rev.2

ICSID (1999) Annual Report. Available at http://www.worldbank.org/icsid/pubs/1999ar/4.htm

International Bank for Reconstruction and Development (1965) Report of the Executive Directors on the Convention on the Settlement of Investment Disputes between States and Nationals of Other States, International Legal Materials, vol. 4

Jack J Coe, Jr (2006) Transparency in The Resolution Of Investor-State Disputes—Adoption, Adaptation, and NAFTA Leadership, University of Kansas Law Review, vol 54

---

[138] Canada-European Union Trade and Investment Enhancement Agreement: Framework for the Agreement, available at http://www.dfait-maeci.gc.ca/tna-nac/rb/tiea-en.asp.

[139] Ann Capling and Kim Richard Nossal (2006), p. 153.

[140] Ann Capling and Kim Richard Nossal (2006), p. 151.

[141] Ann Capling and Kim Richard Nossal (2006), p. 164.

[142] Ann Capling and Kim Richard Nossal (2006), p. 166.

James Mcilroy (2004) Canada's New Foreign Investment Protection and Promotion Agreement—Two Steps Forward, One Step Back? The Journal of World Investment & Trade, vol 5, no 4

Jessica S Wiltse (2003) An Investor-State Dispute Mechanism in the Free Trade Area of the Americas: Lessons from NAFTA Chapter Eleven, Buffalo Law Review, vol 51, Fall

Laurence Norman (2003) Government Reopens 7-year-Old Case Vs Oil Group, Dow Jones Newswires, Oct. 28

Louis Henkin, et al. (1993) International law: Cases and Materials (3rd ed.), West Pub. Co.

Luke Eric Peterson (2008) Ecuador will denounce at least nine bilateral investment treaties, Investment Treaty News (ITN), February 5. Available at http://www.investmenttreatynews.com

Patricia Ranald (2006) The Australia-US Free Trade Agreement: A Contest of Interests, Journal of Australian Political Economy, no. 57

Ray C Jones (2002) NAFTA Chapter 11 Investor-to-State Dispute Resolution: A Shield to Be Embraced or a Sword to be Feared? Brigham Young University Law Review 528

Salacuse J, Sullivan N (2005) Do BITs really work: An Evaluation of Bilateral Investment Treaties and Their Grand Bargain, Harvard International Law Journal, vol 46, Winter

Sornarajah M (1994) The International Law on Foreign Investment, Press Syndicate of the University of Cambridge

UNCTAD (2003-1) Course on Dispute Settlement: ICSID. Available at http://www.unctad.org/en/docs/edmmisc232overview_en.pdf

UNCTAD (2003-2) Dispute Settlement: Investor-State, UNCTAD Series on Issues in International Investment Agreements

UNCTAD (2005) Investor-State Disputes Arising from Investment Treaties: A Review, UNCTAD Series on International Investment Policies for Development

UNCTAD (2006) Latest Developments in Investor-State Dispute Settlement, IIA Monitor, no 4

UNCTAD (2007) Bilateral Investment Treaties 1995–2006: Trends in Investment Rulemaking, United Nations, New York and Geneva

US Democrats Unveil Trade Policy (2007) Days Before Key Deadline, Bridges Weekly Trade News Digest, vol 11, no 11, 28 March

Yanru Wei (2006) On the Impropriety of China's Recent Complete Acceptance of ICSID Jurisdiction in Recent Years (in Chinese), Journal of International Economic Law (China), vol 13

William H Knull III, Noah D Rubins (2000) Betting the Farm on International Arbitration: Is it Time to Offer an Appeal Option? American Review of International Arbitration, vol 11

William S Dodge (2006) Investor-State Dispute Settlement Between Developed Countries: Reflections on the Australia-United States Free Trade Agreement, Vanderbilt Journal of Transnational Law

Won-Mog Choi (2007) The Present and Future of the Investor-State Dispute Settlement Paradigm, Journal of International Economic Law 10(3)

# Chapter 8
# A Chinese Perspective of the ISDS Reform

The legitimacy crisis of investor-state dispute settlement (ISDS) directly leads to the worldwide hot discussion or debate on the ISDS reform. The Working Group III of the United Nations Commission on International Trade Law (UNCITRAL) started to note and then work on the possible ISDS reform since 2015.[1] It is hard for China to decide what type of reform to support at the early stage. China's experience in the WTO dispute settlement may provide many hints, reference and lessons for taking an ISDS reform position. Later in July 2019 and October 2021 respectively, China submitted two submissions to the UNCITRAL regarding its position to the current ISDS reform. Further, China's rich experience in the "arbitration-mediation" model may be its unique contribution to the ISDS reform in a broader sense.

## 8.1 The Background Why it is Difficult for China to Take a Position Toward the ISDS Reform in the Early Stage

The legitimacy crisis of investor-state dispute settlement directly leads to the worldwide hot discussion or debate on the ISDS reform. Suggested reform options range from incremental to systemic and transformative reform.[2] Accordingly, states are

[1] UNCITRAL, Report of Working Group III (Investor-State Dispute Settlement Reform) on the work of its thirty-fourth session (Vienna, 27 November–1 December 2017) Part I, A/CN.9/930/Rev.1, 19 December 2017, p. 2.

[2] Anthea Roberts (2018).

A summary of parts of this chapter was first published in the title of Reforming ISDS: A Chinese Perspective in the book *China, the EU and International Investment Law: Reforming Investor-State Dispute Settlement*, published by Routledge, 2019. This chapter was updated in 2024.

 
H. Chen, *China's Practice in International Investment Law*, Modern China and International Economic Law, https://doi.org/10.1007/978-981-96-5016-3_8

characterized into loyalists, reformists and revolutionaries and undecideds.[3] The US represents the loyalists, the EU represents the reformists and South Africa represents the revolutionaries, while China belongs to the undecideds.[4]

The US is the first state in the world to respond to the ISDS legitimacy crisis, and takes the incremental approach from the very beginning. The term "legitimacy crisis" of ISDS was first proposed and discussed by Susan Frank in 2005 due to the many cases brought before international arbitration on the basis of international investment agreements (IIAs) including bilateral investment treaty, investment chapter in free trade agreement (FTAs) as well as treaty with investment provisions (TIPs),[5] the major critiques of the ISDS include lack of transparency, inconsistency in decisions, critiques on arbitrators, lack of a review mechanism, etc.[6] However, the US realized the ISDS problems when it was challenged by two Canadian investors—Loewen Group and Mondev Group International in 1998 and 1999, respectively, based on the NAFTA.[7] It responded very quickly to the critiques in the FTAs that it was negotiating with other countries such as Singapore and Chile by limiting investor rights, preventing frivolous claims,[8] requires transparency in disclosing relevant documents, and suggesting the use of an appellate body if such a body is established by a separate multilateral agreement.[9] The NAFTA cases directly put the US second wave of BIT policy to an end by reexamining the model BIT negotiating text and commenced the third wave.[10] The US amended its model BIT to follow the investment chapter style in its FTAs and released its 2004 Model BIT.[11] The 2004 Model BIT responded substantially to the ISDS legitimacy crisis by limiting the scope of claims that investors may make,[12] creating mechanisms to eliminate frivolous claims,[13] promoting transparency[14] and providing for the possibility of establishing a bilateral appellate body or similar mechanism.[15] Then since 2009 the US reviewed its model BIT again and published its 2012 Model BIT, improving the ISDS mechanism again. For example, it further limits the scope of claim,[16] and increases transparency requirement.[17] Ever

[3] Anthea Roberts (2017).

[4] Anthea Roberts (2017).

[5] Susan D. Franck (2005).

[6] Susan D. Franck (2005).

[7] Kenneth J. Vandevelde (2009), p. 64.

[8] Kenneth J. Vandevelde (2009), p. 71.

[9] Examples include U.S.-Central American Free Trade Agreement, June 1, 2004, at annex 10-F, United States-Chile Free Trade Agreement, June 6, 2003, ch. 22, United States-Singapore Free Trade Agreement, May 6, 2003, Chapter 15.

[10] Kenneth J. Vandevelde (2009), p. 64.

[11] Kenneth J. Vandevelde (2009), p. 72.

[12] The US 2004 Model BIT, Art.24.

[13] The US 2004 Model BIT, Art. 28.6.

[14] The US 2004 Model BIT, Art.29.

[15] The US 2004 Model BIT, Art.28.10, and Annex D Possibility of a Bilateral Appellate Mechanism.

[16] The US 2012 Model BIT, Art.24.

[17] The US 2012 Model BIT, Art. 29.4.

since 2000, almost all the BITs and FTAs that the US concludes with other countries follow the US model, and thus the US is leading successfully the ISDS reform on its side by its own way. Although the proposed appellate body was not eventually established, the US still believes it an effective way to rectify and remedy arbitral awards.

It could be said that China generally follows the US approach in ISDS. The Chinese Government and the US Government launched negotiations on a bilateral investment treaty (BIT) in 2008. The US side used the 2004 Model BIT as the template before the release of its 2012 Model BIT, as usual.[18] China also proposed its own negotiating text. The negotiation stepped into the "substantive stage" in 2013 after Chinese President Xi Jinping took office. China agreed to negotiate on the basis of pre-establishment national treatment with a negative list approach.[19] This is the first time that China has agreed to do so with another country. Then the negotiation went on much more smoothly. At the end of 2016, the text of the China-US BIT was almost completed. Unfortunately, the China-US BIT was not finally concluded and the negotiations were terminated. Although the text of the BIT was not released, it seems that China accepted most of the US-proposed ISDS provisions with some changes proposed by China. Therefore, it can be said that the almost completed China-US BIT generally takes the US approach of incremental reform concerning both substantive provisions and ISDS.

The EU also took the incremental approach to the ISDS at the beginning. For example, the Consolidated Text of Canada–EU Comprehensive Trade and Economic Agreement (CETA) published on September 26, 2014 adopted the traditional ISDS mechanism with some incremental improvements.[20] However, since 2015 the European Commission has been working to establish a Multilateral Investment Court. The EU made a complete shift from the incremental approach to the systemic approach with a two-tier permanent investment court in its document *Concept Paper: Investment in TTIP and beyond—the path for reform*.[21] Then EU proposed the investment court system in the negotiation with the US the Transatlantic Trade and Investment Partnership (TTIP).[22] Then the ISDS provisions of the CETA was replaced by EU's new proposed investment court system.[23] Eventually both the EU-Vietnam Free Trade Agreement (EUVFTA) and the EU-Singapore Free Trade Agreement (EUSFTA) take the investment court system.

When China was negotiating with the EU a BIT in the early period, EU strongly proposed its two-tier permanent investment court. China did not give any definite

[18] Karl P. Sauvant and Huiping Chen (2012) http://www.vcc.columbia.edu/content/china-us-bilateral-investment-treaty-template-multilateral-framework-investment

[19] Xinhuanet (2013).

[20] European Commission (2014), Chapter 10.

[21] Concept Paper (2015)

[22] European Parliament resolution of 8 July 2015 containing the European Parliament's recommendations to the European Commission on the negotiations for the Transatlantic Trade and Investment Partnership (TTIP) (2014/2228(INI)), available at http://www.europarl.europa.eu/sides/getDoc.do?type=TA&reference=P8-TA-2015-0252&format=XML&language=EN.

[23] European Commission—Press release (2016).

response to this proposal; the major reason being that China has not yet decided what approach to take.

South Africa started to review its BITs in 2012. It took a transformative approach. It started to terminate many 54321'BITs in 2012 (but keeps the China-South African BIT), and refused to conclude any more BITs. Instead, it takes national law approach (Protection of Investment Act of 2015) to deal with foreign investment by local remedies, precluding international arbitration. South Africa is located within the domain of the Belt and Road Initiative (BRI) advocated by China. The BRI has greatly promoted huge amount of Chinese outbound investment in South Africa.

More than 70 countries in various regions and economic groupings are located in the Belt and Road domain.[24] Between 2014 and 2021, Chinese investment in the domain had reached 164 billion USD,[25] and would continue to increase. India and Indonesia are located in the domain. However, India takes the systemic approach for ISDS in its 2015 Model BIT, requiring the exhaustion of local remedy before referring to international arbitration, and began to terminate BITs in 2016, including its BITs with China. Another important state in the Belt and Road domain is Indonesia. Since 2014, Indonesia also terminated its BITs with many states including the one with China. Although many other states in the domain have not yet showed any preference to the IIAs reform, actually they are waiting and seeing. In addition, until May 2024, China has concluded 154 IIAs including BITs and TIPs (treaty with investment provisions) that are in force,[26] most of which belong to the undecided category in terms of ISDS reform.

To sum up, in the early stage, it was difficult for China to take a definite position to the ISDS reform.

## 8.2 China May Learn Lessons from Its Experience in the WTO When Considering Its Position to the ISDS Reform

Although it is difficult for China to take a definite position to the ISDS reform, China is pushed to do so because UNCITRAL entrusted Working Group III with a broad mandate to work on the possible reform of ISDS in 2017.[27] The work would be government-led with high-level input from all governments.[28] When assessing

[24] For the list of the states, please refer to the website for the Belt and Road: https://www.yidaiyilu.gov.cn/info/iList.jsp?cat_id=10037&cur_page=1.

[25] MOFCOM (2021), p. 19.

[26] The data is searched through UNCTAD International Investment Agreements Navigator at http://investmentpolicyhub.unctad.org/IIA/CountryBits/42#iiaInnerMenu, last visit September 30, 2018.

[27] Official Records of the General Assembly, Seventy-second Session, Supplement No. 17 (A/72/17), paras. 263 and 264.

[28] UN General Assembly (2017), p. 3.

UNCITRAL's work and considering China's possible position, China may learn both positive and negative lessons from its experience in the WTO dispute settlement.

UNCITRAL admits that options for possible reform range from relatively minor adjustments to the existing ISDS regime to institutionalizing that regime further through the creation of a permanent adjudicatory body (such as a permanent investment court or dispute settlement body).[29] However, it seems that UNCITRAL prefers the institutionalizing and multilateralizing approach by setting up a permanent and stand-alone appellate body, or a permanent international investment court with an appellate mechanism.[30] The idea of an appellate body actually borrows from the US IIAs practice. The idea of an investment court in turn follows the EU proposal.

### *8.2.1 China's Possible Attitude Toward the Current UNCITRAL Reform Work Based on Its WTO Experience*

The author suggests, based on China's experience in the WTO, that China should participate in the current UNCITRAL ISDS reform actively from the very beginning.

Firstly, whether China should actively participate in the current UNCITRAL works? Discussing the ISDS reform in the UNCITRAL platform is actually **internationalizing** the reform. The ISDS reform is on longer unilateral, or bilateral, or scattered, but international and across the board. The UNCITRAL work will be a rule-making process concerning a new ISDS regime. In this case, China needs to take part in to be a rule-maker, otherwise, China would be rule-taker once the reform is done and set. China had bitter lessons in this regard with the WTO and its dispute settlement mechanism.

China (ROC) was one of the founding states for GATT 1947. Unfortunately, China (PRC) quitted from GATT in 1950s. Therefore, China missed the whole process of the establishment and the rule-making of WTO and its dispute settlement mechanism. China became a member of WTO in 2001 after 15 years of negotiation at high price. China had to be the rule-follower of the WTO dispute settlement mechanism. Learning lesson from this, China would actively participate in the ongoing UNCITRAL work on ISDS reform, trying to offer its ideas and make rules.

Secondly, since the UNCITRAL proposal would eventually be developed into a multilateral mechanism, China should participate in it at the very beginning. The Working Group III is mandated to consider whether ISDS reform was desirable, and if it is concluded to be desirable, to develop a new mechanism.[31] The new mechanism, if could not be accepted on a multilateral basis at the beginning, would take the

---

[29] UN General Assembly (2017), p. 50.

[30] UN General Assembly (2017).

[31] UN General Assembly (2017), p. 3.

Mauritius Convention model to be on a plural basis.[32] The Mauritius Convention would come into force with only three states ratify, accept, approve or accede to it. On October 18, 2017, it came into force with Canada, Switzerland and Mauritius ratifying it. With more and more states ratify or accede to the Convention, it will eventually become a multilateral treaty. Therefore, the current Working Group III's work is very important and has profound significance. This means China should not neglect it but should participate from the very beginning.

In this regard, China should also learn lessons from its WTO experience. The current WTO dispute settlement was evolved from the **provisional** application of the GATT 1947. Because the ITO Charter could not be finished as expected, GATT 1947 was decided to be put into provisional application among eight of the twenty-three countries that had negotiated the GATT 1947.[33] No one expected that the provisional application lasted for almost fifty years, and GATT acted as a de facto international organization for trade. It conducted eight negotiating rounds between 1947 and 1994 on tariff reduction, and set rules on trade. The last Uruguay Round is the most important one and ended up with the establishment of the WTO. The decisions, procedures and customary practices of the GATT 1947 guide the WTO in its actions.[34] Further, the WTO dispute settlement system was not a novel system, but is based on and has taken on board almost fifty years of experience in the resolution of trade disputes in the context of the GATT 1947.[35] However, because China quitted from the GATT, it lost opportunities in the GATT period and the setting up of the WTO.

Third, the global treaty-based institutionalized regimes proposed by UNCITRAL have advantages over the current investment arbitration regime. Either the two-tier permanent investment court or the stand-alone appellate body means setting up a global treaty-based institution for investment dispute settlement. The current investment arbitration has brought up a lot of critiques especially the inconsistency of decisions, parallel proceedings, lack of transparency, etc. The two-tier investment court can overcome the generation of most of the problems, while the appellate body provides remedies to address and correct the problems. Both the two proposed institutionalized regimes borrow elements from the current WTO dispute settlement system, but keep differences. The two-tier investment court approach has the structure of WTO DSB (panel and AB), but different in the panel. The appellate body approach takes only the form of the WTO AB, but different arbitral tribunals are set up for different disputes based on different IIAs. The global institutionalized regime has its advantages over the current investment arbitration regime.

The WTO dispute settlement regime, the "crown jewel" of the WTO system, fully shows the advantages. For China, being the second largest state in both capital-import

---

32 The Mauritius Convention is also called the "Mauritius Convention on Transparency", its full title is United Nations Convention on Transparency in Treaty-based Investor-State Arbitration.

33 Peter Van den Bossche (2005), p. 80.

34 Peter Van den Bossche (2005), p. 78.

35 Peter Van den Bossche (2005), p. 174.

and export, and having 154 IIAs in force, multilateral institutionalized regime would prevail over the current arbitration regime.

Fourth, although China is a late comer and rule-taker with the WTO dispute settlement, China still successfully benefits from the regime to protect its national rights and interests. China has recommended several experts to be listed on the Indicative List of panelists, including Prof. Zhu Lanye, Prof. Han Liyu, etc. In June 2007, Prof. Zhang Yuqing (Chinese) was appointed by the Director General of the WTO as a member of the Panel to hear the banana dispute.[36] China also owns a position in the WTO Appellate Body (AB) as an important state within the WTO. Ms. Zhang Yuejiao, a Chinese national, was elected to be member of the Appellate Body for two terms. Now, Dr. Zhao Hong, another Chinese national, is a member in the Appellate Body. If the future investment court is established, and if China is the founding member of the Court Statue, China could have a position in the appellate mechanism. Otherwise, China would lose the opportunity.

Further, China has successfully used the WTO dispute settlement mechanism to resolve many disputes with other countries. At the beginning of China's accession to the WTO, China was reluctant or even afraid to use the dispute settlement system. However, now China is increasingly confident and skillful in using the dispute settlement system to advance its legitimate interests.[37] Until May 2024, China has brought 24 cases as complainant, and China was sued in 49 cases as respondent. China also participates in 195 cases as third party.[38] By winning some cases, China protects its national interests. Using the dispute settlement mechanism to defend its rights and interests is an important benefit of China's WTO membership.[39] When losing in the cases, China gained an external driving force to promote its internal trade governance regime reforms.[40] China takes the opportunity to adjust and improve its related national law and policy toward rule of law and market economy. Participating in the WTO cases also train Chinese officials and lawyers, and cultivate a talent pool for the WTO dispute settlement. China's experience in the WTO dispute settlement will also enhance its confidence and capacity in future investment dispute settlement.

Lastly, realizing that it missed the rule-setting opportunities for the WTO dispute settlement, after China acceded to the WTO, it pays special attention to the DSU negotiations provided in the Doha Ministerial Declaration. China has consistently attended almost all formal meetings, informal consultations and small group discussions that take place within or outside the WTO and contribute proposals from time to time.[41] China has played and will continue to play an important role in the WTO dispute settlement. In the same token, China will also continue to pay special attention to the current ISDS reform.

---

[36] European Communities (2007).

[37] Tong Qi (2012), p.143.

[38] The data is available at https://www.wto.org/english/tratop_e/dispu_e/dispu_by_country_e.htm.

[39] Wenhua Ji and Cui Huang (2011), p. 2.

[40] Tong Qi (2012), p.144.

[41] Wenhua Ji and Cui Huang (2011), p. 29.

### 8.2.2 *China's Possible Contribution to UNCITRAL's Reform Work*

Being a major capital-import and export country, China has substantial interest in the ISDS reform. China may make substantial contribution the current UNCITRAL's ISDS reform.

Firstly, China may contribute its value of "building a human community with shared destiny" in designing the framework and specific rules of the future appellate body or permanent court.

Secondly, China should accept the future co-existing of the current arbitration regime and the global institutionalized regime and be careful with the possible retrospective effect of the appellate body or permanent court. Since it is not yet consensus to take the institutionalized reform approach, the UNCITRAL works could take the plural model as applied in the Mauritius Convention on Transparency. This means that for a long time in future, the current arbitration regime will continue to work, co-existing with the appellate body or permanent court. On the other hand, the Mauritius Convention has retrospective effect, which means that it would apply to all previous IIAs. China should be careful with the retrospective effect of the future concluded appellate body or permanent court since most of the Chinese IIAs were concluded in the 1980 and 1990s that are far from perfect in substantive provisions. This leads to the next point.

Thirdly, China should insist that ISDS reform should be accompanied by the reform of the substantive investment protection standards. One of the major reasons for the legitimacy crisis of ISDS is the defect provisions of the substantive standards. An ISDS reform without correspondent substantive standard reform is unimaginable and unworkable. For China, it is also necessary to review and update most of its current IIAs.

To sum up, it is reasonable to estimate that China will benefit from and play important role in the future appellate body or permanent investment court, just as what it got from the WTO dispute settlement mechanism.

## 8.3 China's Position to the ISDS Reform in the UNCITRAL

China submitted two submissions to the UNCITRAL regarding its position to the ISDS reform in July 2019 and October 2012, respectively. Generally speaking, China's position was partly affected by its experience in the WTO dispute settlement, as discussed above.

In its first submission, China supports the ISDS mechanism as one that is generally worth maintaining.[42] China welcomes the UNCITRAL reform initiative.[43] Although

[42] China (2019), p. 2.

[43] China (2019), p. 2.

the ISDS mechanism has played a major role in protecting the rights and interests of foreign investors and promoting transnational investment, it has also created many problems in practice, including that arbitral awards lack an appropriate error-correcting mechanism, arbitral awards lack stability and predictability, arbitrators' professionalism and independence are questioned, third-party funding affects the balance between parties' rights, and time frames are overly long and costs overly high.[44]

China makes some proposals for improving the ISDS mechanism, including setting up a permanent appellate mechanism, retaining the right of the parties to appoint arbitrators, improving rules relating to arbitrators, allowing alternative dispute resolution measures such as conciliation, including pre-arbitration consultation procedures, and stipulating transparency discipline for third-party funding.[45]

From the first submission, we can see that China supports the permanent appellate mechanism option.

The second submission is actually a summary of the inter-sessional meeting on ISDS reform held on 28 and 29 October 2021 in Hong Kong. The theme of the inter-sessional meeting is the use of mediation as an alternative measure in ISDS.[46] This submission is a further specific explanations regarding mediation as an alternative proposed in China's first submission.

China is promoting the idea of mediation as an effective way to resolve various international disputes including investor-state disputes. It proposes to set up an International Court of Conciliation as a worldwide intergovernmental organization, parallel to the International Court of Justice and the Permanent Court of Arbitration. As such, litigation, arbitration and mediation could be the major three options for the settlement of international disputes. So far China has drafted and reached a joint statement with countries with similar point of views and decided to initiate and establish the international court of conciliation, specializing in providing mediation services and offering friendly, flexible, economic and convenient solutions to all kinds of international disputes.[47] A preparatory office for the establishment of an international court of conciliation was set up in Hong Kong in February 2023 to carry out intergovernmental negotiations over international conventions about the court. It is expected that with the final establishment of the International Court of Conciliation, conciliation could become a competing option to arbitration in ISDS.

---

[44] China (2019), pp. 2–3.

[45] China (2019), pp. 4–5.

[46] China (2021).

[47] Qiongfang Du, Qingqing Chen (2022).

## 8.4 China May also Share Its Best Practice of "Arbitration + Mediation" Model in ISDS Reform in a Broader Sense

In addition to the ISDS reform in terms of arbitration, in recent years, mediation is strongly proposed to resolve investment dispute on a voluntary basis serving as an alternative means to arbitration. The recently proposed mediation in ISDS is a separate procedure, while China has good practice in combining arbitration and mediation ("arbitration + mediation" model) which proves to be efficient and effective. This model could be good experience deserved to be borrowed in the ISDS reform.

### *8.4.1 The Newly Proposed Mediation Intends to be a Separate Procedure as an Alternative to Arbitration*

In response to the legitimacy crisis of investment arbitration, mediation is proposed by scholars and experts as an alternative to arbitration in the ISDS reform.[48] Some recent bilateral and multilateral treaties with an investment chapter start to include mediation provisions.[49] Various organs related to investment dispute settlement proposed mediation-related rules to promote the use of mediation in ISDS. International Bar Association adopted its IBA Rules for Investor-State Mediation on October 4, 2012.[50] The Energy Charter Conference adopted a Guide on Investment Mediation recognizing mediation as a helpful instrument to facilitate the amicable resolution of investment dispute in July 2016.[51] ICSID as the major arbitration institutions dealing with investment disputes introduced a new set of mediation rules in

---

[48] For example, Early in 2010, UNCTAD and Washington and Lee University (W&L) School of Law organized jointly a Joint Symposium on International Investment and Alternative Dispute Resolution, brought together a unique group of experts to focus on the use of alternative dispute resolution including mediation in the context of international investment law. UNCTAD, Investor-State Disputes: Prevention and Alternatives to Arbitration (II), UNCTAD/WEB/DIAE/IA/2010/8, 2011, available at https://unctad.org/en/Docs/webdiaeia20108_en.pdf, last visit September 26, 2018, p. iii. For scholar articles, examples are Silvia Constain (2013); Nancy A. Welsh and Andrea Kupfer Schneider (2013); Susan Franck (2014).

[49] For example, Art. 10.15 of the Dominican Republic-Central America FTA (CAFTADR) (2006–7); Art. 26 of the Investment Agreement for the COMESA Common Investment Area, Ch. 10, and Art. 9.18 of the Comprehensive and Progressive Agreement for Trans-Pacific Partnership (CPTPP), Annex 29-C on Mediation in the CETA, Chap. 8(II)(3)(2), Art. 5 of the EU-Vietnam FTA, Chap. 3, Art. 3.4, and Annex 6 of the EU-Singapore FTA.

[50] IBA Rules for Investor-State Mediation, https://icsid.worldbank.org/en/Documents/process/IBA%20Rules%20for%20Investor-State%20Mediation%20(Approved%20by%20IBA%20Council%204%20Oct%202012).pdf, last visit September 26, 2018.

[51] Energy Charter Secretariat (2016), 1. WHAT IS MEDIATION?

2018.[52] To assist selection of competent and suitable mediators, International Mediation Institute proposed IMI Competency Criteria for Investor-State Mediators on September 19, 2016.[53] UNCITRAL amended its 2002 Model Law on International Commercial Conciliation to be Model Law on International Commercial Mediation and International Settlement Agreements Resulting from Mediation in 2018 (hereinafter referred to as "Model Law").[54] To make sure the enforcement of the settlement agreements resulting from mediation, UNCITRAL creates an international regime by Draft convention on international settlement agreements resulting from mediation (2018) (hereinafter referred to as "Draft Convention"),[55] which is broadly akin to the 1958 New York Convention for the enforcement of arbitral awards.

Even with the differences among different treaties and organs, the common features of the above new rules are as follows.

Firstly, mediation is regarded the same as conciliation and becomes more commonly accepted term. Energy Charter Conference uses "Mediation" intending to cover both the concepts of mediation and conciliation.[56] Although UNCITRAL thinks that the terms "conciliation" and "mediation" were interchangeable, in its previously adopted texts and relevant documents, it used the term "conciliation". In preparing this Model Law and Model Convention, the Commission decided to replace the term "conciliation" by "mediation" throughout the draft instruments, in an effort to adapt to the actual and practical use of the terms and with the expectation that this change will facilitate the promotion and heighten the visibility of the Model Law. This change in terminology does not have any substantive or conceptual implications.[57] In contrast, According to the ICSID Secretariat Working Paper,

---

[52] The Mediation Rules of the Additional Facility. ICSID Secretariat, Proposals for Amendment of the ICSID Rules—Consolidated Draft Rules (on August 2, 2018), ANNEX E: ADDITIONAL FACILITY RULES OF PROCEDURE FOR MEDIATION PROCEEDINGS, https://icsid.worldbank.org/en/Documents/Amendments_Vol_Two.pdf, last visit September 26, 2018.

[53] https://www.imimediation.org/download/104/investor-state-mediation-task-force/1472/investor-state-mediation-competency-criteria.pdf, last visit September 26, 2018.

[54] Note by the Secretariat on International commercial mediation: draft model law on international commercial mediation and international settlement agreements resulting from mediation, UNCITRAL Fifty-first session, New York (June 25-July 13, 2018), A/CN.9/943 (Mar. 2, 2018), http://www.uncitral.org/pdf/english/commissionsessions/51st-session/ACN9-943_advance_copy_website.pdf, last visit September 25, 2018.

[55] Note by the Secretariat on International commercial mediation: draft convention on international settlement agreements resulting from mediation, UNCITRAL Fifty-first session, New York (June 25-July 13, 2018), A/CN.9/942 (Mar. 2, 2018), http://www.uncitral.org/pdf/english/commissionsessions/51st-session/ACN9-942_Draft_convention_advance_copy_website.pdf, last visit September 25, 2018.

[56] Energy Charter Secretariat (2016).

[57] Note by the Secretariat on International Commercial Mediation: Draft Convention on International Settlement Agreements Resulting from Mediation, UNCITRAL Fifty-first session, New York

although there are similarities between mediation and conciliation framework, they are different from each other.[58] ICSID takes mediation as different from conciliation which has been an ICSID conventional means along with arbitration, though it is scarcely used.

Secondly, mediation is a separate dispute resolution means. Mediation is often seen as a process to be used at the outset of a dispute, but can be initiated at any time, and can take place while arbitration is ongoing. For example, in some treaties, mediation has been introduced as a pre-condition to the commencement of investor-state arbitration.[59] In other treaties, mediation has been introduced as a stand-alone mechanism for dispute resolution, providing an alternative to arbitration or conciliation.[60] According to IBA Rules for Investor-State Mediation, mediation under these rules may take place at any time, regardless of whether court, arbitration or other dispute resolution proceedings have been initiated.[61] The Energy Charter Conference also encouraged its 53 Contracting Parties to consider mediation as a possible option at any stage of the dispute to facilitate an amicable resolution. It is completely separate from arbitration. It is not a necessary prerequisite to arbitration and does not replace arbitration. Once it fails, the dispute may be referred to arbitration. ICSID mediation rules provide an investment dispute-specific mediation framework, apt for use either independently of, or in conjunction with, arbitration or conciliation proceedings.[62] Mediation may also be conducted in parallel with an ICSID arbitration proceeding. One professor suggested the use of mediation in the investor-state disputes process as an adjunct to arbitration, and called this combination by the shorthand CMA (Concurrent Med-Arb). The basic notion is that one or more mediators would "shadow" the arbitral process (concurrently), applying mediation techniques at various junctures

(June 25-July 13, 2018), A/CN.9/943 (Mar. 2, 2018), http://www.uncitral.org/pdf/english/commissionsessions/51st-session/ACN9-943_advance_copy_website.pdf, last visit September 25, 2018, Footnote 2, p. 3; Note by the Secretariat on International commercial mediation: draft convention on international settlement agreements resulting from mediation, UNCITRAL Fifty-first session, New York (June 25-July 13, 2018), A/CN.9/942 (Mar. 2, 2018), http://www.uncitral.org/pdf/english/commissionsessions/51st-session/ACN9-942_Draft_convention_advance_copy_website.pdf, last visit September 25, 2018, p. 9.

[58] Proposals for Amendment of the ICSID Rules—Working Paper, Volume 3, ICSID Secretariat, August 2, 2018, https://icsid.worldbank.org/en/Documents/Amendments_Vol_Three.pdf, last visit September 26, 2018, para. 1328, p. 750.

[59] For example, Art. 26 of the Investment Agreement for the COMESA Common Investment Area requires a six month amicable settlement period, during which the parties "shall seek the assistance of a mediator", unless an alternative method of dispute settlement is agreed upon (*see also* Ch. 10, and Art. 9.18 of the Comprehensive and Progressive Agreement for Trans-Pacific Partnership (CPTPP).

[60] *See, e.g.*, Annex 29-C on Mediation in the CETA (not yet in force), Chap. 8(II)(3)(2), Art. 5 of the EU-Vietnam FTA, Chap. 3, Art. 3.4, and Annex 6 of the EU-Singapore FTA.

[61] IBA Rules for Investor-State Mediation, https://icsid.worldbank.org/en/Documents/process/IBA%20Rules%20for%20Investor-State%20Mediation%20(Approved%20by%20IBA%20Council%204%20Oct%202012).pdf, last visit September 26, 2018 Article 2.

[62] Proposals for Amendment of the ICSID Rules—Working Paper, Volume 3, ICSID Secretariat, August 2, 2018, https://icsid.worldbank.org/en/Documents/Amendments_Vol_Three.pdf, last visit September 26, 2018, para. 1323, p. 749.

throughout that process with a view to helping generate a settlement that might then be embodied in an award on agreed terms.[63]

Thirdly, mediation is conducted on a voluntary basis which needs consent from both parties. According to IBA Rules for Investor-State Mediation, The mediator shall not have the authority to impose on the parties any partial or complete settlement of the differences or disputes.[64] The mediator does not have the authority to impose upon the parties a solution to the dispute.[65] Therefore, mediation is only an ADR to arbitration and happens before arbitration. Relying to mediation does not affect the later relying on arbitration.

Fourthly, in principal, mediators for one case cannot act as arbitrator of the same case once mediation fails. The mediator agrees not to act in any other role, including that of counsel, arbitrator, expert or witness.[66] "Unless otherwise agreed by the parties, the mediator shall not act as an arbitrator in respect of a dispute that was or is the subject of the mediation proceedings or in respect of another dispute that has arisen from the same contract or legal relationship or any related contract or legal relationship.[67]

Fifthly, if the parties reach an amicable settlement through mediation during arbitration under the ICSID Convention, such settlement may then be embodied in an award.[68]

Mediation is rule-oriented and procedure-oriented, just as arbitration. All the arbitration institutions make specific rules and procedures for the applying of mediation. The mediation procedure is not mingled or combined with arbitration procedures.

The mediation mechanism design intends to resolve dispute quickly, less expensively and more efficiently, which are the original purposes of the creation of arbitration to replace litigation. However, investors would be hesitated to take the mediation

[63] Jack J. Coe (2011), p. 43.

[64] IBA Rules for Investor-State Mediation, https://icsid.worldbank.org/en/Documents/process/IBA%20Rules%20for%20Investor-State%20Mediation%20(Approved%20by%20IBA%20Council%204%20Oct%202012).pdf, last visit September 26, 2018 Article 7.

[65] Note by the Secretariat on International commercial mediation: draft model law on international commercial mediation and international settlement agreements resulting from mediation, UNCITRAL Fifty-first session, New York (June 25-July 13, 2018), A/CN.9/943 (Mar. 2, 2018), http://www.uncitral.org/pdf/english/commissionsessions/51st-session/ACN9-943_advance_copy_website.pdf, last visit September 25, 2018, Article 1.

[66] IBA Rules for Investor-State Mediation, https://icsid.worldbank.org/en/Documents/process/IBA%20Rules%20for%20Investor-State%20Mediation%20(Approved%20by%20IBA%20Council%204%20Oct%202012).pdf, last visit September 26, 2018 Article 7.

[67] Note by the Secretariat on International commercial mediation: draft model law on international commercial mediation and international settlement agreements resulting from mediation, UNCITRAL Fifty-first session, New York (June 25-July 13, 2018), A/CN.9/943 (Mar. 2, 2018), http://www.uncitral.org/pdf/english/commissionsessions/51st-session/ACN9-943_advance_copy_website.pdf, last visit September 25, 2018, Article 13.

[68] Proposals for Amendment of the ICSID Rules—Working Paper, Volume 3, ICSID Secretariat, August 2, 2018, https://icsid.worldbank.org/en/Documents/Amendments_Vol_Three.pdf, last visit September 26, 2018, para. 1327, p. 749.

procedure for concerns of extra cost and time. And the author doubts that the rigidly rule-oriented mediation will eventually follow the crisis of arbitration.

### 8.4.2 China's "Arbitration + Mediation" Model Combining Arbitration and Mediation Proves to Be Best Practice

Mediation is not China's "innovation" or "patent". Actually mediation as a traditional form of dispute resolution can be found in societies around the globe and can be traced back to the earliest history of mankind.[69] But China is the country that mediation is used the most commonly and popularly. Mediation is also a possible way to resolve international investment disputes in China. Prof. Wang Guiguao discussed that whether mediation can serve as an alternative for resolving investment disputes.[70] Actually, mediation as an alternative to arbitration is already accepted in state practice, arbitration institutions and scholars. However, the author thinks that China's contribution would be the "arbitration + mediation" model.

In China, mediation is not only used as an independent means to dispute settlement parallel to litigation and arbitration, but also combined to litigation and arbitration as "litigation + mediation" model and "arbitration + mediation" model, which is the features and value-added points of mediation, but does not receive sufficient attention in the world.

Mediation in China has a long history majorly based on Chinese philosophy and culture basis. In ancient China, two philosophical concepts were developed and established in China. One is Li (Confucianism) and the other is Fa (Legalism). Some scholars compare Li and Fa to Natural Law and Positive Law, respectively.[71] In ancient China, most civil cases were decided in accordance with Li rather than Fa,[72] because ancient Chinese "law" referred exclusively to criminal law.[73]

Confucianism's core idea is harmonious society and stopping suits. This culture greatly affects people's thinking and acts. Non-litigation methods for resolving disputes, such as consultation and mediation, are the culturally preferred means and are better suited to the Chinese environment.[74] Ordinary people perceive disputes and social order as being in opposition to each other, and they often consider suits to be shameful and litigation to be synonymous with demoralization and breakdown in morality.[75] When there is any dispute, people will see how to resolve it and maintain the original good relations. Even if the dispute is referred to litigation, people

69 Jacob Bercovitch (2002).

70 Guiguo Wang (2012), p. 216.

71 Junwu Pan (2011), p. 233.

72 Junwu Pan (2011), p. 235.

73 Junwu Pan (2011), p. 234.

74 Guiguo Wang, Xiaoli He, (2012), p. 220. Gao Jun et al. (2005).

75 Guiguo Wang, Xiaoli He, (2012), p. 223.

will find ways to stop it. Therefore, mediation plays an important role both before litigation and during litigation.

In history, disputes over civil matters or minor criminal cases are majorly mediated first by neighbors, clan authentic people or village communities, and if fails, then mediated by competent authorities. Only criminal cases are referred to court for punishment. In ancient China until 1911 when the Qing Dynasty was overthrown, nearly all civil and minor criminal cases were resolved by mediation, and only if mediation failed were these cases adjudicated by the relevant laws and rules.[76] Mediation, however, could not be applied to serious cases such as robbery, murder and so on. Mediation continued to be the major means of resolving disputes in the Republic of China during 1911–1949. Mediation was formally introduced into New China and was paid high attention.

Mediation is commonly and broadly used in current China. It is used as one of the major means for dispute settlement. Mediation is used in civil society as a non-legal informal means. Any person and any entity can offer mediation assistance aiming to resolve disputes. Here the people majorly refer to friends, relatives or lawyers of the disputing parties. The enterprise where the disputing parties work for, or the association where disputing parties are members of a group, often play important roles in mediation. These people or entities do not have the legal obligation to mediate but voluntarily do it. However, the agreement reached by this type of mediation cannot be enforced but rely on voluntary compliance by parties.

In China, there are many grass-rooted people's mediation committees. These committees are sub-committees organized within residents or villagers committees, or enterprises or professional associations. People's mediation is based on voluntary consent and the parties shall comply with the resulted agreement. If one party refuses to comply with it, the other party may refer the agreement to competent court for confirmation and enforcement. This kind of mediation is legalized and institutionalized quite maturely in China.[77]

For local administrative governments, public security organs, industrial and commercial administration organs and other public organs, when they deal with disputes within their business scope, including civil disputes, traffic accident disputes and contractual disputes, they will conduct mediation during the dispute settlement process. Legal basis of this type of mediation scatters in many different laws and regulations.[78]

For labor disputes, since it is closely related to human relations, and to avoid breaking up the relations, all labor disputes are strongly encouraged to be resolved by mediation by labor dispute mediation committee established within the enterprise,

---

[76] Hong Lian (2005), at 89, 91 (original in Chinese). Guiguo Wang, He Xiaoli (2012), p. 221.

[77] It is recognized and stipulated in China's Constitution (Article 111) and China's Civil Procedure Law (Article 194). It is governed by People's Mediation Law (2010).

[78] Examples include Regulation on the Organization of People's Mediation Committee, Measures for the Resolution of Civil Disputes, Water Law, Law on Public Security Administration and Punishment, Implementing Regulation on the Road Traffic Safety Law, Implementing Regulation on Administrative Review Law, etc.

or grass-rooted people's mediation committee, or other local organizations with the function of mediation.[79]

Mediation is also used as parallel to negotiation, litigation and arbitration. According to China's Contract Law, contractual disputes may be resolved by mediation. If it fails, the dispute may be referred to arbitration or litigation.[80] For commercial disputes, mediation is a separate but optional dispute resolution means. CCPIT/ CCOIC Mediation Centre is specially established for this purpose.[81] It has many branches in many provinces. This type of mediation is similar to the recently proposed mediation discussed above.

A unique type of mediation in China is mediation connected to litigation. This type of mediation is conducted during the litigation proceedings, where judge(s) act as mediator(s). This type of mediation is a combination of litigation and mediation, which the author calls it as "litigation + mediation" model. Another unique type of medication is that arbitrator(s) may conduct mediation during the whole proceedings of arbitration. This is also a combination of arbitration and mediation, which the author calls it "arbitration + mediation" model. The "litigation + mediation" model and "arbitration + mediation" model share similar features. Both "litigation + mediation" model and "arbitration + mediation" model are recognized, encouraged, regulated and institutionalized in China.[82] As discussed in Part II, China has started to try to create its own ISDS mechanisms. Both CIETAC and SCIA expand their business scope to cover ISDS. In both of their arbitration rules, they follow the tradition of "arbitration + mediation" model.[83] That means, the "arbitration + mediation" model will be applied to international investment disputes.

Unique features of China's "arbitration-mediation" models are as follows.

Firstly, arbitrator acts as mediator. The tribunal may conduct mediation if both dispute parties intend so, or either party intends so and gets consent from the other party through the tribunal.[84] This means that arbitrator(s) of the tribunal will act as mediator. If the tribunal has only one arbitrator, he/she serves as sole mediator. If the tribunal has three arbitrators, the three can act as mediators, or only one of

---

79 China's Labor Dispute Mediation and Arbitration Law (2007).

80 Article 128 of China's Contract Law.

81 Mediation Rules of the China Council for the Promotion of International Trade/China Chamber of International Commerce (2012).

82 The "litigation + mediation" model is stipulated majorly in Chapter Eight "Mediation" of China's Civil Procedure Law (modified in 2017). The "arbitration + mediation" model is provided in Articles 51 and 52 of China's Arbitration Law (modified in 2017). It is more specifically provided in arbitration rules of various arbitration institutions such as the Arbitration Rules of China International Economy and Trade Arbitration Commission (CIETAC)/China International Commercial Chamber. Article 47 of the CIETAC Arbitration Rules is named "the combination of arbitration with mediation".

83 Article 43 "The Combination of Arbitration and Mediation" of CIETAC International Investment Dispute Arbitration Rules (2017); Chapter 7 "Mediation and Settlement" of the SCIA Arbitration Rules.

84 Article 47(1) of CIETAC Arbitration Rules, Article 43(1) of CIETAC International Investment Arbitration Rules; Article 45(1) of SCIA Arbitration Rules.

them to conduct mediation. This is totally different from the international mediation rules discussed above. If the parties wish to mediate the dispute, but worry about the arbitrators acting as mediators, the arbitration institution may conduct the mediation.[85] The purpose is to relax worries of foreigners about the same person of arbitrator and mediator. Generally speaking, the arbitrator-mediator will continue the arbitration proceedings if mediation fails. But due to the fact that for international investment arbitration, many people challenge the arbitrator-mediator arrangement, Chinese international investment arbitrations rules provide that if the parties agree otherwise, they can request to change the arbitrator,[86] but the extra expenses will be borne by them.[87]

Secondly, mediation could be used in any stage of the arbitration proceedings. Mediation could be raised in any stage of the proceedings, including the case filing stage, pre-hearing stage, hearing stage and even after hearing but before the award announcement stage. This seems similar to the international practice. However, there are differences. Chinese mediation process mingled and intertwined with the arbitration proceedings, but the international mediation discussed above is a separate process parallel to arbitration proceedings.

Thirdly, if the parties come to a settlement agreement as a result of mediation, they may withdraw from their arbitral claims or counter-claims, or they may request the tribunal to make mediation record or arbitral awards,[88] both of which are final and binding. Once the mediation is received by signature by both parties, it is binding and enforceable on both parties as arbitral awards.[89] The mediation record could be recognized and enforced by Chinese court, but not by foreign court. Therefore, many parties prefer making arbitral award.

Fourthly, if mediation succeeds, the arbitration proceedings stop. Once mediation fails, arbitration proceedings resume. Any party expresses its idea not to continue with mediation, the mediator should stop mediation and resume the arbitration proceedings. If either party goes back to the mediation record before it is received with signature, the arbitral tribunal should decide the case in due time.[90]

Fifthly, there are not clear required procedures for mediation to follow. The disputing parties may negotiate to decide the scope of mediation, the procedural rules of mediation, the number and constitution of mediators, etc. Or the tribunal may conduct mediation in a proper way.[91] This is very flexible and greatly different from the rigidly rule-based mediation.

---

[85] Article 47 (8) of CIETAC Arbitration Rules; Article 43(7) of CIETAC International Investment Arbitration Rules.

[86] Article 43(6) of CIETAC International Investment Arbitration Rules; Article 45(1) of SIAC Arbitration Rules.

[87] Article 43(6) of CIETAC International Investment Arbitration Rules.

[88] Article 47(5) of CIETAC Arbitration Rules.

[89] Articles 51 and 52 of China's Arbitration Law.

[90] Article 51 of China's Arbitration Law.

[91] Article 47(2) of CIETAC Arbitration Rules.

Sixthly, there is no extra cost for mediation in addition to arbitration cost.[92]

CIETAC started the "arbitration + mediation" model in 1950's, which is extended to other arbitration institutions in China later on.[93] After 60 years of practice and improvement, it has now been recognized and stated as an outstanding feature of CIETAC and other commercial arbitration institutions in China.[94] According to China Academy of Arbitration Law's annual report, in China, 56,659 cases were resolved by this model accounting for 21.61% of all cases in 2015,[95] 121,527 cases were resolved by this model accounting for 58% of all cases in 2016.[96]

A foreign scholar observed that in China, med-arb (mediation-arbitration) is "used frequently and enjoys a high degree of success". China's arbitration laws already allow for a mediator to also play the role of arbitrator in the same proceeding, combining arbitration and mediation in one process.[97] This model works very well because it has various advantages: Mediation is not used as a separate procedure with a separate mediator, but is integrated into arbitration proceedings, thus, the parties take only one proceedings and thus save another procedure. This will result in the reduction of both time and cost if two procedures are used. Agreement is easier to conclude between parties through mediation since mediation does not have a specific governing law, but only on fair and equitable basis and party consent. Mediator does not have to comply with the rigid procedure rules, therefore it is more flexible, and will save a lot of time. Both time and cost will be saved through "arbitration + mediation" model since the higher chances to conclude a mediation agreement. The chance for the mediation agreement or awards made based on the mediation agreement is higher to be complied with by both parties than normal arbitration awards. Normally there is no such thing as annulment or judicial review or the recognition and enforcement of the awards. The friendly business relations between parties is easier to be maintained through mediation than arbitration.

This model is an established practice not only in China, but also in other countries such as Germany, Switzerland and the Netherlands, and learned and borrowed by some other countries such as Canada, Australia and Singapore.[98]

In terms of ISDS, it is feasible to adopt this model. According to statistics, many investment arbitration cases are finally resolved by settlement. As of December 31, 2017, there are 548 decided cases, among which 125 cases was settled, accounting for 22.8%.[99] This means that many parties would like to resolved disputes flexibly and

---

[92] Neither China's Civil Procedure Law nor Arbitration Law nor CIETAC Arbitration Rules provide any extra cost for the mediation conducted during litigation or arbitration. Also See Qiulan Wang et al. (2014), p. 143.

[93] Shengchang Wang (2001), p. 79.

[94] China Academy of Arbitration Law (2014), pp. 40–41.

[95] China Academy of Arbitration Law (2015), p. 9.

[96] China Academy of Arbitration Law (2016), p. 13.

[97] Tiffany M Lin (2016), p. 612.

[98] Shengchang Wang (2001), pp.131–132, 138–139.

[99] UNCTAD, Concluded original arbitration proceedings, http://investmentpolicyhub.unctad.org/ISDS?status=4, last visit September 30, 2018.

quickly. If mediation is used during the arbitration process, the chances of concluding agreement would be high.

## 8.5 Conclusion

Although it is not easy for China to adopt a definite position toward the ISDS reform in the early stage, China may learn lessons from its experience in the WTO dispute settlement in assessing the UNCITRAL ISDS reform work. Currently China has clearly expressed its support to the setting up of a separate appellate body proposed by UNCITRAL. China has rich experience and mature law in "arbitration + mediation" model which could be its contribution to the ISDS reform in a broader sense.

## References

Anthea Roberts (2017) The shifting landscape of investor-state arbitration: loyalists, reformists, revolutionaries and undecideds. www.ejiltalk.org/the-shifting-landscape-of-investor-state-arbitration-loyalists-reformists-revolutionaries-and-undecideds/, published on June 15, 2017

Anthea Roberts (2018) Investment treaties: the reform matrix, AJIL Unbound

China (2019) Recommendations of China regarding investor-State Dispute settlement reform, Annex to the Possible reform of investor-State dispute settlement (ISDS) Submission from the Government of China, Note by the Secretariat, A/CN.9/WG.III/WP.177, 19 July 2019

China (2021) Summary of the inter-sessional meeting on investor-State dispute settlement (ISDS) reform submitted by the People's Republic of China, A/CN.9/WG.III/WP.210, 10 November 2021

China Academy of Arbitration Law (2014) Annual report of China's international commercial arbitration.

China Academy of Arbitration Law (2015) Annual report of China's international commercial arbitration.

China Academy of Arbitration Law (2016) Annual report of China's international commercial arbitration.

Concept Paper (2015): Investment in TTIP and beyond—the path for reform. http://trade.ec.europa.eu/doclib/docs/2015/may/tradoc_153408.PDF

Energy Charter Secretariat (2016) Guide on Investment Mediation, Brussels, 19 July 2016

European Commission (2014) Consolidated CETA text published on 26 September 2014

European Commission (2016) Press release, CETA: EU and Canada agree on new approach on investment in trade agreement, Brussels, 29 February 2016. http://europa.eu/rapid/press-release_IP-16-399_en.htm

European Communities (2007) Regime for the importation, sale and distribution of bananas, Recourse to Article 21.5 of the DSU by Ecuador, Constitution of the Panel, WT/DS27/82

Guiguo Wang, Xiaoli He (2012) Mediation and international investment: a Chinese perspective, 65 Me L Rev 215

IBA Rules for Investor-State Mediation. https://icsid.worldbank.org/en/Documents/process/IBA%20Rules%20for%20Investor-State%20Mediation%20(Approved%20by%20IBA%20Council%204%20Oct%202012).pdf

ICSID (2018) Proposals for amendment of the ICSID rules—Working Paper, vol 3, ICSID Secretariat. https://icsid.worldbank.org/en/Documents/Amendments_Vol_Three.pdf

ICSID (2018) The mediation rules of the additional facility. ICSID Secretariat, Proposals for Amendment of the ICSID Rules—Consolidated Draft Rules (on August 2, 2018), Annex E: Additional Facility Rules of Procedure For Mediation Proceedings. https://icsid.worldbank.org/en/Documents/Amendments_Vol_Two.pdf

Jack J. Coe, Jr. (2011) Concurrent Med-Arb (CMA)—Some Further Reflections on a Work in Progress, in: UNCTAD, Investor-State Disputes: Prevention and Alternatives to Arbitration (II), UNCTAD/WEB/DIAE/IA/2010/8

Jacob Bercovitch (2002) Introduction: putting mediation in context, in studies in international mediation: essays in honor of Jeffrey Z. Rubin 3, 4 (Jacob Bercovitch, ed. 2002)

Jun Gao, Yiping Long, Hongwei Xu (2005) Revelations of traditional Chinese non-legal-dispute culture on construction of contemporary harmonious Chinese Society, 23 Journal of Hubei Institute for Nationalities (Philosophy and Social Sciences), no. 4, 2005 (original in Chinese)

Junwu Pan (2011) Chinese philosophy and international law. Asian J Intern Law 1

Karl P Sauvant, Huiping Chen (2012) A China—US bilateral investment treaty: a template for a multilateral framework for investment?, Columbia FDI Perspectives, no 85

Kenneth J Vandevelde (2009) U.S. international investment agreements, Oxford University Press

Hong Lian (2005) Harmonious concept of Confucianism and Chinese traditional mediation system, 18 Chang Chun University of Science and Technology (Social Sciences), no 2 (original in Chinese)

MOFCOM (2021) Statistical bulletin of China's outward foreign direct investment, China Commerce and Trade Press

Nancy A Welsh, Andrea Kupfer Schneider (2013) The thoughtful integration of mediation into bilateral investment treaty arbitration, 18 HARV NEGOT L REV 71

Peter Van den Bossche (2005) The law and policy of the world trade organization: text, cases and materials, Cambridge University Press

Qiongfang Du, Qingqing Chen (2022) Chinese central govt to set up preparatory office for intl court of mediation in HK, published on Nov 02, 2022. Available at https://www.globaltimes.cn/page/202211/1278518.shtml

Qiulan Wang, Xingmei Qiu, Jinhua Liu, Li Wang (2014) A study on the issues related to legislation, theory and practice of mediation in China, CUPL Press (original in Chinese)

Shengchang Wang (2001) The theory and practice of combining arbitration with conciliation, Law Press (original in Chinese)

Silvia Constain (2013) Mediation in investor–state dispute settlement: government policy and the changing landscape, 29 ICSID Review—Foreign Invest Law J 25–40

Susan D Franck (2005) The legitimacy crisis in investment treaty arbitration: privatizing public international law through inconsistent decisions, 73 Fordham L. Rev. 1521

Susan Franck (2014) Using investor-state mediation rules to promote conflict management: an introductory guide, 29 ICSID Review—Foreign Invest Law J 66–89

The US 2004 Model BIT

The US 2012 Model BIT

Tiffany M Lin (2016) Chinese attitudes toward third-party dispute resolution in international law, 48 N.Y.U. J. Int'l L & Pol 581

Tong Qi (2012) China's first decade experience in the WTO dispute settlement system: practice and prospect, 7 Asian J. WTO & Int'l Health L & Pol'y 143

UN General Assembly (2017) Possible future work in the field of dispute settlement: reforms of investor-State dispute settlement (ISDS): Note by the Secretariat, A/CN.9/917

UN General Assembly (2017) Possible reform of investor-State dispute settlement (ISDS): Note by the Secretariat, A/CN.9/WG.III/WP.142

UNCITRAL (2017) Report of Working Group III (Investor-State Dispute Settlement Reform) on the work of its thirty-fourth session (Vienna, 27 November–1 December 2017) Part I, A/CN.9/930/Rev.1, 19 December 2017

UNCITRAL (2018) Note by the Secretariat on International commercial mediation: draft model law on international commercial mediation and international settlement agreements resulting

from mediation, UNCITRAL Fifty-first session, New York (June 25-July 13, 2018), A/CN.9/943
UNCTAD (2011) Investor-state disputes: prevention and alternatives to arbitration (II), UNCTAD/WEB/DIAE/IA/2010/8
Wenhua Ji, Cui Huang (2011) China's experience in dealing with WTO dispute settlement: a Chinese perspective. J World Trade 45(1)
Xinhuanet (2013) Fruitful achievements of the China-U.S. strategic and economic dialogue. http://news.xinhuanet.com/world/2013-07/13/c_116520838.htm

# Chapter 9
# Chinese Practice in ISDS Cases

## 9.1 Introduction

China started to attract foreign investment since the end of the 1970s, and eventually became the second largest FDI recipient in the world in 2022, behind the US.[1] China started to encourage outbound investment since 2000, and eventually became the second major home economy of FDI in the world, behind the US.[2] In addition, China is the country who has the concluded largest amount of investment agreements, next to Germany. Currently, it has concluded 123 BITs and 29 treaties with investment provisions (TIPs).[3] Before 2020, China was not involved in many ISDS cases: there were only 15 investor-state investment disputes, among which in four cases that the Chinese Government acted as respondent before ICSID, in 11 cases that Chinese investors acted as claimant to sue host states before various fora.[4]

However, since China continues to be the second largest state to attract foreign investment in the world, the risk it would be subject to disputes with foreign investors is increasing. Further, with the increase of the amount of Chinese outward investment as a result of the Belt and Road Initiative (BRI) could increase the number of investor-state disputes between Chinese investors and the host governments. Moreover, with the increasing number of China's second generation of BITs which allows "any investment dispute" instead of "the dispute over the amount of compensation for expropriation" to be resolved by international arbitration, the investment disputes would be expected to increase. Although Chinese culture prefers harmony and does not encourage legal resolution of disputes, with the increase of Chinese

---

[1] UNCTAD (2022) , p.8.

[2] UNCTAD (2022), p.8.

[3] The data is searched through UNCTAD International Investment Agreements Navigator, available at http://investmentpolicyhub.unctad.org/IIA/CountryBits/42#iiaInnerMenu, last visited on November 30, 2023.

[4] The data was collected by the author based on several sources including UNCTAD, ICSID, italaw.com, etc.

 
H. Chen, *China's Practice in International Investment Law*, Modern China and International Economic Law, https://doi.org/10.1007/978-981-96-5016-3_9

**Chart 9.1** China as respondent state

**Chart 9.2** Chinese investor as claimant

OFDI, investment disputes will get more, and thus more arbitration cases are estimated in the future. The following Chart 9.1 shows the number of cases that Chinese Government is challenged as host state in chronological order of year, while Chart 9.2 shows the number of cases that Chinese investors challenge host states as claimants in chronological order of year.

Actually, the cases that China acted as respondent and Chinese investors acted as claimants have already increased drastically ever since 2020: There are four new cases that China is respondent, and 14 new cases that Chinese investors are claimants.[5]

[5] The data was collected by the author based on several sources including UNCTAD, ICSID, italaw.com, etc.

In the following two parts, the author will discuss the cases the China acts as respondent state and the cases that Chinese investors act as claimants.

## 9.2 Cases that China is the Respondent State

Till August 30, 2023, there have been eight cases that China is challenged by foreign investors to international investment arbitration. This number does not cover those that notice of intent is sent out but not formally registered.

### *9.2.1 Overview of the Cases that China is Respondent State*

The following table shows the current ISDS cases that China is challenged (Table 9.1).

The above table shows some characteristics of the cases that China is respondent state.

First, in terms of the year of initiation, it shows the increasing trend in recent years.

Second, in terms of the legal basis of the cases, all cases are based on bilateral investment agreements (BIT), and most of them were concluded in the 1980s or 1990s, which belong to the old generation of BIT.

Third, in terms of the forum that the cases are referred to, ICSID is the major choice, but ad hoc arbitration based on UNCITRAL Arbitration Rules is another choice. For ad hoc arbitration, most cases are administered by the Permanent Court of Arbitration (PCA).

Fourth, in terms of the outcome of original proceedings, half are pending, and half are resolved. In no case that China lost.

Fifth, in terms of the home state of the investor, all except one is developed countries.

Sixth, in terms of the industry that the case is involved, most except two is involved with real estate development. This is because the development of real estate in China is very active and China's policy regarding real estate is changing. China should learn lessons from this fact.

### *9.2.2 Case Study of Some Major Cases*

In the above eight cases, four of them have been resolved, among which information of three is available. For the rest four still pending cases, information of only one of them is available. This section will review the three cases, namely Ekran v. China, Hela Schwarz v. China and AsiaPhos v. China. The case of Ansung Housing v. China

**Table 9.1** Basic information of the cases that China is respondent state

| No | Year of initiation | Short case name | Legal basis | Forum | Outcome of original proceedings | Home state of investor | Industry involved |
|---|---|---|---|---|---|---|---|
| 1. | 2011 | Ekran v. China[6] | China-Malaysia BIT (1988) | ICSID | Settled | Malaysia | Real estate development |
| 2. | 2014 | Ansung Housing v. China[7] | China-Korea BIT (2007) | ICSID | In favor of State (No jurisdiction) | Republic of Korea | Real estate development |
| 3. | 2017 | Hela Schwarz v. China[8] | China-Germany BIT (2003) | ICSID | Pending | Germany | Real estate development |
| 4. | 2019 | Jason v. China[9] | China-UK BIT (1986) | Administered by PCA | Pending | United Kingdom | Not available |
| 5. | 2020 | Macro v. China[10] | China-Japan BIT (1988) | ICSID | Discontinued | Japan | Real estate development |
| 6. | 2020 | Goh Chin Soon v. China[11] | China-Singapore BIT (1985) | Administered by PCA | Pending | Singapore | Real estate development |

(continued)

[6] Ekran Berhad v. People's Republic of China (ICSID Case No. ARB/11/15) https://icsid.worldbank.org/en/Pages/cases/casedetail.aspx?CaseNo=ARB/11/15, last visited on May 11, 2023.

[7] Ansung Housing Co., Ltd. v. People's Republic of China (ICSID Case No. ARB/14/25), https://icsid.worldbank.org/en/Pages/cases/casedetail.aspx?CaseNo=ARB/14/25, last visited on May 11, 2023.

[8] Hela Schwarz GmbH v. People's Republic of China (ICSID Case No. ARB/17/19), https://icsid.worldbank.org/en/Pages/cases/casedetail.aspx?CaseNo=ARB/17/19, last visited on May 11, 2023.

[9] Jason Yu Song (United Kingdom) v. People's Republic of China (PCA Case No. 2019–39), https://pca-cpa.org/en/cases/241/, last visited on April 25, 2023.

[10] Macro Trading Co., Ltd. v. People's Republic of China (ICSID Case No. ARB/20/22), https://icsid.worldbank.org/cases/case-database/case-detail?CaseNo=ARB/20/22, last visited on April 25, 2023.

[11] Mr. Goh Chin Soon (Singapore) v. People's Republic of China (PCA Case No. 2021–30) https://pca-cpa.org/en/cases/269/, last visited on April 25, 2023.

**Table 9.1** (continued)

| No | Year of initiation | Short case name | Legal basis | Forum | Outcome of original proceedings | Home state of investor | Industry involved |
|---|---|---|---|---|---|---|---|
| 7. | 2021 | AsiaPhos v. China[12] | China-Singapore BIT (1985) | Administered by ICSID | In favor of State (No jurisdiction) | Singapore | Mining |
| 8. | 2021 | Eugenio Montenero v. China[13] | China-Switzerland BIT (2009) | Ad hoc UNCITRAL Rules | Pending | Switzerland | Entertainment |

[12] AsiaPhos Limited and Norwest Chemicals Pte Ltd v. People's Republic of China (ICSID Case No. ADM/21/1) https://icsid.worldbank.org/cases/case-database/case-detail?CaseNo=ADM/21/1, last visited on April 25 2023.

[13] EUGENIO MONTENERO V. CHINA https://www.iareporter.com/arbitration-cases/eugenio-montenero-v-china/, last visited on April 25, 2023.

has been discussed in Chapter 2 and thus would not be repeated hereby. After the case study, the author tries to analyze some lessons that could be learned.

#### 9.2.2.1 Ekran v. China

Ekran Berhad (hereinafter "Ekran") is a Malaysian company. On May 24, 2011, it instituted an arbitration proceeding at ICSID against the Chinese Government based on China-Israel BIT (1995) and Malaysia-China BIT (1988). This is the first case that China was challenged as respondent and thus both the relevant Chinese officials and the government were uncomfortable and anxious about it. China seemed not yet ready for an investment arbitration case and thus negotiated with the claimant for peaceful settlement of the case. The two parties agreed to suspend the arbitration proceedings in July 2011. In about two years of negotiation and bargaining, the two parties eventually came to a settlement agreement without disclosing details. On May 16, 2013, the parties filed a request to the ICSID for the discontinuance of the proceedings.

Claims arising out of the local government's revocation of claimant's subsidiary rights to a leasehold land due to an alleged failure to develop the land as stipulated under local legislation. In 1993, Ekran registered a subsidiary, Sino-Malaysia Culture & Art Co. Ltd. (Culture Co.), in Wanning-Xian, Hainan Province in China, in which Ekran holds a 70% equity interest. To develop its business of arts and cultural facilities, the Culture Co. entered into a land lease agreement involving 900 hectares of land with the Wanning local government of Hainan Province, which has a 70-year leasehold from 1993 to 2063. However, for over 15 years, the Culture Co. had not developed any project on that piece of land.

Since 2007, the real estate had risen very fast in China and the Chinese Government issued several rules and regulations to regulate the development of real estate and the prices of real estate. Accordingly, Hainan Province also amended its Regulation on the Land Administration of the Hainan Special Economic Zone in 2008 (2008 Amended) (hereinafter "the Regulation"). Article 44(2) of the Regulation provides that the right to use the land will be taken back without any compensation when the land is kept idle for more than two years. Therefore, in 2009, the Hainan Government revoked the Culture Co.'s rights to the leasehold land due to its failure to develop the land.

Ekran, then, brought the claim before ICSID claiming for expropriation. In all the BITs that China concluded in the 1980s and 1990s until the one with Barbados in 1998, China only consented to refer the dispute with a foreign investor over the amount of compensation for expropriation to international arbitration. Moreover, when China-Malaysia BIT was concluded in 1988, China had not yet joined the ICSID Convention (China signed the ICSID Convention in 1990 and it entered into force for China in 1993), therefore, the China-Malaysia BIT provides that an investor may request an International Arbitral Tribunal (not ICSID) to review the amount of compensation. According to this, Ekran is not entitled to bring the case before

ICSID. Therefore, Ekran relied on the Most-Favored Nation Provisions of the China-Malaysia BIT and thus based on the China-Israel BIT (1995) which clearly allows a dispute over the amount of compensation in the case of expropriation be submitted to ICSID.

The case was eventually settled. No award or decision is made and thus not available data online.

Ekran v. China was the first case that China acted as a respondent in ICSID arbitration. This dispute is related to China's first generation of BITs which only allows the "dispute over the amount of compensation of expropriation" to be resolved by international arbitration. However, the claimant asserted expropriation, which is obviously exceeding the scope of dispute in the BIT. Although the claimant relied on the MFN clause and invoked China-Israel BIT (1995), this BIT also belongs to the first generation with the same scope of ISDS. The reason that the claimant invoked the China-Israel BIT is to justify its submission the case to ICSID. Therefore, this case would not be a big deal for China, but since this is the first case, and China showed too much worry and non-self-confidence about ISDS and the result of tribunals, China decided to settle with the claimant.

Though due to discontinuance of the proceeding, the merits part hasn't been judged, the case still has some important legal significance especially concerning China's BITs. The key question is concerning arbitration jurisdiction which involves the subject matter of the case and whether the MFN treatment applies. Firstly, Ekran claims expropriation of its investment, while the China-Malaysia BIT only permits the dispute over the amount of compensation of the expropriation be submitted for international arbitration. Secondly, the China-Malaysia BIT allows the MFN treatment be given to the investments (substantive treatment), whether it could be expanded to the disputes over the investment (procedural treatment)? And whether referring a dispute to ICSID is a better treatment than referring it to an International Arbitral Tribunal? These questions are not answered in this case since it is settled.

#### 9.2.2.2 Hela Schwarz v. China

Hela Schwarz GmbH ("Hela" or "Claimant") is a German company. On May 2, 2017, it instituted an arbitration proceeding against China before ICSID on the basis of China-Germany BIT (2003). This is the third case that China was challenged as respondent. Now China seemed to be accustomed to the investment arbitration and responded in a regular manner. A tribunal was constituted on January 8, 2018. China filed a memorial on jurisdiction, including a request to address the objections to jurisdiction as a preliminary question on October 1, 2018. The tribunal decided to join the objections to jurisdiction to the merits of the dispute. On December 5, 2022, the tribunal met to hear both the jurisdiction and merits. So far no award is made public.

Claims arose out of the Claimant's investment in China through a wholly owned subsidiary, Ji'nan Hela Schwarz Food Co., Ltd. ("JHSF"), which was established in

1996. Hela is a German-owned spice and food additive manufacturer. It has been operating in the city of Jinan since 1996, as a joint venture with a local meat processing company. In 1999, it was transferred to German ownership. In 2001, JHSF was granted the legal right to use a parcel of state-owned industrial land in Shandong Province (the "Land") for 50 years, until July 29, 2051. After receiving this right, JHSF built a series of buildings on 4821.18 square meters of the Land (the "Buildings"). On September 11, 2014, the Jinan Municipal Government issued a Housing Expropriation Decision to expropriate the Land and the Buildings (the "Expropriation Decision"). According to the Respondent, this expropriation measure was implemented as part of the Huashan area renovation project, a program aimed at improving environmental and living conditions along the river Xiaoqing. On March 1, 2017, the Jinan Municipal Government notified JHSF that it was required to collect its compensation and vacate the Buildings. According to Hela, Jinan Government deprived its investment by expropriating the land which is necessary for its operation. After losing domestic administrative proceedings in China, Hela brought the claim before ICSID under the China-Germany BIT.

This is the third case that China is challenged. This case arose from the second generation of China's BIT. China showed usual mind to ISDS now, though the award is yet to be made.

#### 9.2.2.3 AsiaPhos v. China

On August 7, 2020, Singaporean companies AsiaPhos Limited ("First Claimant" or "AsiaPhos") and its wholly owned Chinese subsidiary Norwest Chemicals Pte Ltd ("Second Claimant" or "Norwest Chemicals", collectively referred as "Claimants") instituted an ad hoc arbitration proceeding against China on the basis of the Agreement between the Government of the People's Republic of China and the Government of the Republic of Singapore on the Promotion and Protection of Investments dated November 21, 1985 (the "Treaty"). On February 16, 2023, the Tribunal rendered an award in favor of China granting its Bifurcated Jurisdictional Objection and finding that the Tribunal does not have jurisdiction over any of Claimants' claims.[14]

The dispute concerns the alleged violation of Respondent's obligations under the Treaty with respect to alleged investments made by Claimants in the phosphate industry in China. Prior to Respondent's alleged unlawful acts, Claimants held, through their wholly owned Chinese subsidiary Sichuan Mianzhu Norwest Phosphate Chemical Co. ("Mianzhu Norwest"), mining and exploration licenses for two phosphate mines, i.e., the Cheng Qian Yan mine ("Mine 1") and the Shi Sun Xi mine ("Mine 2"). Claimants further own two plants which produced yellow phosphorus using phosphate rocks extracted from Mines 1 and 2. In addition, First Claimant directly or indirectly holds a 55% equity interest in Deyang Fengtai Mining Co. Ltd ("Deyang Fengtai"), a Chinese company which held an exploration license and exploration rights for the Yingxiongya barite mine ("Mine 3", together with Mine 1

[14] AsiaPhos v. China, Award (2023).

and Mine 2 the "Mines"). Mines 1, 2 and 3 are located in and around the Jiudingshan Nature Reserve. Sichuan Province and Mianzhu City permitted extensive mineral exploration and exploitation in the Jiudingshan Nature Reserve and surrounding areas. However, in the course of 2016 and 2017, Respondent developed and adopted a new policy that prohibited mining in and around the Jiudingshan Nature Reserve and the national panda park that was to be created. According to Claimant, this new policy led to the shutdown, sealing and mandatory "exit" of Mines 1, 2 and 3 and their associated mineral rights in 2017. Claimant asserted that Mine 1 was not within the Jiudingshan Nature Reserve but the Mianzhu City Government nonetheless sealed Mine 1 in July 2017. According to the Claimant, despite Respondent's repeated recognition of its obligation to provide compensation as a result of its measures, Mianzhu Norwest and Deyang Fengtai have received no compensation for the "exit" of their mineral rights or for their downstream operations. In contrast, Respondent argued that the Mianzhu City Government did not order the sealing of Mine 1 or 2 and the mining licenses held by Mianzhu Norwest and Deyang Fengtai simply expired.

In this arbitration, Claimants raised four categories of claims, which could be classified as Expropriation Claim and Non-Expropriation Claims. Respondent argued that the Tribunal lacks jurisdiction because the dispute was not within the scope of Respondent's consent to arbitration. Respondent submitted that the arbitration clause contained in Article 13(3) of the Treaty is limited to disputes over the amount of compensation for expropriation, thus excluding disputes involving whether an expropriation has occurred and accordingly disputes on whether an obligation to compensate has arisen. While the Claimant argued that each of the seven expressions "involving", "the amount of compensation", "resulting from", "expropriation", "nationalization", "other measures having effect equivalent to nationalization or expropriation", and "mentioned in Article 6" in Article 13(3) of the Treaty confirms that the consent to arbitration extends to disputes involving both the responsibility for expropriation and the quantification of compensation. The Tribunal concluded that Respondent's arbitral consent provided in Article 13(3) of the Treaty does not cover Claimants' Expropriation and Non-Expropriation Claim; rather, the scope of the arbitration clause is limited to disputes regarding the amount of compensation and the scope of Respondent's consent also cannot be expanded by virtue of the MFN clause in Article 4 of the Treaty. The Tribunal concludes that Respondent's arbitral consent provided in Article 13(3) of the Treaty does not cover Claimants' Expropriation and Non-Expropriation Claims. Rather, the scope of the arbitration clause is limited to disputes regarding the amount of compensation. The scope of Respondent's consent also cannot be expanded by virtue of the MFN clause in Article 4 of the Treaty. The award is made in a 2 to 1 majority decision. Arbitrator Stanimir A. Alexandrov gave his dissenting opinion.

The Claimant disagreed with the decision and filed a petition to the Swiss Supreme Court seeking to *inter alia* set aside the Tribunal's jurisdictional award. According to the IA Reporter, the Swiss Federal Tribunal made a judgment dismissing the Claimants' request to set aside the award.

#### 9.2.2.4 Common Features of the Cases and Lessons Learned

In the above cases that China is acting as respondent, we can find some common features:

Firstly, all the first three cases are related to real estate development and expropriation and brought before ICSID for arbitration. The fourth case is related to the extension of concession for mining.

Secondly, the counsels representing China consist of both foreign lawyers and Chinese lawyers, while foreign lawyers play a major role. This is the model China used in its WTO cases, and in this way, Chinese lawyers get to practice and will eventually become more experienced and sophisticated.

Thirdly, the actions challenged by foreign investors are conducted by local governments, instead of the Central Government. This gives warning to the Chinese Government that the major risks of being challenged would come from its vast amount of local governments. China is a huge country with 34 provincial governments and about 2800 local governments. Many officials of these local governments lack the mindset of rule of law, and do not know much about BITs and ISDS.

Fourthly, the subjects of all the three cases are related to land, especially the change of the policy regarding real estate. In over the past ten years, the real estate sector has developed steadily, and housing prices have been increasing very fast as well. This led to the dramatic change of relevant policies on both the central government level and local government level, which caused the investment disputes. Frequently changing its policy is a problem in China, and the ISDS cases would warn China to keep stable policies and laws.

## 9.3 Cases that China is Home State of Investors

Till August 30, 2023, 25 international investment arbitration and conciliation cases (excluding cases in which the notice of arbitration was issued but not formally registered) had been formally initiated by Chinese investors (including foreign-funded enterprises incorporated in Chinese mainland, Hong Kong and Macao) pursuant to international investment agreements signed between China (including Hong Kong) and other countries or investment contracts signed between the investors and foreign governments.

### *9.3.1 Overview of the Cases that China is the Home State of Claimant*

The following table shows the current ISDS cases that Chinese investors referred to international arbitration for resolution (Table 9.2).

**Table 9.2** Basic information of the cases that Chinese investors are claimant

| No | Year of initiation | Short case name | Legal basis | Forum | Outcome of original proceedings | Host STATE | Industry involved |
|---|---|---|---|---|---|---|---|
| 1. | 2007 | Tza Yap Shum v. Peru[15] | China—Peru BIT (1994) | ICSID | Decided in favor of investor | Peru | Manufacturing |
| 2. | 2010 | Beijing Shougang and others v. Mongolia[16] | China—Mongolia BIT (1991) | Administered by PCA | Decided in favor of State | Mongolia | Mining and quarrying |
| 3. | 2010 | SCB HK v. Tanzania Electric[17] | Power Purchase Agreement | ICSID | Decided in favor of investor | Tanzania | Electric Power & Other Energy |
| 4. | 2011 | Philip Morris v. Australia[18] | Australia—Hong Kong, China SAR BIT (1993) | Ad hoc Arbitration (Administered by PCA) | Decided in favor of State | Australia | Manufacturing |

(continued)

[15] Tza Yap Shum v. Republic of Peru (ICSID Case No. ARB/07/6) https://icsid.worldbank.org/en/Pages/cases/casedetail.aspx?CaseNo=ARB/07/6, last visited on May 5, 2023.

[16] Beijing Shougang and others v. Mongolia (PCA Case No. 2010–20) https://pca-cpa.org/en/cases/48/, last visited on May 11, 2023.

[17] Standard Chartered Bank (Hong Kong) Limited v. Tanzania Electric Supply Company Limited (ICSID Case No. ARB/10/20) https://icsid.worldbank.org/en/Pages/cases/casedetail.aspx?CaseNo=ARB/10/20, last visited on May 11, 2023.

[18] Philip Morris Asia Limited (Hong Kong) v. The Commonwealth of Australia (PCA Case No. 2012–12) http://www.pcacases.com/web/view/5, last visited on May 11, 2023.

**Table 9.2** (continued)

| No | Year of initiation | Short case name | Legal basis | Forum | Outcome of original proceedings | Host STATE | Industry involved |
|---|---|---|---|---|---|---|---|
| 5. | 2012 | Ping An v. Belgium[19] | BLEU (Belgium-Luxembourg Economic Union)—China BIT (1984)<br>BLEU (Belgium-Luxembourg Economic Union)—China BIT (2005) | ICSID | Decided in favor of State | Belgium | Financial service activities, except insurance and pension funding |
| 6. | 2013 | Sanum Investments v. Laos (I)[20] | China—Laos BIT (1993) | PCA | Discontinued | Laos | Accommodation; Gambling and betting activities |
| 7. | 2014 | Beijing Urban Construction v. Yemen[21] | China—Yemen BIT (1998) | ICSID | Discontinued due to settlement | Yemen | Construction of buildings |

(continued)

[19] Ping An Life Insurance Company of China, Limited and Ping An Insurance (Group) Company of China, Limited v. Kingdom of Belgium (ICSID Case No. ARB/12/29) https://icsid.worldbank.org/en/Pages/cases/casedetail.aspx?CaseNo=ARB/12/29, last visited on May 11, 2023.

[20] Sanum Investments Limited v. Lao People's Democratic Republic (PCA Case No. 2013–13) https://www.italaw.com/cases/2050, last visited on May 11, 2023.

[21] Beijing Urban Construction Group Co. Ltd. v. Republic of Yemen (ICSID Case No. ARB/14/30) https://icsid.worldbank.org/en/Pages/cases/casedetail.aspx?CaseNo=ARB/14/30, last visited on May 11, 2023.

**Table 9.2** (continued)

| No | Year of initiation | Short case name | Legal basis | Forum | Outcome of original proceedings | Host STATE | Industry involved |
|---|---|---|---|---|---|---|---|
| 8. | 2015 | SCB HK v. Tanzania[22] | Power Purchase Agreement | ICSID | Decided in favor of investor | Tanzania | Electric Power & Other Energy |
| 9. | 2017 | Sanum Investments v. Laos (II)[23] | China—Laos BIT (1993) | Ad hoc Arbitration (Administered by ICSID) | Pending | Laos | Accommodation; Gambling and betting activities |
| 10. | 2018 | Zhongshan Fucheng v. Nigeria[24] | China—Nigeria BIT (2001) | Ad hoc Arbitration | Decided in favor of investor | Nigeria | Construction |
| 11. | 2019 | Jetion and T-Hertz v. Greece[25] | China—Greece BIT (1992) | None (no administering institution) | Discontinued | Greece | Electricity, gas, steam and air conditioning supply |

(continued)

22 Standard Chartered Bank (Hong Kong) Limited v. United Republic of Tanzania (ICSID Case No.ARB/15/41) https://icsid.worldbank.org/en/Pages/cases/casedetail.aspx?CaseNo=ARB/15/41, last visited on May 11, 2023.

23 Sanum Investments Limited v. Lao People's Democratic Republic (ICSID Case No. ADHOC/17/1) https://icsid.worldbank.org/en/Pages/cases/casedetail.aspx?CaseNo=ADHOC/17/1, last visited on May 11, 2023.

24 Zhongshan Fucheng Industrial Investment Co. Ltd. v. Federal Republic of Nigeria https://jusmundi.com/en/document/decision/en-zhongshan-fucheng-industrial-investment-co-ltd-v-federal-republic-of-nigeria-final-award-monday-1st-march-2021, last visited on May 11, 2023.

25 Jetion Solar Co. Ltd and Wuxi T-Hertz Co. Ltd. v. Hellenic Republic https://investmentpolicy.unctad.org/investment-dispute-settlement/cases/975/jetion-and-t-hertz-v-greece, last visited on May 11, 2023.

**Table 9.2** (continued)

| No | Year of initiation | Short case name | Legal basis | Forum | Outcome of original proceedings | Host STATE | Industry involved |
|---|---|---|---|---|---|---|---|
| 12. | 2020 | Barrick v. Papua New Guinea[26] | Investment Contract | ICSID | Concluded (Conciliation) | Papua New Guinea | Oil, Gas & Mining |
| 13. | 2020 | Min v. Korea[27] | China—Korea, Republic of BIT (2007) | ICSID | Decidedin favor of State (no jurisdiction) | Korea | Real estate activities |
| 14. | 2020 | Wang Jing et al. v. Ukraine[28] | China-Ukraine BIT (1992) | Ad hoc Arbitration (Administered by PCA) | Pending | Ukraine | Manufacturing |
| 15. | 2020 | Shift Energy v. Japan[29] | Hong Kong-Japan BIT (1997) | Ad hoc Arbitration (Administered by ICSID) | Decided in favor of State | Japan | Electricity, gas, steam and air conditioning supply |

(continued)

[26] Barrick (Niugini) Limited v. Independent State of Papua New Guinea (ICSID Case No. CONC/20/1) https://icsid.worldbank.org/cases/case-database/case-detail?CaseNo=CONC/20/1, last visited on January 22, 2024.

[27] Fengzhen Min v. Republic of Korea (ICSID Case No. ARB/20/26) https://icsid.worldbank.org/cases/case-database/case-detail?CaseNo=ARB/20/26, last visited on May 11, 2023.

[28] Till April 2023, the PCA has not made the case public, and the information above regarding the case is summarized based on IA Reporter's relevant reports instead of official information released by the tribunal. See WANG JING ET AL. V. UKRAINE https://www.iareporter.com/arbitration-cases/wang-king-et-al-v-ukraine/, last visited on May 11, 2023.

[29] Till April 2023, the ICSID has not made the case public, and the information above regarding the case is summarized based on IA Reporter's relevant reports, see SHIFT ENERGY V. JAPAN https://www.iareporter.com/arbitration-cases/shift-energy-v-japan/, last visited on May 11, 2023.

**Table 9.2** (continued)

| No | Year of initiation | Short case name | Legal basis | Forum | Outcome of original proceedings | Host STATE | Industry involved |
|---|---|---|---|---|---|---|---|
| 16. | 2021 | Wang Jiazhu v. Finland[30] | China—Finland BIT (2004) | Ad hoc Arbitration | Discontinued due settlement | Finland | Trade; Land Transportation, Logistics & Storage |
| 17. | 2021 | Qiong Ye and Jianping Yang v. Cambodia[31] | ASEAN-China Investment Agreement (2009) | ICSID | Pending | Cambodia | Telecommunications |
| 18. | 2021 | Alpene v. Malta[32] | China—Malta BIT (2009) | ICSID | Pending | Malta | Financial service activities, except insurance and pension funding |
| 19. | 2021 | Everyway v. Ghana[33] | China—Ghana BIT (1989) | Ad hoc Arbitration (Administered by PCA) | Decided in favour of State | Ghana | Specialized construction activities |

(continued)

30 Wang Jiazhu v. Finlnad https://www.iareporter.com/arbitration-cases/wang-jiazhu-v-finland/; https://jusmundi.com/en/document/other/en-wang-jiazhu-v-the-republic-of-finland-request-for-arbitration-friday-22nd-january-2021; https://jusmundi.com/en/document/other/en-wang-jiazhu-v-the-republic-of-finland-response-to-the-notice-of-arbitration-friday-19th-february-2021#other_document_22076, https://jusmundi.com/en/document/other/en-wang-jiazhu-v-the-republic-of-finland-discontinuance-order-tuesday-24th-october-2023#other_document_35501, last visited on April 21, 2024.

31 Qiong Ye and Jianping Yang v. Kingdom of Cambodia (ICSID Case No. ARB/21/42) https://icsid.worldbank.org/cases/case-database/case-detail?CaseNo=ARB/21/42, last visited on May 11, 2023.

32 Alpene Ltd v. Republic of Malta (ICSID Case No. ARB/21/36) https://icsid.worldbank.org/cases/case-database/case-detail?CaseNo=ARB/21/36, last visited on May 11, 2023.

33 Everyway Traffic and Lighting Company Limited v. Ghana (PCA 2021–15) https://www.italaw.com/cases/10145, last visited on May 11, 2023.

**Table 9.2** (continued)

| No | Year of initiation | Short case name | Legal basis | Forum | Outcome of original proceedings | Host STATE | Industry involved |
|---|---|---|---|---|---|---|---|
| 20. | 2022 | Huawei v. Sweden[34] | China—Sweden BIT (1982) | ICSID | Pending | Sweden | Telecommunications |
| 21. | 2022 | PCCW v. Saudi Arabia[35] | China—Saudi Arabia BIT (1996) | ICSID | Pending | Saudi Arabia | Telecommunications |
| 22. | 2022 | Junefield v. Ecuador[36] | China—Ecuador BIT (1994) | Data not available | Pending | Ecuador | Mining of metal ores |
| 23. | 2022 | PowerChina and China Railway v. Viet Nam (I)[37] | ASEAN—China Investment Agreement (2009) | ICSID | Pending | Viet Nam | Civil engineering |

(continued)

[34] Huawei Technologies Co., Ltd. v. Kingdom of Sweden (ICSID Case No. ARB/22/2) https://icsid.worldbank.org/cases/case-database/case-detail?CaseNo=ARB/22/2, last visited on May 11, 2023.

[35] PCCW Cascade (Middle East) Ltd. v. Kingdom of Saudi Arabia (ICSID Case No. ARB/22/20) https://icsid.worldbank.org/cases/case-database/case-detail?CaseNo=ARB/22/20, last visited on May 11, 2023.

[36] Junefield Gold Investments Limited v. Republic of Ecuador (Information on administering institution, case number, etc. not available) https://globalarbitrationreview.com/article/chinese-mining-investor-brings-claim-against-ecuador;https://investmentpolicy.unctad.org/investment-dispute-settlement/cases/1260/junefield-v-ecuador, last visited on May 11, 2023.

[37] PowerChina HuaDong Engineering Corporation and China Railway 18th Bureau Group Company Ltd v. Socialist Republic of Viet Nam (ICSID Case No. ARB(AF)/22/7), https://icsid.worldbank.org/cases/case-database/case-detail?CaseNo=ARB(AF)/22/7, last visited on May 11, 2023.

**Table 9.2** (continued)

| No | Year of initiation | Short case name | Legal basis | Forum | Outcome of original proceedings | Host STATE | Industry involved |
|---|---|---|---|---|---|---|---|
| 24. | 2023 | PowerChina and others v. Viet Nam (II)[38] | China—Viet Nam BIT (1992) | Ad hoc Arbitration (Administered by ICSID) | Pending | Viet Nam | Civil engineering |
| 25. | 2023 | China Machinery v. Trinidad and Tobago[39] | China—Trinidad and Tobago BIT (2002) | ICSID | Pending | Trinidad and Tobago | Manufacture of basic metals |

[38] PowerChina HuaDong Engineering Corporation and China Railway 18th Bureau Group Company Ltd v. Socialist Republic of Viet Nam (ICSID Case No. ADM/23/1),https://icsid.worldbank.org/cases/case-database/case-detail?CaseNo=ADM/23/1, last visited on May 11, 2023.

[39] China Machinery Engineering Corporation v. Republic of Trinidad and Tobago (ICSID Case No. ARB/23/8), https://icsid.worldbank.org/cases/case-database/case-detail?CaseNo=ARB/23/8.

The above table shows some characteristics of the cases that Chinese investors are claimants.

First, in terms of the year of initiation, it shows the increasing trend in recent years.

Second, in terms of the legal basis of the cases, most of the cases are based on BITs, most of which were concluded in the 1990s or early 2000s, belonging to the old generation of BITs, while three cases among them were initiated under agreements between the relevant parties.

Third, in terms of the forum that the cases are referred to, ICSID is the major choice, but ad hoc arbitration based on UNCITRAL Arbitration Rules is another choice. For ad hoc arbitration, most cases are administered by the PCA or the ICSID.

Fourth, in terms of the industries involved in these cases, most are involved with manufacturing, electricity and telecommunication.

## *9.3.2 Case Study of Some Major Cases*

In the above 25 cases, 15 of them have been concluded. Due to the fact that the information of some cases is not available, this section will review some selected cases. After the case study, the author tries to analyze some lessons that could be learned.

### 9.3.2.1 Tza Yap Shum v. Peru

On February 12, 2007, Mr. Tza Yap Shum, a citizen of Hong Kong Special Administrative Region of China, instituted arbitration proceedings at ICSID against Peru under the China-Peru BIT (1994). Peru challenged the jurisdiction but the tribunal confirmed its jurisdiction and competence in the Decision on Jurisdiction and Competence dated June 19, 2009.[40] On July 7, 2011, the Tribunal rendered its award in favor of the claimant.[41] On November 9, 2011, Peru filed an application for annulment of the decision and award, and on February 12, 2015, the ad hoc Committee issued its decision on annulment dismissing Peru's claims in its entirety and upholding the original tribunal's award.[42]

Claims arose out of the seizure of the bank account of claimant's enterprise due to tax debt and other alleged actions undertaken by Peruvian tax authorities that resulted in the substantive deprivation of claimant's investment. Mr. Tza Yap Shum is the major shareholder of the Peruvian company TSG Perú S.A.C. company ("TSG") which engaged in the manufacturing of food products derived from fish. According to

[40] Tza Yap Shum v. Peru, Decision (2009).

[41] Tza Yap Shum v. Peru, Award (2011).

[42] Tza Yap Shum v. Peru, Decision (2015).

Mr. Tza Yap Shum, in 2004, the Peruvian National Superintendence of Tax Administration ("SUNAT") started to conduct a series of actions that destroyed the commercial operations and the economic viability of TSG. SUNAT considered TSG as an industrial company rather than as a service company operating as a financing source for the Peruvian industrial fisheries.

The audit of TSG conducted by SUNAT in 2004 resulted in the issuance in 2005 of 95 retroactive taxation decisions, resolutions and fines arising from breaches of the income tax and general sales tax laws totaling approximately US$ 45 million. On January 28, 2005, SUNAT issued an Enforcement Resolution to freeze TSG's bank accounts up to the amount of S/. 3,535,791 and notified fifteen Peruvian banks of its decision. Under the circumstances described, on September 29, 2006, Mr. Tza Yap Shum together with TSG submitted a Request for Arbitration against the Republic of Peru before ICSID. The Request for Arbitration claimed that Peru violated the fair and equitable treatment, expropriation, transfer of capital and returns and others provided in the Peru-China BIT.

Peru challenged the tribunal's jurisdiction for two reasons: Firstly, the China-Peru BIT was concluded in 1995 when Hong Kong was not yet returned to China, therefore, the China-Peru BIT did not apply to Hong Kong and Hong Kong citizens. Secondly, the BIT only allows the dispute over the amount of compensation of expropriation to be resolved in arbitration. The tribunal decided that the China-Peru BIT applies to Tza Yap Shum who is a Chinese national and thus falls into the definition of "investor" of the BIT, and that the dispute "involving" the amount of compensation of expropriation covers the dispute over expropriation, and therefore rendered its decision confirming its jurisdiction over the dispute over expropriation but dismissed other claims. Finally, the tribunal decided that Peru violated its obligation under China-Peru BIT by indirectly expropriated Mr. Tza Yap Shum's investment and awarded 0.78 million USD for compensation. Then Peru filed an application for annulment of the award claiming that the Arbitral Tribunal committed a manifest excess of powers, Failure to State Reasons and Serious Departure from a Fundamental Rule of Procedure, but the ad hoc Committee dismissed all the claims in its Decision on Annulment.

This is the first case that Chinese investor challenged a host state under a Chinese BIT. But this case also showed two serious problems in Chinese BITs: Firstly, whether Chinese BITs apply to Hong Kong and Macao Special Administrative Regions; and secondly, whether the dispute involving the amount of compensation of expropriation covers disputes over expropriation. The Tribunal's affirmative decision received critical criticisms from the opponents. Professor An Chen, a high-profile Chinese scholar in the field of international economic law, asserted that the China-Peru BIT could not be directly applied to Hong Kong Special Administrative Region because under China's "One Country, Two Systems" policy, Hong Kong has high autonomy and has concluded several of its own BITs. The tribunal's broad interpretation of the dispute "involving" the amount of compensation over expropriation showed its tendency to expand its jurisdiction. Nevertheless, the tribunal's decision has a profound impact on future cases related to Chinese BITs, such as the case of Sanum v. Laos, which will be elaborated later on.

#### 9.3.2.2 Beijing Shougang and Others v. Mongolia

On February 12, 2010, three companies organized under the laws of China, Beijing Shougang Mining Investment Company Ltd., China Heilongjiang International Economic & Technical Cooperative Corp. and Qinhuangdaoshi Qinlong International Industrial Co. Ltd, brought a case before the Permanent Court of Arbitration (PCA) against Mongolia for arbitration according to the UNCITRAL Arbitration Rules under China-Mongolia BIT (1991). The tribunal rendered an award in favor of the state on June 30, 2017 deciding that it lacked jurisdiction over the dispute.[43] On September 28, 2017, the claimants filed a petition at the United States District Court Southern District of New York to vacate the tribunal's arbitral award declining to exercise arbitral jurisdiction and compel arbitration. This petition was finally rejected.

Claims arose out of Mongolian Government's cancellation of licenses held by the claimants in the Tumurtei iron ore mine. In 2002, the claimants formed a joint venture with a Mongolian company who held a license to exploit certain iron ore deposits located in Mongolia to commercially develop these deposits. In 2006, a new government took power in Mongolia. Due to the increased price of iron ore, the new Mongolian Government ultimately revoked the license. Claimants asserted that the revocation constituted expropriation and referred the case to PCA. The tribunal interpreted the dispute "involving" the amount of compensation for expropriation as the dispute over the amount and thus it lacked jurisdiction over the dispute over expropriation.

In contrast to the Tza Yap Shum case, this tribunal took a different approach to the interpretation of the scope of disputes and strictly restricted its jurisdiction to dispute only about the amount of expropriation.

#### 9.3.2.3 SCB HK v. Tanzania Electric

On October 1, 2010, the ICSID Secretary-General registered a request for the institution of ICSID arbitration proceedings by Standard Chartered Bank (Hong Kong) Limited ("SCB HK" or "Claimant") against Tanzania Electric Supply Company Limited ("TANESCO" or the "Respondent") under a Power Purchase Agreement (the "PPA"). In this arbitration SCB HK claimed for various tariff payments and other sums owed to Independent Power Tanzania Limited ("IPTL") by TANESCO. On April 13, 2012, the Respondent filed a request to address the objections to jurisdiction as a preliminary question. On August 24, 2012, the Respondent filed a counter-memorial on jurisdiction and the merits. On February 12, 2014, the Tribunal issued a decision on jurisdiction and liability, deciding that IPTL's rights had been validly assigned to SCB HK under the PPA and that the Tribunal had jurisdiction over SCB HK and TANESCO (collectively the "Parties") as well as the dispute.[44] On September 12, 2016, the Tribunal rendered an award in favor of the investor, deciding that the

[43] Beijing Shougang and others v. Mongolia, Award (2017).

[44] SCB HK v. Tanzania Electric, Decision (2014).

tariff should be determined on the basis of an Internal Rate of Return of 22.31% applied to a shareholder loan and that amounts paid by TANESCO into the Escrow Account, payment out of the Escrow Account to IPTL/PAP did not and payments made to IPTL/PAP since August 2013 did not discharge TANESCO's obligation to SCB HK under the PPA and thus could not be used to reduce the amount that TANESCO owed SCB HK. The Tribunal ordered TANESCO to pay to SCB HK the amount of US$ 148.4 million with simple interest. All the other claims were dismissed.[45] While on January 13, 2017, the Secretary-General registered an application for annulment of the award filed by TANESCO. On August 22, 2018, the ad hoc Committee issued its decision on annulment, deciding that the Application for Annulment of the Award rendered on September 12, 2016, submitted by TANESCO was dismissed in its entirety.[46]

The dispute arose out of the PPA entered into by the Respondent and IPTL in 1995. TANESCO is the entity designated as an agency of Tanzania pursuant to Article 25(1) of the ICSID Convention. Since 1998, there had been ongoing disputes between IPTL and TANESCO over the equity contribution, tariff and payment of electricity. During this period, IPTL went through debt restructurings. Further to an auction of distressed debt, in August 2005, SCB HK acquired Term Loans 1 and 2, and became the sole lender to IPTL. Under that transaction, SCB HK was assigned a number of contracts, including the 1997 Security Deed, the Implementation Agreement and the Guarantee Agreement concluded between IPTL and the government of Tanzania. And in 2009, SCB HK became the Security Agent of IPTL. SCB HK claimed that as Security Agent, SCB HK held all of IPTL's "right, title and interest in and to the Assigned Contracts, including all monies which may at any time be or become payable to the Borrower".

#### 9.3.2.4 Philip Morris v. Australia

On June 22, 2011, Philip Morris Asia Limited ("PM Asia" or the "Claimant") served upon the Commonwealth of Australia ("Australia" or the "Respondent") a Notification of Claim in accordance with Article 10 of the Australia-Hong Kong, China SAR BIT (1993) ("BIT"). Without any settlement reached, the Claimant served a Notice of Arbitration dated November 21, 2011 on the Respondent, submitting the dispute to arbitration under the UNCITRAL Arbitration Rules of 2010 (the "UNCITRAL Rules") before the PCA in accordance with Article 10 of the BIT. The Tribunal rendered an award in 2015 in favor of the state deciding that the claims raised are inadmissible.[47]

---

[45] SCB HK v. Tanzania Electric, Award (2016).

[46] SCB HK v. Tanzania Electric, Decision (2018).

[47] Philip Morris v. Australia, Award (2015).

The claim arose out of the Respondent's enactment and enforcement of the Tobacco Plain Packaging Act 2011 (the "TPP Act") and the implementing regulations known as the Tobacco Plain Packaging Regulations 2011 (the "TPP Regulations") (collectively the "Plain Packaging Measures") which affected the Claimant's investments in Australia. The Claimant was incorporated in Hong Kong in 1994 and is the Asia regional headquarter of Philip Morris International Inc. ("PMI") which produces several top cigarette brands in the world. After restructuring of PMI, the Claimant owns 100% of the shares of Philip Morris (Australia) Limited ("PM Australia"), a holding company incorporated in Australia that in turn owns 100% of the shares of Philip Morris Limited ("PML"). In August 2009, a senator introduced the Plain Tobacco Packaging Bill 2009 in the Australian Senate, which proposed to remove "brands, trademarks and logos from tobacco packaging". On November 21, 2011, the TPP Act was enacted and the Claimant served the Respondent with a Notice of Arbitration. On December 7, 2011, the TPP Regulations were promulgated. Under the terms of the Plain Packaging Measures, all tobacco packages had to be manufactured in compliance with the plain packaging requirements as of October 1, 2012 and all tobacco products sold at retail outlets had to comply with the Plain Packaging Measures as of December 1, 2012. Before the Plain Packaging Measures went into effect, PML's Director of Corporate Affairs reiterated PML's opposition to plain packaging in the Australian Financial Review, stating that the Plain Packaging Measures were "an unconstitutional expropriation of our valuable intellectual property and violate[d] a variety of Australian international trade obligations".

The Claimant requested the Tribunal order Respondent to withdraw the [Plain Packaging] Measures or refrain from applying them against Claimant's investments; or award damages and other fees. In Procedural Order No. 8, the Tribunal ordered the bifurcation of the proceedings. On December 17, 2015, the Tribunal issued an Award on Jurisdiction and Admissibility in favor of the state, in which it addressed 3 objections to the jurisdiction of the Tribunal and to admissibility of claims. The first two objections centered on the question whether, in the period between Australia's announcement of a decision to introduce the Plain Packaging Measures and the enactment of these measures into legislation, the Claimant properly became an investor in Australia when it acquired equity in PML in the context of a corporate restructuring in 2011. While the Tribunal rejected Australia's first two preliminary objections, it upheld the third objection concluding that, "the initiation of this arbitration constitutes an abuse of rights, as the corporate restructuring by which the Claimant acquired the Australian subsidiaries occurred at a time when there was a reasonable prospect that the dispute would materialize and as it was carried out for the principal, if not sole, purpose of gaining the Treaty protection (i.e., the BIT protection). Accordingly, the claims raised in this arbitration are inadmissible and the Tribunal is precluded from exercising jurisdiction over this dispute". The Tribunal then rendered a Final Award Regarding Costs on March 8, 2017.[48]

[48] Philip Morris v. Australia, Final Award (2017).

#### 9.3.2.5 Ping An v. Belgium

On September 19, 2012, Ping An Life Insurance Company of China, Limited and Ping An Insurance (Group) Company of China, Limited (Ping An) instituted arbitration proceedings at ICSID against Belgium under the BLEU (Belgium-Luxembourg Economic Union)-China BIT (1984) and the BLEU (Belgium-Luxembourg Economic Union)-China BIT (2005). On December 20, 2013, the Respondent filed a notice of intent to file objections to jurisdiction and later the proceeding on the merits is suspended. On April 30, 2015, the Tribunal rendered its award in favor of Belgium declining its jurisdiction.[49]

Ping An is the largest shareholder in the Belgian-Dutch financial institution Fortis. Claims arose out of the Belgium Government's bailout, and subsequent nationalization and sale to a third party, of the financial institution in which the claimants had invested, in the context of the 2008 financial crisis. Between October 2007 and July 2008, the Claimants acquired shares in Fortis in the open market and became Fortis Bank's single largest shareholder. On September 15, 2008 Lehman Brothers collapsed, and the interbank lending market dried up. On September 28, 2008 Belgium acquired a 49.93% stake in Fortis Bank in return for a payment of €4.7 billion. Finally, Belgium transferred 75% of the shares in Fortis to BNP Paribas, which caused huge losses to Ping An. After failing consultations with Belgium, Ping An brought the case before ICSID, alleging that Belgium's behavior was a direct expropriation and violated other provisions of the 1984 BITs.

The Claimants relied on the 1984 BLEU-China BIT for the substance of their claim and on the 2005 BLEU-China BIT for the jurisdiction of this Tribunal, probably because the former BIT has a narrow scope of the dispute while the latter has a broader scope for international arbitration. The 1984 BIT entered into force on October 5, 1986, while the 2005 BIT entered into force on December 1, 2009. The 1984 BIT allows a dispute on an amount of compensation for expropriation to be submitted for international arbitration, while the 2005 BIT allows a legal dispute to be submitted to ICSID for resolution. The 2005 BIT also provides for the "transition" of the two BITs, and the new BIT shall not apply to any dispute or any claim concerning an investment which was already under judicial or arbitral process before its entry into force. Such disputes and claims shall continue to be settled according to the old BIT. Belgium challenged the jurisdiction of the tribunal majorly based *on Ratione Temporis* and others, because the dispute between the parties arose before the entry into force of the 2005 BIT. The Tribunal accepted the respondent's argument and declined its jurisdiction.

Again, this case involved the first generation and the second generation of Chinese BITs, and especially concerning the scope of dispute for international arbitration and the transition of the old and the new BITs.

---

[49] Ping An v. Belgium, Award (2015).

#### 9.3.2.6 Beijing Urban Construction v. Yemen

On December 3, 2014, Beijing Urban Construction Group Co. Ltd. (Beijing Urban), a Chinese state-owned enterprise, instituted an arbitration proceeding at ICSID against Yemen on the basis of the China-Yemen BIT (1998). Yemen challenged the tribunal's jurisdiction by asserting that state-owned enterprises cannot bring claims before ICSID and that the dispute is not concerning the amount of compensation for expropriation. The Tribunal rendered a decision on jurisdiction dated May 31, 2017 in favor of the claimant.[50] Then the parties settled the case and the arbitration proceedings declared discontinued on June 7, 2018.

Claims arose out of the alleged forced deprivation of claimant's assets and contract concerning a project for the construction of an airport terminal in Sana'a, Yemen. Beijing Urban won the tender by the Sana'a International Airport project (phase 2) for selection of the construction contractor for a new International Terminal Building. On February 28, 2006, Beijing Urban entered into a construction contract with the Yemen Civil Aviation and Meteorology Authority (CAMA). Beijing Urban alleged that in July 2009, Yemen Government unlawfully deprived it of its investment in Yemen by employing its military forces and security apparatus to assault and detain its employees and forcibly deny its access to the Project site and thus its ability to perform its contractual obligations. On July 22, 2009, Beijing Urban alleged, following weeks of state orchestrated harassment and intimidation, CAMA gave notice of its intention to terminate the Contract on the basis of its failure to return to the site to complete the works. Beijing Urban said it was prevented from performing the Contract by CAMA and the Yemen Government.

Yemen challenged the tribunal's jurisdiction by asserting that Beijing Urban is a state-owned entity and did not qualify as a "national of another Contracting State". Further, it asserted that the China-Yemen BIT only allows any dispute relating to the amount of compensation for expropriation to be brought to ICSID for resolution, and the MFN clause of the BIT did not apply to dispute settlement provisions. Both Parties accepted the Broches test which was formulated by Aaron Broches, the first Secretary-General of ICSID, that government-owned corporation should not be disqualified as a "national of another Contracting State" unless it is acting as an agent for the government or is discharging an essentially governmental function. The tribunal decided that Beijing Urban met the *Broches test*, took the broad interpretation approach as to the dispute concerning the amount of compensation and denied the application of MFN clause to dispute settlement, and finally affirmed its jurisdiction overt hose claims related to the Claimant's allegations of expropriation.

This case raised three critical issues for Chinese investors. Firstly, the scope of the dispute is whether the dispute involving the amount of compensation, or any dispute. Secondly, whether the MFN clause applies to the dispute settlement provisions. And thirdly, whether the state-owned enterprise qualifies as national of another contracting state. China has a large number of state-owned enterprises accounting for 18% in

[50] Beijing Urban Construction v. Yemen, Decision (2017).

the whole world, which state-owned enterprises have played a key role in China's outbound investment.[51]

#### 9.3.2.7 SCB HK v. Tanzania

In 2015, Standard Chartered Bank (Hong Kong) Limited ("SCB HK" or the "Claimant") instituted an ICSID arbitration proceeding against the United Republic of Tanzania ("Tanzania" or "GoT" or the "Respondent", and the Claimant and the Respondent are collectively referred to as the "Parties") on the basis of the Implementation Agreement between the Government of the United Republic of Tanzania and Independent Power Tanzania Limited ("IPTL") dated June 8, 1995 ("Implementation Agreement" or "IMA"). On October 11, 2019, the Tribunal rendered its award deciding in favor of the investor.[52] The Tribunal found that Claimant was the lawful assignee under Article 15.2 of the Implementation Agreement and had the title and interest to pursue its claims against the Respondent for breach of Articles 15.3, 16.1 and 16.2 of the Implementation Agreement and entitled the Claimant to compensation.

This dispute relates to the Claimant's allegations against the Respondent of breach of Articles 15 and 16 of the Implementation Agreement and the validity of the Claimant's termination of the Implementation Agreement. On November 1, 1994, the company IPTL was incorporated in Tanzania as a joint venture company between Mechmar Corporation (Malaysia) Berhad ("Mechmar") and VIP Engineering and Marketing Limited ("VIP"). IPTL was formed to apply for the operating license to build, construct and operate a 100 megawatts ("MW") power plant for 20 years pursuant to the Memorandum of Understanding signed between Mechmar and the Tanzanian Ministry of Water Energy and Minerals dated August 27, 1994. By Implementation Agreement dated June 8, 1995 signed by IPTL and GoT, the GoT gave various undertakings and assurances in favor of IPTL and "its permitted successors and assigns", including undertakings against discriminatory action and expropriation, and granted IPTL the exclusive right to design, finance, insure, construct, complete, own and operate. SCB HK brought the claims in this arbitration proceeding in its capacity as the assignee of IPTL's right under several contracts concluded between IPTL and the GoT.

In the October 2019 Award, the Tribunal found that the assignment of IPTL's rights under the IMA to SCB HK was lawful under the IMA, and it therefore upheld jurisdiction over the Claimant. The Tribunal also decided that the project did not cease to be an investment solely because IPTL assigned its rights to the Claimant. Thus, the arbitrators concluded that a legal dispute arising out of an investment existed, and that they had jurisdiction under Article 25 of the ICSID Convention. With respect to the merits, the Tribunal decided that the GoT violated Article 16 of the IMA when indirectly and directly expropriating the investment (notably by transferring control

[51] UNCTAD (2017), p. 31.

[52] SCB HK v. Tanzania, Award (2019).

over IPTL to a local company, Pan Africa Power Solutions (T) Limited, or "PAP"), and by discriminating against IPTL and in favor of PAP. The Tribunal also found that Tanzania violated Article 15 of the IMA by failing to provide a security for payments owed to TANESCO. Considering these findings, the arbitrators decided that the Claimant was entitled to unilaterally terminate the IMA, and that it had faithfully adhered to the procedural steps for termination provided for by the IMA.

#### 9.3.2.8 Sanum Investments v. Laos (I) and Sanum Investments v. Laos (II)

Sanum Investments is involved in two cases based on interrelated facts.

The general facts are as follows: Mr. John Baldwin and Mr. Shawn Scott, two US entrepreneurs who were experienced in a number of businesses including gambling facilities, became involved in casinos and slot machines in Laos in 2007. For this purpose, they caused two companies to be incorporated in Aruba, the Netherlands Antilles Lao Holdings NV ("LHNV"), and a subsidiary Sanum Investments ("Sanum") in Macau. Based on the same events happened to them by the Laos government, both Sanum and LHNV initiated arbitrations against Laos. Sanum challenged Laos before PCA under the UNCITRAL Arbitration Rules according to the bilateral investment treaty (BIT) between Laos and China (Macau is the Special Administrative Region of China). The case number is PCA Case No. 2013–13. While LHNV challenged Laos before ICSID under ICSID Additional Facility Rules according to the BIT between Laos and the Netherlands. The case number is d ICSID Case No. ARB(AF)/12/6. In June 2014, Sanum and LHNV concluded a settlement agreement with Laos.[53] In 2017, Sanum alleged that Lao Government's actions breached the settlement agreement, and commenced a new arbitration proceeding (ICSID Case No. ADHOC/17/1).

<u>**Sanum Investments v. Laos (I)**</u>

The Claimant is Sanum Investments Limited ("Sanum" or "Claimant"), an entity incorporated in the Macao Special Administrative Region of China ("Macao"). On August 14, 2013, the Claimant commenced arbitration proceedings using the UNCITRAL Arbitration Rules at PCA against the Laos on the basis of the China-Laos BIT (1993). Claims arose out of an alleged series of measures by the Government of Laos, including its courts and provincial authorities, that affected claimant's bundle of rights for the construction and operation of two hotels and casinos, among other gaming facilities in which the claimant had invested.

The Respondent challenged the tribunal's jurisdiction by asserting among others that: Firstly, the BIT does not apply to Macao which was handed over to China and established as a special administrative region in 1999, much later than the conclusion of the BIT; secondly, the BIT only allows the dispute involving the amount of compensation for expropriation to be submitted to an ad hoc arbitral tribunal;

---

[53] Deed of Settlement between LHNV, Sanum and Laos.

and thirdly, the MFN clause does not apply to dispute settlement provisions. After analysis, the tribunal concluded that the China-Laos BIT is applicable to the Macao SAR. The tribunal also took the broad interpretation of the scope of dispute to cover dispute over expropriation, not only the dispute over the amount of compensation for expropriation. The Tribunal rendered its award on jurisdiction on December 13, 2013, in Singapore affirming its jurisdiction to arbitrate only the expropriation claims of Sanum.[54]

On January 7, 2014, the Laotian Ministry of Foreign Affairs sent a letter to the PRC Embassy in Vientiane, Laos stating its view that the China-Laos BIT did not extend to Macau, and on January 9, 2014, received a letter from the PRC Embassy in Vientiane, Laos stating its view that the PRC-Laos BIT did not apply to Macau "unless both China and Laos make separate arrangements in the future".

On January 10, 2014, Laos filed an application to the Singapore High Court in Singapore, the seat of the arbitration. The application requested to vacate the tribunal's decision on jurisdiction. Laos' two submissions concern the applicability of China-Laos BIT to the Macau SAR and the interpretation of the scope of dispute for international arbitration. Finally, the Singapore High Court made its judgment on January 20, 2015 concluding that the China-Laos BIT does not apply to Macau, and the Tribunal did not possess subject matter jurisdiction over the defendant's expropriation claims because only disputes over the amount of compensation for expropriation can be submitted to arbitration.[55]

On June 5, 2014, Sanum and the LHNV concluded a settlement agreement with Laos to resolve the treaty claims, during the merits hearing in Singapore. Shortly after the Settlement, the Sanum alleged that the Government had committed a material breach of its terms which entitled it to a revival of the treaty arbitration.

On July 20, 2015, Sanum appealed against the Judgment made by the Singapore High Court to the Court of Appeals of Singapore. During the proceedings, China's Ministry of Foreign Affairs replied to Laos' letter on November 18, 2015 confirming that the letter from the PRC Embassy in Vientiane, Laos stating that the China-Laos BIT did not apply to Macau had been sent with its authorization. However, the Court of Appeals of Singapore rendered its judgment on September 29, 2016 reversing the High Court's decision and concluding that the PRC-Laos BIT does apply to Macau and secondly, that the Tribunal has subject matter jurisdiction over the claims brought by Sanum.[56]

Less than one month after the judgment, on October 21, 2016, China's Foreign Ministry Spokesperson responded to the judgment in a Regular Press Conference. It stressed again that the geographical scope of application of the China-Laos investment agreement is a question of fact concerning acts of state, which is up to the contracting parties to decide. China has confirmed twice in diplomatic notes that the

[54] Sanum Investments v. Laos, Award (2013).

[55] Government of the Lao People's Democratic Republic v. Sanum Investments Ltd, Judgement of the Singapore High Court (2015) .

[56] Sanum Investments v. Government of the Lao People's Democratic Republic, Judgment of the Court of Appeals of Singapore (2016).

China-Laos investment agreement does not apply to Macao SAR. The ruling made by the Singaporean court on this question of fact is incorrect.[57]

The Chinese side handles the application of treaties to Hong Kong and Macao SARs in line with the "one country, two systems" policy and the Basic Laws in Hong Kong and Macao. To be specific, the Chinese central government decides whether or not the international treaties to which the People's Republic of China is or becomes a party apply to the SARs based on the circumstances and their needs after seeking the views of the governments of the SARs. The SARs can conclude agreements with foreign countries on their own in the appropriate fields, including economy, finance, trade and investment, in accordance with the Basic Laws or under specific authorization of the central government. Therefore, as a principle, the investment agreements between the central government and foreign countries do not apply to SARs, unless otherwise decided by the central government after seeking the views of the SAR governments and consulting with the other contracting parties of the agreement.[58]

Eventually, on August 6, 2019, the Tribunal issued the Award concluding that the Claimants have failed to meet the evidentiary onus of establishing facts necessary to support their legal arguments, and thus dismissed the claims.[59]

**Sanum Investments v. Laos (II)**

In 2017, Sanum alleged that the Laotian Government breached the settlement agreement concluded by the claimant and Lao Holdings N.V. with the Government in 2014, and thus commenced a new arbitration proceedings again Laos. On April 27, 2017, the Tribunal is constituted in accordance with the ICSID Arbitration (Additional Facility) Rules because Laos is not a contracting state of ICSID Convention. The Respondent challenged the tribunal's jurisdiction but agreed that it would not seek bifurcation with respect to any jurisdictional objections in this case. So far, the case is still pending.

#### 9.3.2.9 Barrick v. Papua New Guinea

On July 22, 2020, the Secretary-General registered a request from Barrick (Niugini) Limited ("Claimant") for the institution of conciliation proceedings against Papua New Guinea ("Respondent"). On January 19, 2021, a Commission was constituted in accordance with Article 29(2)(b) of the ICSID Convention. On April 9, 2021, the Commission declared the proceeding closed in accordance with Article (34)(2) of the ICSID Convention and ICSID Conciliation Rule 30(3), and issued its Report.

---

[57] Embassy of the People's Republic of China in the United States of America, Foreign Ministry Spokesperson Hua Chunying's Regular Press Conference on October 21, 2016, http://www.china-embassy.org/eng/fyrth/t1407743.htm, last visited March 28, 2019.

[58] Embassy of the People's Republic of China in the United States of America, Foreign Ministry Spokesperson Hua Chunying's Regular Press Conference on October 21, 2016, http://www.china-embassy.org/eng/fyrth/t1407743.htm, last visited March 28, 2019.

[59] Sanum Investments v. Laos, Award (2019).

The Claimant, Barrick Niugini Limited, has two major shareholders: the Canadian Barrick Gold Corporation and the Chinese Zijin Mining Group, each with 47.5% of the shares. The Claimant applied to the Papua New Guinea Government for a 20-year extension of its gold mining rights after they expired in August 2019, but was denied. The Claimant then filed a request for conciliation with the ICSID based on its previous contract with the government. Neither details about the case nor the Conciliation Report is available for public.

This is the first case that Chinese investor is involved regarding the use of conciliation instead of arbitration. Further, this case is initiated on the basis of investment contract, instead of a BIT or other IIA.

#### 9.3.2.10 Alpene v. Malta

On July 2, 2021, the ICSID Secretary-General registered a request from a Chinese bank Alpene Ltd ("Claimant") for the institution of arbitration proceedings against Republic of Malta ("Respondent") under Malta-China BIT (2009). It was reported that the Claimant claimed that Malta had breached the Malta-China BIT (2009). This is the first time that Malta appears as a respondent in an ICSID arbitration.

Claims arose out of the Malta Government's taking control of Pilatus Bank, a bank owned by the claimant, and the revocation of its banking license, among other alleged acts of mistreatment and discrimination by government officials. It is revealed that the Hong Kong-based Alpene indirectly owns 100% of the Maltese Pilatus Bank. According to a November 5, 2018 communication from the Malta Financial Services Authority (MFSA), upon a proposal from the MFSA, the European Central Bank decided to withdraw the banking authorization of Pilatus Bank as of that date. Reportedly, this decision was prompted by money-laundering investigations against Pilatus' chair in the US (which, however, were reportedly dropped) and the European Union. Notably, this arbitration has triggered a couple of requests for discovery under §1782 of the US Code in aid of the ICSID arbitration. Alpene's first attempt to seek discovery, from a US resident who was appointed as administrator of Pilatus Bank, Lawrence Connell, was unsuccessful. The claimant then sought §1782 discovery from another US court with respect to another resident, Elizabeth McCaul.

Shortly after the Tribunal in this arbitration was constituted, Malta filed preliminary objections on the basis of ICSID Arbitration Rule 41(5), objected to the ripeness of the claims and argued that the claimant had manifestly failed to comply with the BIT's exhaustion of local remedies requirement. (Article 9(3)(b) of the BIT states that: "with respect to Malta the investor concerned shall submit the dispute to a domestic court, tribunal or arbitration so as to exhaust the local procedures before proceeding to international arbitration".) According to IA Reporter, in an as-of-yet unpublished May 23, 2022 decision, the Tribunal unanimously found that the claim did not manifestly lack legal merit, allowing the case to proceed to the next stage. The case is still pending and not much information is available.

#### 9.3.2.11 Huawei v. Sweden

In January 2022, Chinese investor Huawei Technologies Co., Ltd. (the "Claimant" or "Huawei") filed a request for arbitration against Kingdom of Sweden (the "Respondent" or "Sweden") to the ICSID under Sweden-China BIT (1982) (the "BIT"), arguing that the Swedish Government's decision to prohibit Huawei from participating in the rollout of Sweden's 5G network had seriously impaired the interests of Huawei and its local subsidiaries.[60]

The dispute relates to Huawei's indirect investment in Swedish 5G market, which is claimed to be impaired by Sweden. Huawei owned its alleged investment in Sweden (shares in Huawei Technologies Sweden AB or "Huawei Sweden") indirectly through a Dutch entity (Huawei Technologies Coöperatief U.A or "Huawei NL"). It is alleged by the Claimant that Sweden mandated removal of Huawei's 3G and 4G infrastructure from the 2.3 and 3.5 GHz bands and Huawei was also excluded from the future 6G and 7G markets.

On February 13, 2023, the Respondent raised objections to jurisdiction as a preliminary question. The two preliminary objections regard the existence of a protected investment and the rights underlying Huawei's claims. The Respondent raised the first objection on jurisdiction by arguing that the BIT does not protect indirect investments by Chinese investors. Defining a Chinese investor under Article 1(2) of the BIT as "any company, other legal person or citizen of China authorized by the Chinese Government to make an investment", the Respondent contended that, by leaving out the notion of "predominant" ownership in the definition of Chinese investors, which appears in the definition of Swedish investors, the BIT excludes Chinese investors from "owning a protected investment indirectly". While the Claimant stressed that Article 1(2) of the BIT is silent on whether only direct or also indirect investments are protected and that the exclusion of investors with indirect investments from the scope of the BIT needs explicit language, which is missing in this case.

As for the second objection, that is, existence of the alleged rights underlying the claims, the Respondent raised two arguments: First, the Claimant has not established that such a right exists. Although Huawei Sweden allegedly entered into supply contracts for 3G and 4G with Swedish mobile network operators ("MNOs"), the Claimant has not filed the frame contracts that it allegedly concluded with certain MNOs concerning the 5G networks. Second, there is no evidence showing that the Claimant has met the requirement set in Article 1(2) of the BIT, according to which the Chinese Government must have authorized the Claimant to make a 5G-related investment in Sweden. In contrast, the Claimant contended that Huawei Sweden entered into contracts to provide equipment and services to Sweden's MNOs, including with respect to the upcoming 5G networks. Sweden's actions in breach of the BIT prevented Huawei Sweden from performing those contracts, thereby destroying Huawei Sweden's carrier network business and affecting the value of Huawei's shareholding in Huawei Sweden (held through Huawei NL).

---

[60] Huawei Technologies Co., Ltd. v. The Kingdom of Sweden, Request for Arbitration (2022).

The Tribunal denied the Respondent's bifurcation request. The case is still pending.

### 9.3.3 *Common Features of the Cases and Lessons Learned*

In the above cases that Chinese investors acted as claimant, we can find some common features and learn some lessons.

Firstly, the majority of the cases relate to expropriation and brought before ICSID or administered by PCA.

Secondly, the key issues are concerning: (1) the scope of dispute for international arbitration, for example, whether international investment tribunals have the jurisdiction to decide on the question of expropriation where BITs only provide that disputes regarding amount of compensation for expropriation can be submitted to an arbitral tribunal; (2) the application of the MFN clauses, i.e., whether the MFN clause applies to the dispute settlement provisions.

Thirdly, the tribunals in the above cases gave different interpretation as to the above issues.

Fourthly, BITs of the early generation that limit the scope of dispute for international arbitration regarding expropriation to "amount of compensation for expropriation" can protect China from international arbitration, they also prevent Chinese investors who suffer from foreign expropriation from obtaining relief through international arbitration.

Fifthly, the Chinese Government should learn lessons from the above cases and formulate its own consistent position as to the above two issues and incorporate them in future new BITs.

## 9.4 Conclusion

In light of China's evolution into major home economy of FDI and its increasing encouragement of outbound investment, it is imperative to recognize and respond to the distinct challenges and opportunities associated with this transformative shift.

As indicated by the case practice, none of the current investment dispute cases related to China or Chinese investors are rooted in the BITs concluded in or after 2012. China's old generation of the BITs show the tendency to protect home states and have many defects in design. Despite China has developed a new generation of BITs with comprehensive arbitration clauses and other modified provisions to boost investment liberalization, the majority of the BITs concluded by China still feature restrictive dispute resolution provisions, especially where expropriation is concerned. As Chinese investors are more frequently resorting to international arbitration for relief, it becomes imperative for China to adapt old BITs to align with its status as a major home state of investors. Specifically, China should consider modifying its old

BITs that is still effective to incorporate clearer provisions on key issues such as the scope of dispute for international arbitration, and the application of MFN clauses.

Furthermore, China's transition into a significant outbound investor underscores the importance of enhancing its capacity to navigate international investment disputes effectively. This includes investing in legal awareness and capacity-building initiatives at both the central and local government levels to ensure a comprehensive understanding of BITs and investor-state dispute settlement mechanisms. Additionally, China should consider adopting a more proactive stance in shaping the interpretation of international investment law by participating in relevant international fora and engaging in constructive dialogue with other stakeholders.

By revising its BITs and enhancing its capacity to navigate investment disputes, China can effectively protect the interests of its investors abroad and uphold its commitments under international law, thereby contributing to a more stable and predictable investment environment globally.

## References

AsiaPhos v. China (ICSID Case No. ADM/21/1), Award (2023)
Beijing Shougang and others v. Mongolia (PCA Case No 2010–20), Award (2017)
Beijing Urban Construction v. Yemen (ICSID Case No. ARB/14/30), Decision on Jurisdiction (2017)
Deed of Settlement between LHNV, Sanum and Laos
Embassy of the People's Republic of China in the United States of America, Foreign Ministry Spokesperson Hua Chunying's Regular Press Conference on October 21, 2016
Government of the Lao People's Democratic Republic v. Sanum Investments Ltd, Judgement of the Singapore High Court (2015)
Huawei Technologies Co., Ltd. v. The Kingdom of Sweden, Request for Arbitration (2022)
Philip Morris v. Australia (PCA Case No. 2012–12), Award on Jurisdiction and Admissibility (2015)
Philip Morris v. Australia (PCA Case No. 2012–12), Final Award Regarding Costs (2017)
Ping An v. Belgium (ICSID Case No. ARB/12/29), Award (2015)
Sanum Investments v. Government of the Lao People's Democratic Republic, Judgment of the Court of Appeals of Singapore (2016)
Sanum Investments v. Laos (PCA Case No. 2013–13), Award on Jurisdiction (2013)
Sanum Investments v. Laos (PCA Case No. 2013–13), Award (2019)
SCB HK v. Tanzania (ICSID Case No. ARB/15/41), Award (2019)
SCB HK v. Tanzania Electric (ICSID Case No. ARB/10/20), Award (2016)
SCB HK v. Tanzania Electric (ICSID Case No. ARB/10/20), Decision on Jurisdiction and Liability (2014)
SCB HK v. Tanzania Electric (ICSID Case No. ARB/10/20), Decision on the Application for Annulment (2018)
Tza Yap Shum v. Peru (ICSID Case No. ARB/07/6) (in Spanish), Award (2011)
Tza Yap Shum v. Peru (ICSID Case No. ARB/07/6), Decision on Annulment (2015)
Tza Yap Shum v. Peru (ICSID Case No. ARB/07/6) (in Spanish), Decision on Jurisdiction and Competence (2009)
UNCTAD (2017), World Investment Report 2017
UNCTAD (2022), World Investment Report 2022

# Conclusion

China concluded its first bilateral investment treaties (BIT) with Sweden in 1982. Ever since, China has concluded more than 150 international investment agreements (IIAs) including BIT, trilateral investment treaties, investment chapter of free trade agreements, etc. This book reviews some selected IIAs with typical features including: the BIT that China signed with a region as a whole (ASEAN), the series IIAs that China signed or involved with a specific country (Korea), the BITs that China signed with the countries of the same region (Africa) and the BIT that China (the largest developing country) failed to sign with the US (the most developed country in the world). This book also reviewed some investor-state investment disputes arising from the above-mentioned IIAs: two cases initiated on the basis of China-ASEAN BIT, two cases initiated on the basis of China-Korea BIT and two cases initiated on the basis of China-African BITs (Nigeria and Ghana). Some other selected investment disputes were also discussed that China was challenged as respondent state and Chinese investors acted as claimant. ISDS is an integral part of international investment treaties but its legitimacy was challenged. This book also reviews China's position toward the ISDS reform at the international level and national level. At the end, this book concludes as follows.

The long-lasted negotiations of China-ASEAN Agreement on Investment reflected China's mind change toward IIAs as a result of its status change from the mere receiver of international investment to both receiver and source state of international investment.

The finally concluded Agreement is a high-standard investment agreement for China in the first decade of the twenty-first century. The five IIAs between China and Korean concluded during 1992 and 2020 witnessed the gradual development footprint of IIAs for both China and the world. The China-African BITs fall into the category of South-South cooperation investment agreements, but could not provide sufficient protection to Chinese investors, especially in the context that more and more Chinese investment flows to Africa as a result of the BRI. It is a pity that the China-US BIT negotiations failed in the last minute. Otherwise, it would provide a solution to the



H. Chen, *China's Practice in International Investment Law*, Modern China and International Economic Law, https://doi.org/10.1007/978-981-96-5016-3

challenge of balancing the interests of a given country in its capacity as a (capital-importing) host country with its interests in its capacity of a (capital-exporting) home country. Meeting this challenge would represent a historic compromise between the traditionally quite diverging host and home country positions.

The BRI proposed by China has produced great impacts on China's outward foreign investment law and policy on both national level and international level, and will continue to generate more impacts in the future. To respond to the limited access to investor-state dispute settlement for Chinese investors in the BRI countries, China is innovating its own ISDS at its national level. The tendency that some ICSID tribunals tried to expand their jurisdiction in investment cases also caused the legitimacy crisis of investment arbitration. Some countries implemented a more effective mechanism to limit the tribunals' discretion to expand jurisdiction in the ISDS reform. In the first decade of the twenty-first century, both developing countries and developed countries took measures to reform ISDS by limiting or even abandoning ISDS at their domestic level or treaty practice. The new developments reflect that certain kind of emerging consensus is being reached between developing and developed countries. Regarding the ISDS reform work conducted within the UNCITRAL, China clearly expressed its support to the setting up of a separate permanent appellate body on the basis of a multilateral agreement. The current investment dispute cases related to China or Chinese investors are majorly rooted in China's old generation of the BITs, which show the tendency to protect home states and have many defects in design, including the restrictive dispute resolution provisions, especially where expropriation is concerned. By revising its BITs and enhancing its capacity to navigate investment disputes, China can effectively protect the interests of its investors abroad and uphold its commitments under international law, thereby contributing to a more stable and predictable investment environment globally.

The manufacturer's authorised representative in the EU is Springer Nature Customer Service Centre GmbH, Europaplatz 3, 69115 Heidelberg, Germany. If you have any concerns regarding our products, please contact ProductSafety@springernature.com

Printed and bound by CPI Group (UK) Ltd, Croydon, CR0 4YY
30/09/2026
02225297-0001